Christmas Handcrafts
Book Three

Oxmoor House®

Christmas Handcrafts, Book Three

©1994 by Oxmoor House, Inc.
Book Division of Southern Progress Corporation
P.O. Box 2463
Birmingham, Alabama 35201

Published by Oxmoor House, Inc., Leisure Arts, Inc., and Symbol of Excellence Publishers, Inc.

All rights reserved. No part of this book may be reproduced in any form or by any means without the prior written permission of the publisher, excepting brief quotations in connection with reviews written specifically for inclusion in a magazine or newspaper.

Library of Congress Catalog Card Number: 92-60993
Hardcover ISBN: 0-8487-1189-0
Softcover ISBN: 0-8487-1415-6
ISSN: 1074-8962
Manufactured in the United States of America
First Printing 1994

Oxmoor House, Inc.

Editor-in-Chief: Nancy J. Fitzpatrick
Senior Crafts Editor: Susan Ramey Wright
Copy Editor: Susan Smith Cheatham
Associate Production Manager: Theresa L. Beste
Production Assistant: Marianne Jordan

Symbol of Excellence Publishers, Inc.

Executive Editors: Barbara Cockerham, Phyllis Hoffman
Editor: Diane Kennedy-Jackson
Writer: Amy H. Ryan
Editorial Assistants: Susan Branch, Cindy Housel, Carol Odom, Carol Zentgraf
Production Manager: Wayne Hoffman
Associate Production Manager: Perry James
Creative Director: Mac Jamieson
Executive Art Director: Yukie McLean
Art Director: Michael Whisenant
Graphic Designers: Dottie Barton, Scott Begley, Charles Long, Rick Nance
Photography Stylists: Cathy Muir, Ada Parker, Glenda Parker, Tracey M. Runnion, Jarinda Wiechman

Dear Handcrafters,

Does your idea of the perfect Christmas include decking the halls with handmade treasures? Do you adorn the tree to overflowing with cherished holiday ornaments and fill every corner of your home with works from your hands and heart? Then this array of holiday designs is guaranteed to delight you.

Whether your preference is crafting, quilting, cross stitching, or crocheting, the designs presented here will make you eager to get started. You'll find holiday masterpieces you'll be proud to display in your own home, as well as great, quick-to-complete projects for last-minute decorating and giving. So sit back, turn the pages, and choose your favorites. Then get set for many enjoyable afternoons of handiworking fun.

Merry Christmas!

Diane Kennedy-Jackson

Contents

BERWICK
CHRISTMAS CLASSICS
Perfect For All
Decorating Needs
DMC

CELEBRATE THE SEASON

Whatever your personal celebrations may be, the warmth of handmade items and gifts will heighten the spirit of Christmas. As friends and family meet to celebrate, this collection of crafts and stitchery will convey the heartfelt pleasure of the season. Special family rituals will once again be recorded on the pages of time's photo album as children leave cookies for Santa and hang their stockings in anticipation of Christmas morn. As you prepare to celebrate this festive season, let these handmade treasures add merriment to your family's holiday.

Fireside Cheer

Lit by the glow of a crackling fire, the faces of loved ones smile warmly as they remember Christmas past, celebrate Christmas present, and anticipate Christmas future. Perhaps the family members at the fireside have returned from a long tramp through the woods, victorious in their search for the perfect evergreen. Or maybe they are resting from a day sledding down snowy hills. Nature's beauty plays a leading role in holiday activities and decorations, whether those embellishments come directly from the "great outdoors" or are simply inspired by nature.

The festive trimmings we feature here are from both categories: a wreath and a basket made from organic materials; and stocking designs and a wreath drawn from nature. The ***Pinecone Basket***, shown below, makes a wonderful, rustic accent for your home. Transform it into a centerpiece by adding rosy-red apples and greenery, or use it as a catchall for gift-wrapping gear—scissors, tape, and gift tags will fit easily inside.

If you choose to place the ***Pinecone Basket*** on the hearth, the ideal companion for it is the ***Natural Sweet-Gum Wreath***, shown at right, hanging above the mantel. Made with sweet-gum balls from the sweet-gum tree, the wreath is an inviting, cheerful addition to anyone's decor. Small acorns, dried okra pods painted gold, and a big raffia bow lend country Christmas charm.

For a more ornate look, try our ***Victorian Fruits Wreath***, shown on page 10, as a wall or door decoration with color, texture, and style. The rich greens of the leaves and luscious reds of the fruits will complement other seasonal ornaments, and the opulence of Doe Suede™ and felt will give your home the lavish touch that comes from Victoriana.

Our final foray into the world of nature takes a more whimsical look at some dressed-for-Christmas birds. The ***Feathered Friends Stockings***, shown on page 11, feature cross-stitched designs of a big-eyed cardinal and a pair of winsome wrens, dressed in festive finery. Stitch the perky pals on pre-finished stockings with Aida inserts for quick-to-complete gifts.

Left*—The* Pinecone Basket *is a fresh, natural addition to the holiday hearth. Collect small pinecones and create this versatile basket using the instructions on page 22.*

Opposite*—Transform sweet-gum balls into a* Natural Sweet-Gum Wreath. *Add acorns and dried okra pods to finish the project. Instructions are on page 22.*

Above—*Sumptuous fabrics yield the colorful fruits found on our* Victorian Fruits Wreath. *Instructions are on page 22.*

Above—*Birds in holiday attire make a festive appearance in these cross-stitch designs. Charts for* Feathered Friends Stockings *are on page 25. Color code is on page 24.*

Seasonal Accents

The heart of the Christmas celebration is in the home of every family. Festive evergreen tree and holly boughs, glittering lights and candles, and handmade decorations express the joy and spirit of the season. Decorating one's home is always a family event. Every family has its own, personal style, and the warmth and good feelings of the holidays are always conveyed through the decorating efforts of its members.

Our collection of seasonal accents brings glad tidings to home-decorating enthusiasts everywhere. Among these wonderful wall hangings, pillows, and tree skirt you are certain to find several favorites that will be perfect for your holiday decorating scheme.

The ***Home for Christmas*** ensemble, featured on these two pages, includes a tree skirt, shown at left, and a wall hanging and pillow cover, shown opposite. Because all of the simply-shaped houses and their trimmings—doors, windows, and other details—are machine-appliquéd, each piece can be completed swiftly. Choose holiday prints in muted colors for the houses, and they will remind you of the cozy, secure feeling of going home for Christmas.

Place a patchwork quilt anywhere in a room to add instant color. ***Pines in the Patches***, shown on page 14, conveys thoughts of a down-home holiday when hung above the mantel, as shown, over the headboard of a bed, or just about anywhere. Its simple, geometric shapes—squares, triangles, and rectangles—make it a snap to machine piece, and its small size makes it a quick-to-finish gift that has a special, handmade touch. The red, green, and white prints and solids used to create the pines and patches give a holiday-inspired look to the wall hanging. Join the quilt craze—piece and quilt this little delight for yourself or a friend.

Above—*Make this simple, machine-appliquéd tree skirt, which is part of the* Home for Christmas *ensemble, following the instructions on page 24.*

***Above—**Use muted holiday prints to create an assortment of houses for the* Home for Christmas *wall hanging and pillow. Instructions begin on page 24.*

Here's another quick wall hanging, with a special seasonal message. The ***Real Reason Banner***, shown above, uses words associated with the holiday to create a Christmas-tree shape, complete with a shiny star above and a tree trunk below. The letters are fused onto the background fabric—a super time-saving method. Red-and-green print fabric binds this wall hanging and forms the hanging loops for the wooden rod. For a rustic look, try using a real branch as a hanging rod.

The ***Joy Wall Hanging***, shown on page 16, is the ideal size to enliven a bare interior door, a wall, or the space above a mantel. This machine-appliquéd charmer requires very little fabric or time to complete—you can probably find quite a few of the necessary materials and trims in your scrap basket. Coordinate the wall hanging to the furnishings of the room where it will hang, or choose traditional reds and greens. For a sparkling seasonal touch, complete the colorful angel with silver or gold lamé wings.

Above*—Celebrate the "reason for the season" as you make this banner. Seasonal words, fused to the background, form the Christmas-tree shape. Instructions for* the Real Reason Banner *are on page 29.*

Left*—Add down-home charm to your Christmas decor with a patchwork wall hanging.* Pines in the Patches *is made from scraps of holiday prints that will add a festive touch to seasonal decorating. Instructions are on page 27.*

Crocheters, hold on to your stockings! The ***Bells & Trees Wall Hanging***, shown at right, will change the way you think about holiday crochet. The checkerboard-style design alternates red bell and green tree blocks, and will add a colorful touch to your Christmas decorating. You'll love the decorative loops and "ornaments" on the trees! Ambitious yarn crafters may choose to make an afghan-size version of this design by simply adding bell and tree blocks as needed.

***Left**—Shown displayed on an interior door, the* Joy Wall Hanging *is a wonderful project for using scraps of fabric and trim. Add greenery and a decorative bow atop the hanger for extra "joy." Instructions are on page 29.*

***Above**—Holiday crochet takes a colorful turn in the* Bells & Trees Wall Hanging, *with alternating green trees and red bells. Instructions begin on page 32.*

The six pillow designs featured here and on the following pages vary greatly, both in style and in the techniques used to create them—choose your favorites or make them all!

Fans of cross stitch will enjoy making the pint-sized ***Joy and Noel Pillows***, shown here and on page 19. Both pieces are finished simply, with lace and ruffled, Christmas-print fabric around the edges. Use them both as miniature throw pillows or attach a decorative ribbon and hang them on a doorknob or newel post.

For those who like to work with their sewing machines, the next two pillows will be welcome projects. First, the ***Papercut Snowflake Pillow***, shown at the top of page 20, combines fold-and-cut paper and machine appliqué. Remember cutting out paper snowflakes in elementary school? Relive those memories when making the snowflake design shown here.

Next, the ***Christmas Tree Pillow***, shown at the bottom of page 20, will be incredibly simple to create—in fact, it can be described as fast, fun, and fantastic! Use green felt from your Christmas scraps for the tree; then appliqué the tree to the red, felt background. The tree trunk is embroidered with gold metallic thread, which also serves as some of the tree's "ornaments" when made into French knots. Other adornments sewn onto the felt tree are medium and small pearl beads and small flowers cut from lace trim. The pillow itself is finished with plain red felt as the back and four purchased, green, silky tassels at the corners.

Crafters will love to make the ***Golden Angels and Kings*** pillows, shown on page 21. Begin with plain muslin squares; then, using metallic gold paint and stencils, paint the regal and heavenly scenes onto the background.

Finish the pillows with shirred, gold lamé cording; then display them where they're certain to be noticed. These elegant throw pillows will add a bit of glamour to your holiday decorating scheme.

Above left and right—*What dainty, diminutive, yuletide accents for your home!* The Joy and Noel Pillows, *featuring cross-stitched holly and poinsettias, are quick to stitch and quite versatile: one is finished as a miniature throw pillow; the other includes a decorative, ribbon hanger. Charts and instructions are on pages 34 and 35.*

***Above**—Fold and cut a "snowflake;" then use easy, machine appliqué to create the* Papercut Snowflake Pillow. *Instructions are on page 36.*

***Left**—Have fun with felt this holiday season when you make the* Christmas Tree Pillow. *With its simple tree shape and bead "ornaments," it will be a quick-and-easy project to complete for decorating or for gift giving. Instructions are on page 37.*

***Right**—Use your talents for stenciling and sewing to craft the* Golden Angels and Kings *pillows. Gold paint and gold lamé cording give these accent pieces a touch of elegance. Instructions are on pages 38 and 39.*

Pinecone Basket

Materials:

Round twig basket (approximately 5" tall, not including handle, and 7" in circumference)
60 small pinecones (approximately 1"–1½" long)
3–4 large pinecones
Old scissors **or** wire cutters
Hot glue gun

1. Remove large burs from bottom of large pinecones, using old scissors or wire cutters. Glue three rows of burs around top of basket, extending first row approximately ½" above rim of basket. Overlap second row of burs over first row, and third row over second row.
2. Apply glue to base of small pinecones and glue pinecones to basket. Begin at bottom of basket, work in rows toward top, and complete top row so as to slightly overlap bottom row of pinecone burs at top of basket.
Note: Bottom row of pinecones should be glued slightly above bottom of basket, so that pinecones will not touch surface on which basket is placed.

Natural Sweet-Gum Wreath

Materials:

16" straw wreath
250–300 sweet-gum balls (from sweet-gum tree)
100–150 small acorns
10 pods dried okra
Thirty–forty 50"–60"-long pieces raffia
12" length 19-gauge wire
6" length 26-gauge wire
Hot glue gun
Spray paint, color: gold (optional)

1. Wrap 12" length 19-gauge wire around top center of wreath and twist to form hanger.
2. Spray several pods of okra gold, if desired. Let dry.
3. Glue sweet-gum balls in rows around wreath, placing them close together, beginning with outside rows, continuing with inside rows, and finishing with top rows to make a total of seven rows.
Note: Leave area at bottom-inside center of wreath uncovered.
4. Glue acorns randomly between sweet-gum balls.
5. Glue okra at bottom-inside center of wreath, referring to photo on page **9** for placement. Glue sweet-gum balls and acorns around okra.
6. Remove one strand of raffia from bunch. Set aside. Shape remaining raffia strands into bow and secure center, using 6" length of 26-gauge wire. Wrap strand of raffia around center of bow to cover wire and glue down raffia end to secure. Glue bow at bottom-center front of wreath.

Victorian Fruits Wreath

Materials:

Scraps of velveteen, Doe Suede™, **or** velour fabric, as follows:
- 5" x 10" scrap **each** red, burgundy, medium green (for apples);
- 8" x 9" scrap light yellow (for banana);
- 5" x 10" scrap light purple (for cluster of grapes);
- 4" x 10" scrap light yellow (for lemon);
- 4" x 8" scrap **each** pink, dark tan (for peaches);
- 4" x 8" scrap dark purple (for plum);
- Two 4" x 12" scraps very light brown (for pears);
- Three 4" x 8" scraps red (for strawberries).

12" x 22" piece green Doe Suede™ **or** felt (for leaves and strawberry stems)
2" x 8" scrap brown Doe Suede™ **or** felt (for stems)
11" x 12" piece Pellon® Wonder-Under® Transfer Web
2" x 4" piece Pellon® Wonder-Under® Transfer Web
Polyester filling
Thread to match fabrics
Pinking shears
18" grapevine wreath
12" length 30-gauge hobby wire (for **each** piece of fruit, to wire fruit to wreath) **or** 12" length gold thread (for **each** piece of fruit, for ornament hangers)
Wire cutters
Straight pins
Measuring tape
Pencil
Press cloth
Sewing machine
Iron
Hand-sewing needle (if making ornaments)
Powder blush and brush (optional)

Note: Materials listed will make one *Victorian Fruits Wreath*. Patterns include ¼" seam allowance. Wreath shown features three apples, one banana, one cluster of grapes, one lemon, two peaches, two pears, one plum, and three strawberries.
Option: Pieces of fruit may be used as tree ornaments.

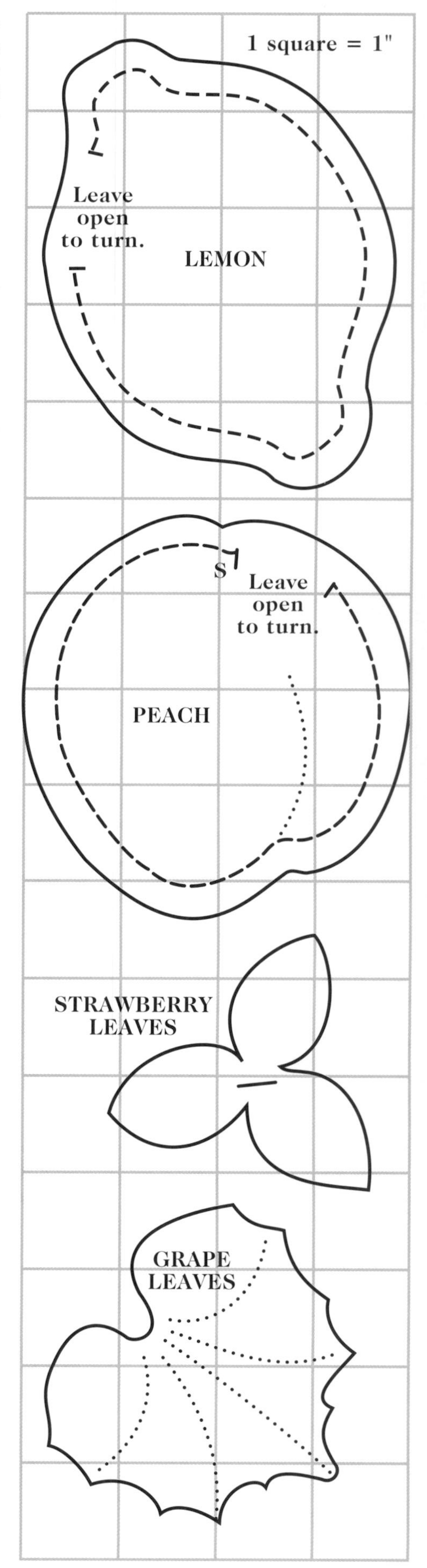

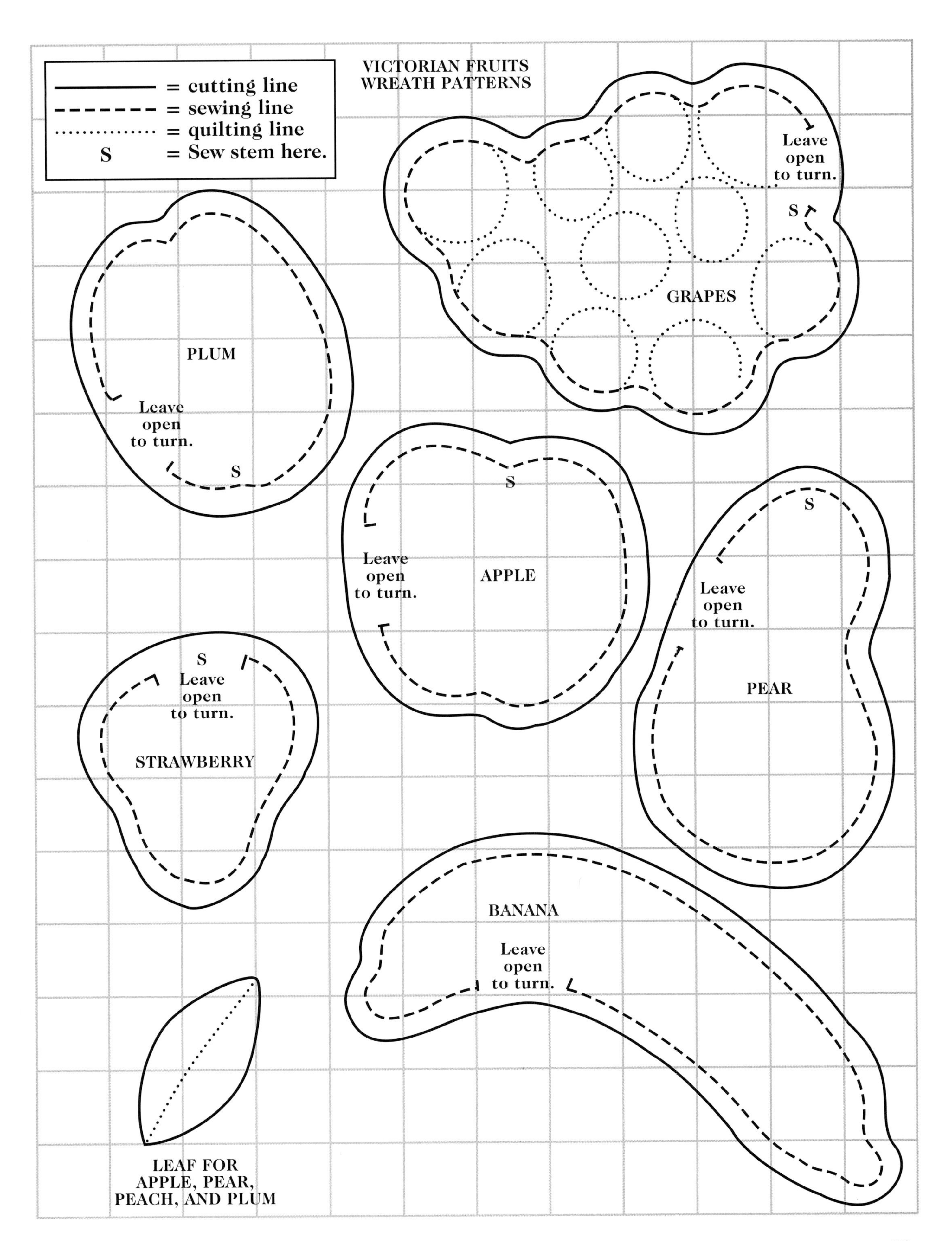

VICTORIAN FRUITS
WREATH PATTERNS
= cutting line
= sewing line
= quilting line
S = Sew stem here.
GRAPES
Leave open to turn.
S
PLUM
Leave open to turn.
S
APPLE
S
Leave open to turn.
PEAR
S
Leave open to turn.
STRAWBERRY
S
Leave open to turn.
BANANA
Leave open to turn.
LEAF FOR
APPLE, PEAR,
PEACH, AND PLUM

1. Enlarge patterns as indicated. Cut out.
2. To make leaves, fuse 11" x 12" piece Wonder-Under® to wrong side of one half of 12" x 22" piece green Doe Suede™, following manufacturer's instructions for fusing. Let cool, peel off paper backing, and fold remaining half of Doe Suede™ over Wonder-Under®. Fuse again, fusing Doe Suede™ to itself and using press cloth between iron and Doe Suede™. Repeat with 2" x 4" piece Wonder-Under® and 2" x 8" piece brown Doe Suede™ to make stems. Cut nine ¼" x 2" strips from brown Doe Suede™ for stems. Cut three strawberry stems and three sets of strawberry leaves from green Doe Suede™. Trim strawberry leaves with pinking shears to serrate edges. Slash center of each set of strawberry leaves as indicated on pattern and pull stem through opening. Cut ten leaves from green Doe Suede™ for fruit. Sew vein lines in leaves, using matching thread. Set leaves and stems aside.
3. To make fruit, fold each piece of velveteen in half, placing right sides of fabric together. Place pattern atop fabric. Lightly trace around pattern and cut out. Pin stems in place at *S* (marked on pattern pieces) on applicable pieces of fruit. Sew around perimeter of each piece of fruit, using a short stitch length (approximately fifteen stitches per inch), matching thread, and leaving an opening for turning. Clip curves. Turn right-side out. Stuff lightly with polyester filling. Whipstitch opening closed. For cluster of grapes, hand-quilt outline of each grape, referring to pattern. For peaches, quilt "dimple" line in each, referring to pattern. (**Option:** Brush blush on peaches along "dimple" lines.) Hand-sew leaves to fruit at stems, referring to photo on page 10 for placement.
4. To add fruit to wreath, pierce back side of each piece of fruit with one end of wire, push wire along inside back of piece of fruit, and pierce fabric again approximately 1" away, bringing wire end back to outside of piece of fruit. Wire fruit to wreath, twisting wire ends together to secure. Cut wire ends, using wire cutters.
Option: To finish each piece of fruit as a tree ornament, thread needle with 12" length gold thread, pierce top of stem with needle, and run needle with thread through top of stem. For pieces of fruit without stems, run needle with thread through top of piece of fruit. Unthread needle. Bring thread ends together and tie in a knot to form hanger. Repeat for remaining ornaments.

Feathered Friends Stockings

	DMC	Color
■	310	black
★	742	tangerine, lt.
◢	904	parrot green, vy. dk.
V	906	parrot green, med.
=	907	parrot green, lt.
/	321	red
◒	498	red, dk.
·	white	white
-	844	beaver gray, ul. dk.
M	840	beige-brown, med.
Z	842	beige-brown, vy. lt.
ı	543	beige-brown, ul. lt.
II	3713	salmon, vy. lt.
+	761	salmon, lt.
X	814	garnet, dk.

Fabric: 14-count Aida cuff on stockings by Charles Craft, Inc.
Stitch count:
Cardinal 56H x 93W
Wrens 56H x 94W
Design size:
Cardinal 4" x 6⅝"
Wrens 4" x 6¾"

Instructions: Cross stitch using three strands of floss. Backstitch using three strands of floss.
Backstitch instructions:
Cardinal
321 beak
310 claws, pinecones
844 remainder of backstitching
Wrens
844 all backstitching

Home for Christmas

Materials:
3 yds. 44/45"-wide natural muslin
3 yds. 44/45"-wide backing fabric of your choice
3 yds. lightweight quilt batting
2 yds. fusible web
2 yds. **total** of assorted 44/45"-wide complementary green and rust prints
¼ yd. 44/45"-wide mustard yellow print
4 pkgs. Coats Extra Wide Double Fold Bias Tape, Art. M890, color: 39B Barberry Red
2 spools **each** Coats Rayon Machine Embroidery Thread, Art. D63, colors: 39B Barberry Red, 177 Kerry Green
1 spool Coats Dual Duty Plus thread, Art. 210, color: 256 Natural
16" square pillow form
20" length ¼"-wide green satin ribbon
Scissors
Pencil
Hand-sewing needle
Sewing machine with zigzag stitch

Note: Use a ¼" seam allowance throughout.
Wall Hanging
1. Cut one 25" square from muslin. Fold to find the vertical and horizontal centers and mark lightly with pencil.
2. Enlarge pattern pieces as indicated. Trace four houses with roofs, windows, doors, and chimneys onto paper side of fusible web, mixing and matching pieces as desired. Fuse shapes to assorted fabrics, following manufacturer's instructions for fusing, and cut out. Fuse windows and doors to houses. Machine satin stitch around doors and windows with red or green thread, running stitching across windows along broken lines indicated on pattern pieces to make window casings. Trace curtain shapes on paper side of fusible web and fuse to fabrics as desired. Cut out shapes, fuse curtains to windows, and machine appliqué in place.
Note: Some of the curtains and doors on model include decorative stitching. Refer to photo on page 13 for ideas.
3. Fuse one house to center of each square marked on the 25" muslin square. Place roof over top of each house and place chimney(s) behind roof, referring to photo for placement. (**Note:** Chimney on house in upper-left corner of quilt is placed on front of roof.) Machine satin stitch houses and roofs to square in same manner used for windows and doors. Press.
4. Cut two 25" x 1½" strips from green print. Stitch one strip to each side of muslin square. Cut two 26½" x 1½" strips from green print and sew to top and bottom of muslin square.
5. Cut two 26" x 3" strips from rust print. Stitch one strip to each side green print strip. Cut two 31" x 3" strips from rust print and sew to top and bottom green print strips.
6. Cut one 35" square **each** from backing fabric and quilt batting. Layer backing fabric right-side down, batting, and assembled quilt top right-side up atop a flat surface. Pin or baste layers together.
7. Machine-quilt in the ditch along seam lines and marked center lines, using green thread. Trim edges of backing and batting even with quilt top and bind quilt with bias tape, folding tape in half lengthwise and mitering at corners.

Pillow Cover
1. Cut one 12½" square from muslin. Assemble one house following instructions for wall hanging and fuse to

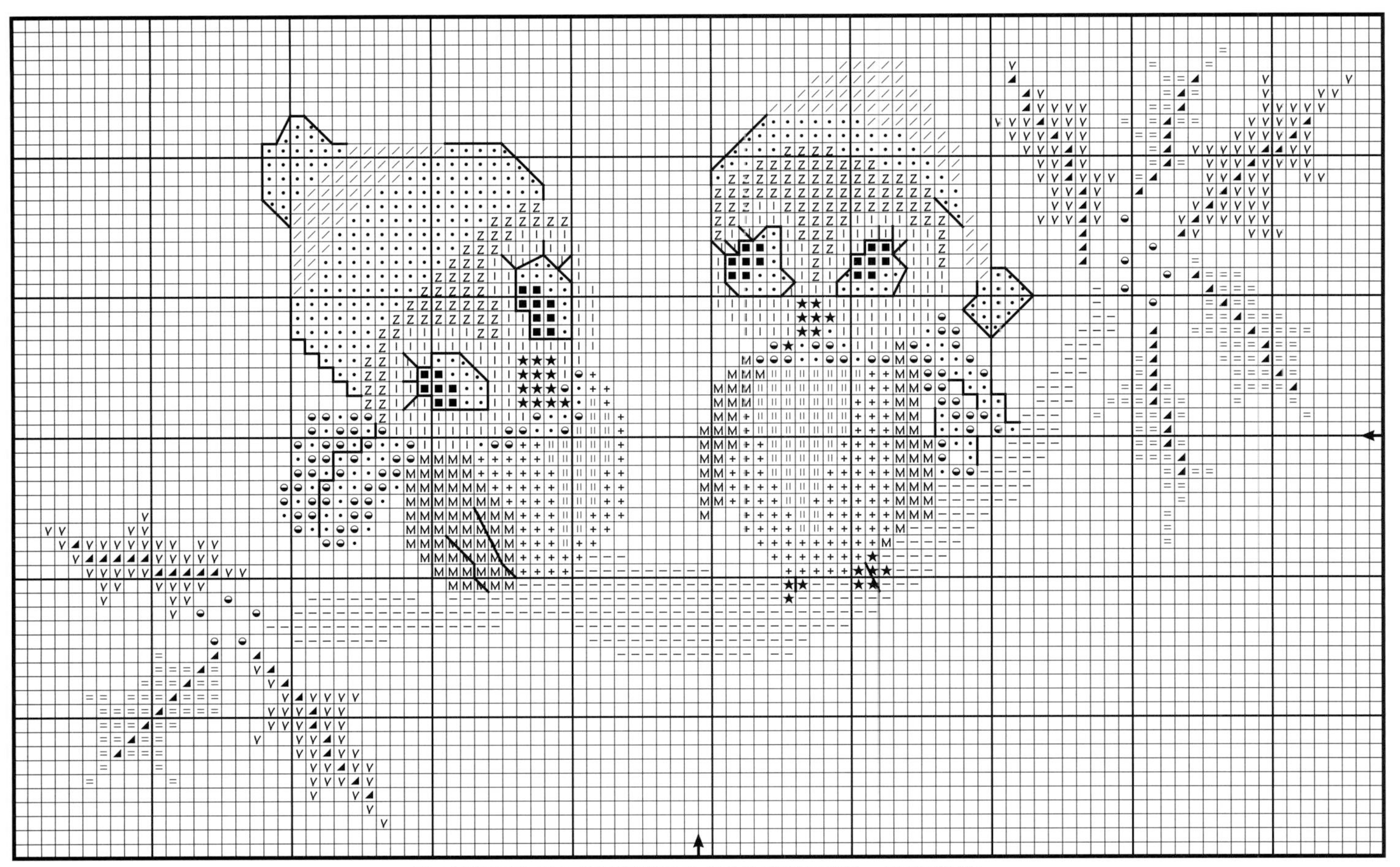

FEATHERED FRIENDS STOCKINGS—WRENS

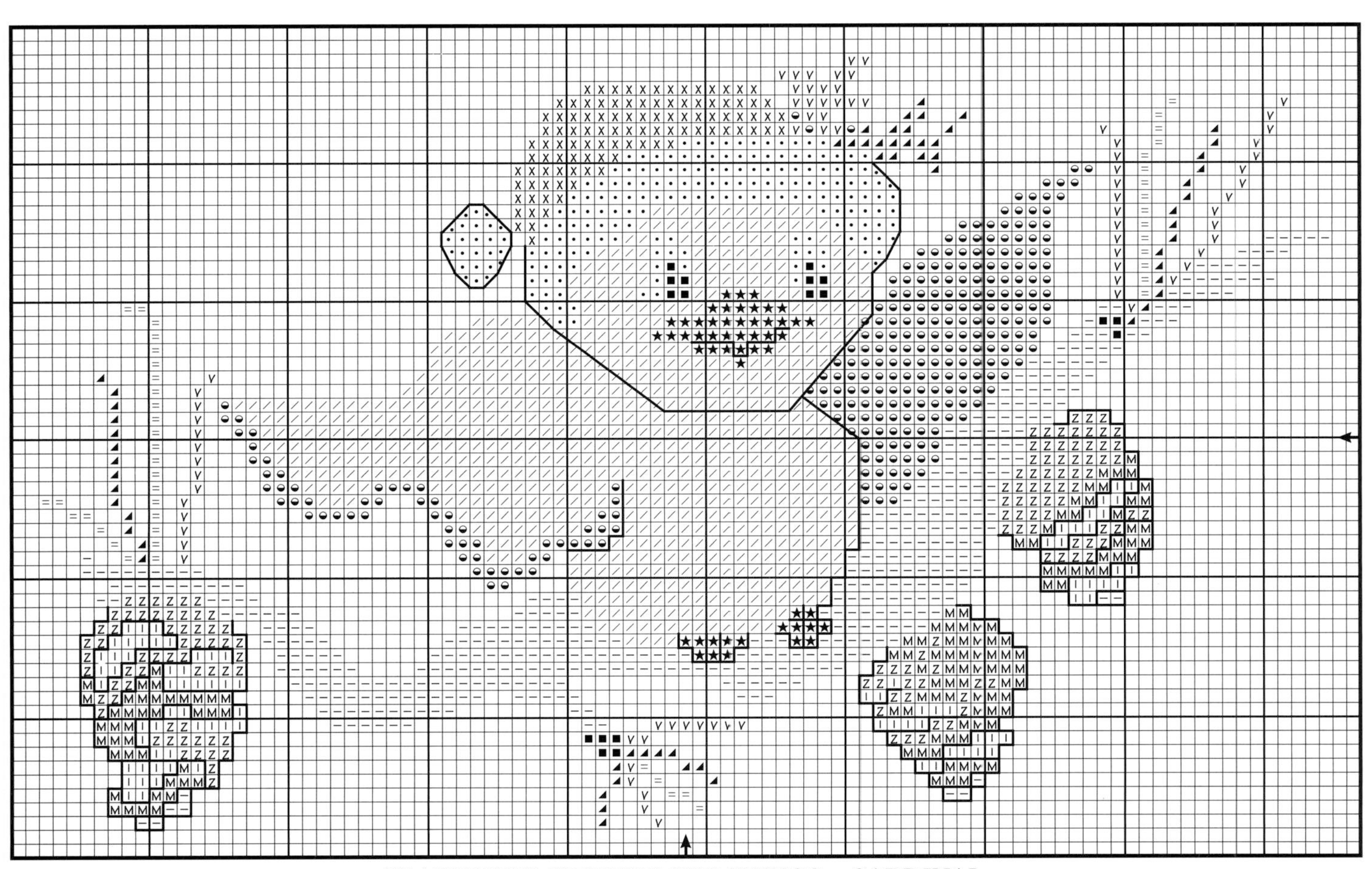

FEATHERED FRIENDS STOCKINGS—CARDINAL

HOME FOR CHRISTMAS PATTERNS

C

B

A

HOUSES

WINDOW

WINDOW

WINDOW

WINDOW

ROOFS B & C

CHIMNEY

DOOR

ROOF A

WINDOW

1 square = 1"

center of muslin. Machine appliqué house to muslin square.
2. Cut two 12½" x 2½" strips from green print and sew to top and bottom of appliquéd muslin square. Cut two 16½" x 2½" strips from green print and sew to sides of muslin square. Press.
3. Cut one 16½" square from batting and baste to wrong side of pillow front.
4. Cut two 16½" x 10" backing pieces from green print fabric. Hem one 16½" side of each piece, turning raw edges under ⅛" and ⅛" again. Lay backing pieces atop appliquéd front, placing wrong sides of fabric together and overlapping hems of backing pieces at center. Baste together close to edges.
5. Bind edges of pillow cover with bias tape, folding tape in half lengthwise and mitering at corners. Slip pillow form in opening in back.
Note: Pillow form can be removed for washing.

Tree Skirt
1. Mark tree-skirt pattern on muslin, referring to Skirt Layout Illustration for dimensions. **Do not cut out.**
2. Assemble three houses following instructions for wall hanging. Fuse houses to tree-skirt outline on muslin. Machine appliqué houses to muslin.
3. Cut one 44" square **each** from backing fabric and batting. Layer backing fabric right-side down, batting, and tree skirt right-side up atop a flat surface. Pin through all layers and machine baste along tree-skirt markings. Cut out skirt close to machine basting.
4. Bind tree skirt with bias tape, folding tape in half lengthwise and mitering at corners.
5. Cut green ribbon in half. Tack one length at each corner of inner circle where skirt splits to go around tree trunk. Machine quilt line between houses, using green thread and referring to photo for placement.

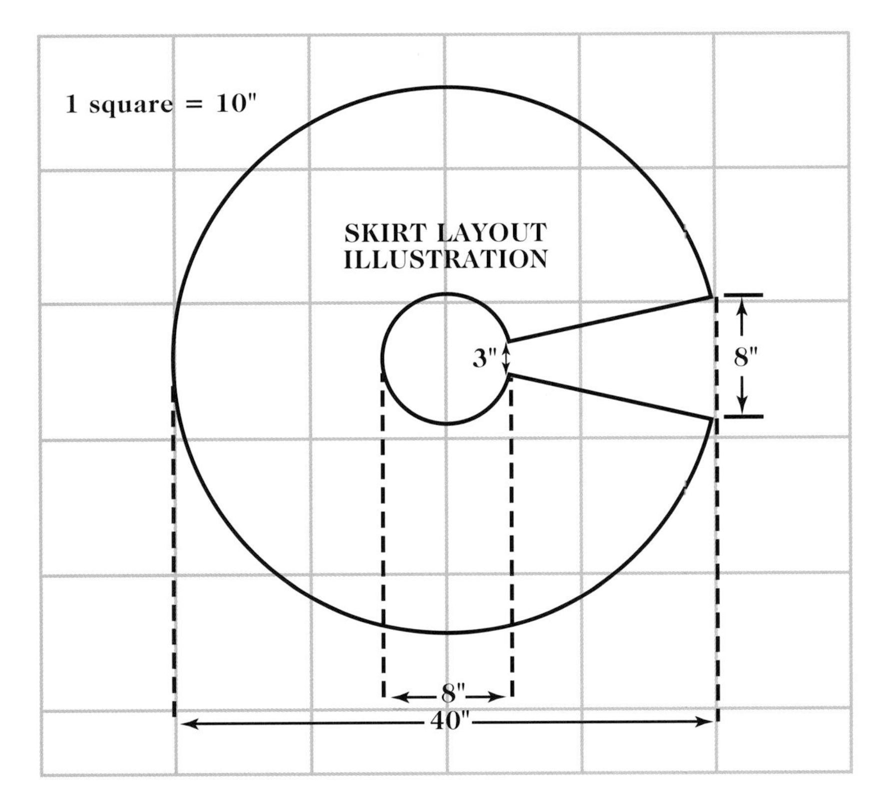

Pines in the Patches

Materials:
¼ yd. 44/45"-wide red solid fabric
¼ yd. 44/45"-wide light print fabric (for background)
¼ yd. **total** 44/45"-wide assorted green print fabrics
⅓ yd. 44/45"-wide green solid fabric (for outer border and binding)
¾ yd. 44/45"-wide complementary print fabric (for backing)
26" square lightweight quilt batting
Thread to match fabrics
White quilting thread
Plastic **or** tracing paper (for templates)
Mechanical pencil
Straight pins
Scissors
Sewing machine
Quilting needles (if hand quilting)
Safety pins (optional)

Finished Size: 24½" x 24½"
Note: Please read instructions carefully before beginning. Use ¼" seam allowances throughout.

1. Trace around patterns on plastic or tracing paper to make templates. Cut out.
2. To make pine-tree blocks, draw around templates on wrong side of fabric, using mechanical pencil for a narrow line and leaving ½" space between each piece. Adding ¼" seam allowances, cut fabric pieces as follows:
Template A: Cut four from light background print. Reverse template and cut four from light background print.
Template B: Cut four from assorted green prints.
Template C: Cut eight from assorted green prints.
Template D: Cut eight from light background print.
Template E: Cut four from red solid.
Sew two *C* pieces to one *B* piece to form tree. Then sew one *A* piece and one *A* piece reversed to sides of tree. Sew *D* pieces at opposite sides of *E* piece. Then sew this unit to bottom of tree to complete one pine-tree block. Make four pine-tree blocks.
3. To make nine-patch blocks, draw around *Template F* on wrong side of fabric, using mechanical pencil for a narrow line and leaving ½" space between each piece. Adding ¼" seam allowances, cut out 20 squares from light background print, 20 squares from assorted green prints, and 5 squares from red solid. Piece nine-patch blocks in three rows of three blocks each, referring to Quilt-Top Schematic. Make five nine-patch blocks.
4. To make quilt top, piece pine-tree and nine-patch blocks together, alternating blocks and referring to Quilt-Top Schematic for placement.
5. To make borders, cut four 1½" x 22" strips from red solid and four 2½" x 25" strips from green solid. Sew a red solid strip to each side of quilt, press borders out, and square up ends. Sew red solid strips to top and bottom of quilt, press borders out, and square up ends. Repeat for green solid strips, pressing borders out and squaring up corners on each side.
6. Layer backing fabric right-side down, batting, and assembled quilt top right-side up atop a flat surface. Safety pin or pin and baste through all layers.
7. Hand or machine quilt around each tree and as desired in a simple grid pattern over blocks. Remove pins. Square up edges of quilt.

8. To make binding, cut 2½"-wide strips from green solid and piece together for a length of at least 112". Fold strip in half lengthwise and pin around perimeter of quilt front, aligning raw edges. Sew binding to quilt. Remove pins. Turn binding to back of quilt and whipstitch in place.

9. Sign and date back of quilt if desired, using a permanent marking pen or embroidery. If you wish to hang your quilt for display, add a sleeve for a dowel or attach a curtain ring for hanging at each top corner.

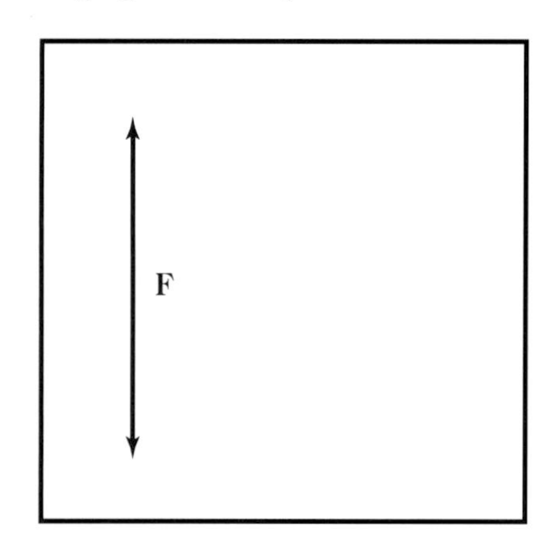

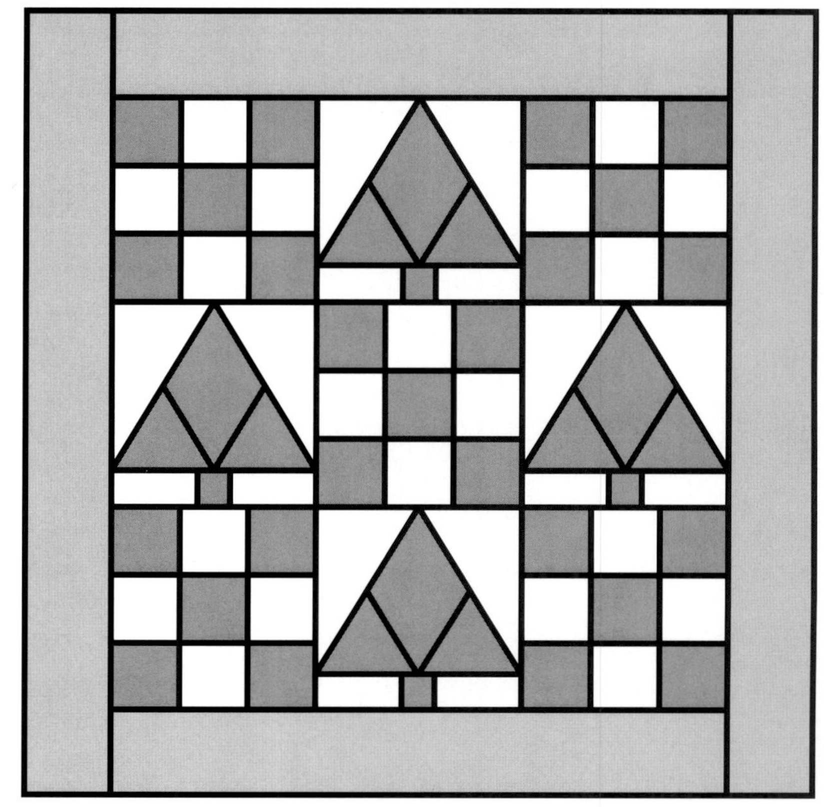

SETTING DIAGRAM

TEMPLATES
Seam allowances not included.

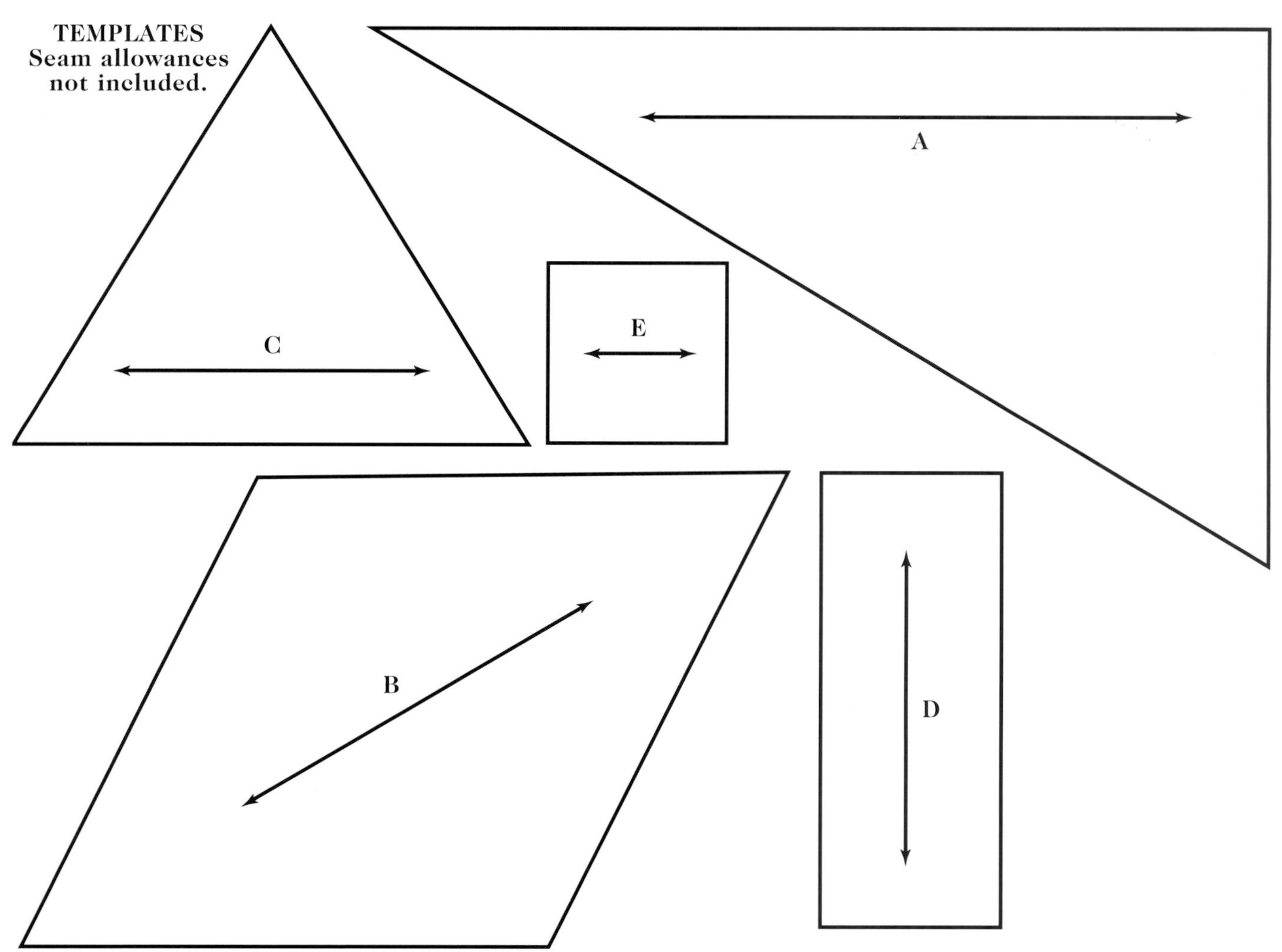

Real Reason Banner

Materials:
18" x 22" piece tan linen fabric
18" x 22" piece muslin
18" x 22" piece Pellon® Fleece
10" x 12" piece Pellon® Wonder-Under® Transfer Web
10" x 12" piece burgundy Doe Suede™ **or** felt
3" square gold tissue lamé
3¼ yds. ¾"-wide double-fold quilt binding to match burgundy fabric
Thread to match binding
Wide ruler
Straight pins
Scissors
Iron
Sewing machine (optional)

1. Enlarge pattern pieces as indicated. Trace patterns onto paper side of Wonder-Under® and cut out. Fuse Wonder-Under® letters, larger star, and tree base to wrong side of burgundy fabric, following manufacturer's instructions for fusing. (**Note:** Place letter patterns right-side up—as they are shown—on paper side of fusible web. Letters will appear backward on fusible web. This is correct, and letters should be used with their right sides up as the process for fusing will reverse the fabric designs from the way they appear on the paper patterns.) Fuse small star to gold lamé. Cut out all pieces. Fuse gold lamé star to center of burgundy star.
2. Layer muslin right-side down, fleece, and linen right-side up atop a flat surface. Find horizontal and vertical center of linen with ruler and mark with straight pins. Place letters on linen, leaving ¾" between rows of letters and approximately ⅝" between letters in each word, referring to photo on page 15 for placement. Center burgundy star at top of word tree and center tree base below *CHRIST* on word tree. Fuse letters, star, and tree base to linen.
3. Pin binding to edges and machine- or hand-sew binding to banner, mitering corners as you sew. Cut four 5"-long pieces from binding. Sew open edge of binding closed. Fold pieces in half to form hanging tabs, folding raw edges to inside. Sew tabs to back of banner at binding, referring to photo for placement.

Joy Wall Hanging

Materials:
14" x 18" piece white broadcloth fabric
17" x 21" piece red-and-white pindot fabric (for backing and binding)
6" x 12" piece light blue gingham fabric (for wings)
7" x 9" piece holiday-print fabric (for dress)
10" x 12" piece green print fabric, different than that used for dress (for sleeves and letters)
Small scrap pale pink fabric (for hands and face)
Small scrap medium pink fabric (for cheeks)
Small scrap bright yellow fabric (for halo)
Small scrap brown print fabric (for hair)
Thread to match fabrics
Embroidery floss, colors: red, blue
15" x 19" piece polyester quilt batting
½ yd. Pellon® Wonder-Under® Transfer Web
12" length ½"–¾"-wide gathered lace
16" length ¼"–⅜"-diameter wood dowel
2 wood beads to fit dowel ends
24" length yarn **or** string (to suspend dowel)
Hand-sewing needle
Straight pins
Scissors
Iron
Sewing machine with zigzag stitch

Note: Please read instructions carefully before beginning.

1. Enlarge pattern pieces as indicated. Trace patterns onto paper side of Wonder-Under® and cut out. Fuse patterns to wrong side of appropriate fabrics, following manufacturer's instructions for fusing. (**Note:** Place letter patterns right-side up—as they are shown—on paper side of fusible web. Letters will appear backward on fusible web. This is correct, and letters should be used with their right sides up as the process for fusing will reverse the fabric designs from the way they appear on the paper patterns.) Cut out pieces along pattern lines.
2. Position letters and angel on white broadcloth rectangle, referring to photo on page 16 for placement and arranging pieces for angel in following order: wings, dress, halo, face, hair, cheeks, sleeves, and hands. By arranging in this order, pieces will overlap each other as needed for this design. Before ironing pieces in place, insert a length of lace, cut to fit, under the chin to form neck edge of dress, and another under hem edge of dress. (**Note:** If halo or top of dress shows through face fabric, cut a second face piece from pink fabric and fuse to wrong side of face piece with features, using Wonder-Under®). Fuse all pieces in place, following manufacturer's instructions for fusing.
3. Satin stitch eyes using three strands of blue floss and backstitch mouth using three strands of red floss, referring to photo for placement.
4. Place backing fabric right-side down atop a flat surface. Center and layer batting and assembled quilt top right-side up atop backing. (**Note:** Backing fabric will extend 1½" beyond batting and front piece around perimeter of wall hanging.) Pin or baste layers together.
5. Machine appliqué around raw edges of letters and angel, using matching thread and a medium-width, closely spaced satin stitch. Straight stitch line between hands, as indicated on pattern.
6. Trim excess batting to within ½" of appliquéd front on sides and bottom of piece. Cut top edge of batting even with top edge of appliquéd front. This will remove extra bulk from casing, which will hold dowel.
7. Fold edges of backing to front, turning raw edges under ¼" and pinning to make an even edge. Machine topstitch along length of sides, close to folded edge of backing fabric. Repeat for top and bottom edges of backing, leaving ends open on top edge to form a casing.
8. Slip dowel through casing. Tie yarn or string to both ends of dowel. Slide wood bead over each end of dowel. Do not glue. This will allow for easy removal of dowel for washing wall hanging.

REAL REASON BANNER PATTERNS
1 square = 1"
I
JOY
LOVE
PEACE
CHRIST

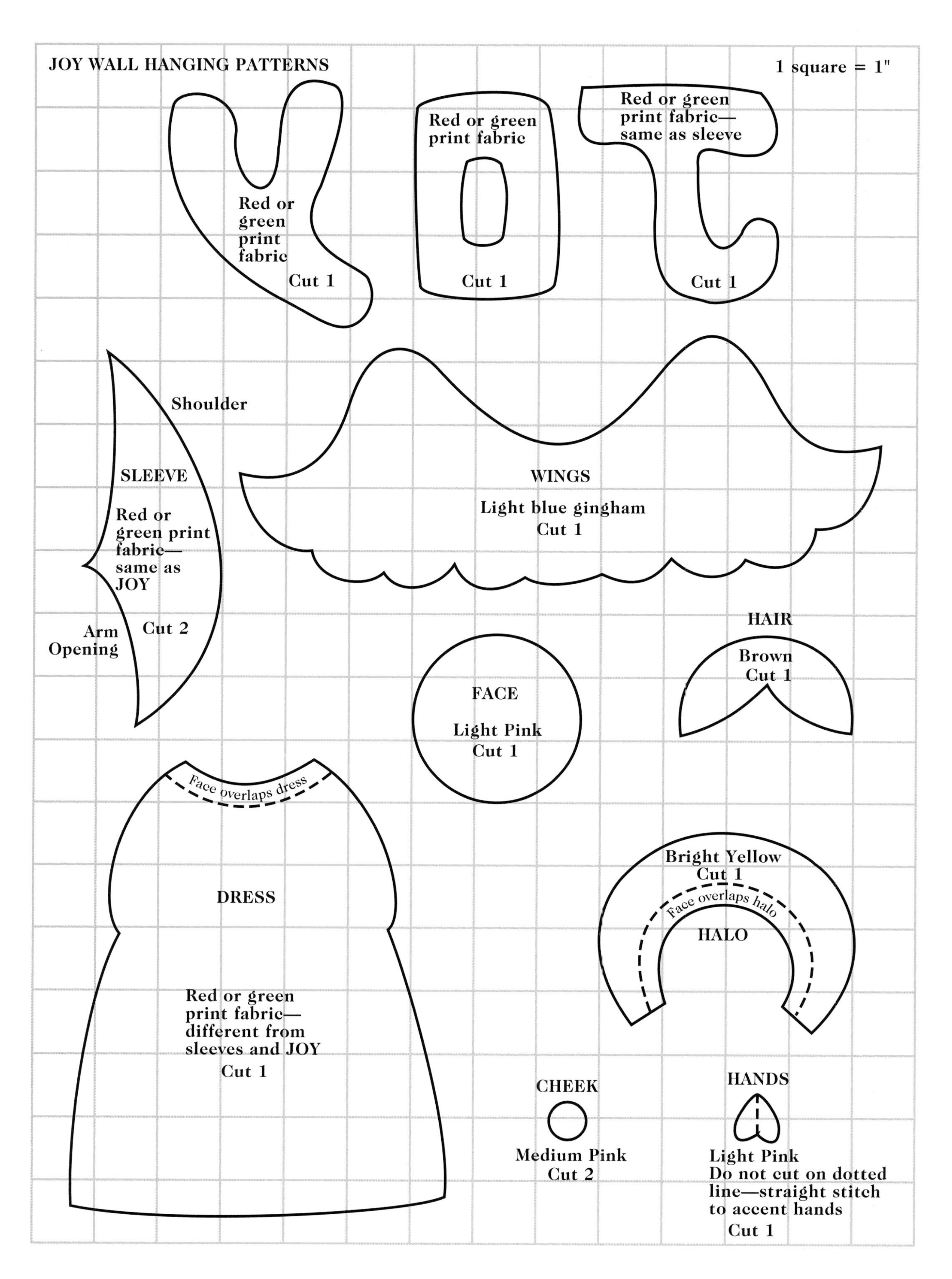
JOY WALL HANGING PATTERNS
1 square = 1"
Red or green print fabric
Cut 1
Red or green print fabric
Cut 1
Red or green print fabric—same as sleeve
Cut 1
Shoulder
SLEEVE
Red or green print fabric—same as JOY
Cut 2
Arm Opening
WINGS
Light blue gingham
Cut 1
HAIR
Brown
Cut 1
FACE
Light Pink
Cut 1
Face overlaps dress
DRESS
Red or green print fabric—different from sleeves and JOY
Cut 1
Bright Yellow
Cut 1
Face overlaps halo
HALO
CHEEK
Medium Pink
Cut 2
HANDS
Light Pink
Do not cut on dotted line—straight stitch to accent hands
Cut 1

Bells & Trees Wall Hanging

Crochet Abbreviations
beg—begin(ning)
bet—between
bhdc—backward half double crochet
bo—bind off
ch—chain stitch
k—knit
lp(s)—loop(s)
MC—main color
nxt—next
p—purl
rep(s)—repeat(s)
rem(s)—remain(s)
rs—right side
sc—single crochet
sk—skip
sl st—slip stitch
st(s)—stitch(es)
tog—together
yo—yarn over

Materials:
Coats & Clark Red Heart Super Sport Yarn, Art E. 271, colors: White #001 (MC) (4 skeins), Peacock Green #508 (A) (2 skeins), Jockey Red #904 (B) (1 skein, divided into 2 balls), Vermillion #918 (C) (1 skein), Yellow #230 (D) (1 skein), Coffee #366 (E) (1 skein)
Size I afghan hook **or** size needed to obtain gauge
Size G crochet hook (for edging)

Gauge: 5 sts and 4 rows = 1 inch
Finished size: 30" x 38"

Basic Afghan St (k):
Row 1—First Half: Working on underside of ch and retaining lps on hook, pick up lp in 2nd ch from hook and in each ch to end.
Row 1 (and all rows)—2nd half: Yo, draw through first lp on hook *yo draw through 2 lps on hook, rep from * to end. One lp rems on hook. This is first lp of nxt row.
Row 2—First Half: Working through vertical bars and retaining lps on hook, draw lp through 2nd bar and through each bar to end.
Purl (p)—First Half: Working on given number of sts, hold yarn in front of work with thumb, insert hook through vertical bar and draw lp through, release yarn and tighten.
Loop St (ls): P nxt st, holding yarn in front of work with thumb, p same st, release yarn and tighten until approximately ½" lp rems, yo draw through 2 lps on hook, work nxt st then pull yarn to tighten both sts.
Bobble: With color as instructed and taking care not to draw lps too tight, draw lp through bar (yo, draw lp through same bar) 2 times, draw MC through 5 lps on hook.

Afghan
Note: Directions and charts are written for First Half of row. Second half is always the same and should be worked as given in basic instructions. When changing colors, pick up new yarn under old yarn to avoid holes. When changing colors on second half of row, draw new color through last lp of old color and first lp of new color. When carrying yarn across back of work, take care not to pull yarn too tight. When working charts, **do not** carry yarn over more than 5 sts. Attach new yarn.
Panels 1, 3, & 5: Leaving end long enough to sew panels (approximately 40"), with MC, ch 31.
Row 1: Working on underside of ch, work afghan st Row 1 (k).
Seed St—Note: First and last st are always k.
Row 2: *P 1, k 1, rep from * to end.
Row 3: *K 1, p 1, rep from * ending k 1.
Row 4: Rep Row 2.
Row 5: (K 1, p 1) 2 times, k to last 5 sts, (p 1, k 1) 2 times, k last st.
Rows 6–26: Keeping 6 edge sts in seed st as established, work Chart I over center 19 sts.
Rows 27 & 28: With MC, seed st 5 sts, k 19 sts seed st 5 sts, k last st.
Rows 29–31: Work seed st across row.
Row 32: P.
Row 33: K.
Rows 34–60: Work Chart II.
Rows 61 & 62: With MC, k.
Row 63: P.
Rep from Row 2 until 3rd rep of Chart I is completed, ending with Row 31. Bo (draw lp through bar and lp on hook).
Panels 2 & 4: Leaving end (approximately 40"), with MC, ch 32.
Row 1: Working on underside of ch, work afghan st Row 1.
Beg with Row 33, work same as Panel 1 through Row 63, then beg with Row 2 work same as Panel 1 until 3 reps of Chart II are complete. Work Rows 61 and 62. Bo.
Finishing: Draw in all ends. Sew Panels tog as follows: 1, 2, 3, 4, 5.

CHART I

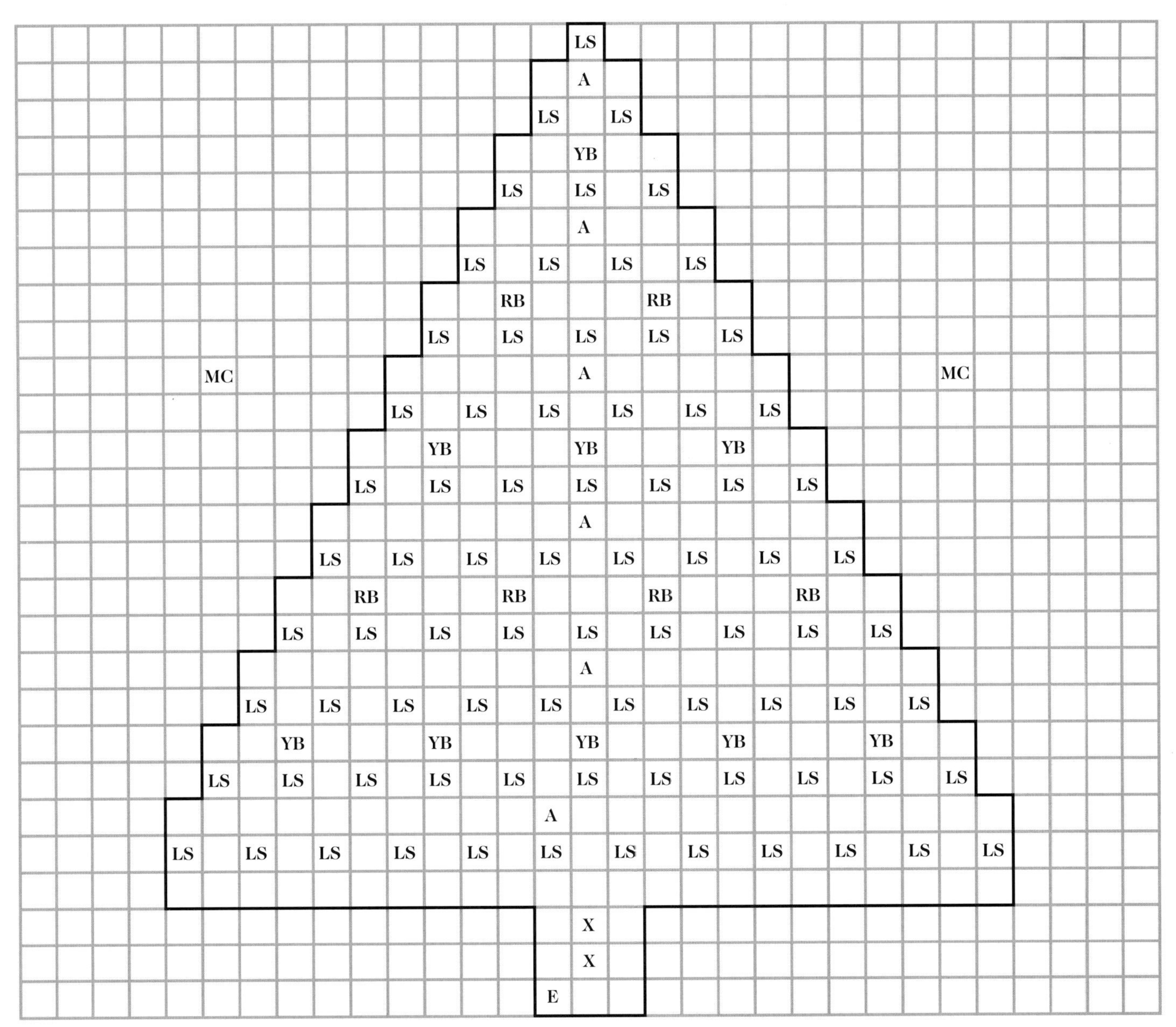

CHART II

Edging—Row 1: With rs of work facing, MC and G hook, beg in first st of bottom row edge, work 2 sc in first st (corner st), *sk nxt st, sc in nxt st, rep from *, ending 2 sc in last st, 2 sc in edge of first row [last 2 sts are corner sts, *sk nxt row, sc in nxt row, rep from *, ending 2 sc in last row], rep bet [ ] once, join with a sl st. **Do not turn.**

Row 2: Working from left to right, yo, insert hook in first st to right of hook, draw lp through, yo, draw through 3 lps on hook (backward half double crochet made-bhdc), ch 1, *bhdc in nxt sc, ch 1, sk nxt sc, rep from * around, working 1 bhdc in each of 4 corner sc. Join with a sl st. Fasten off. Wet block.

CHART SYMBOLS

X = P st

LS = Loop st (worked with A)

YB = Yellow Bobble

RB = Red Bobble

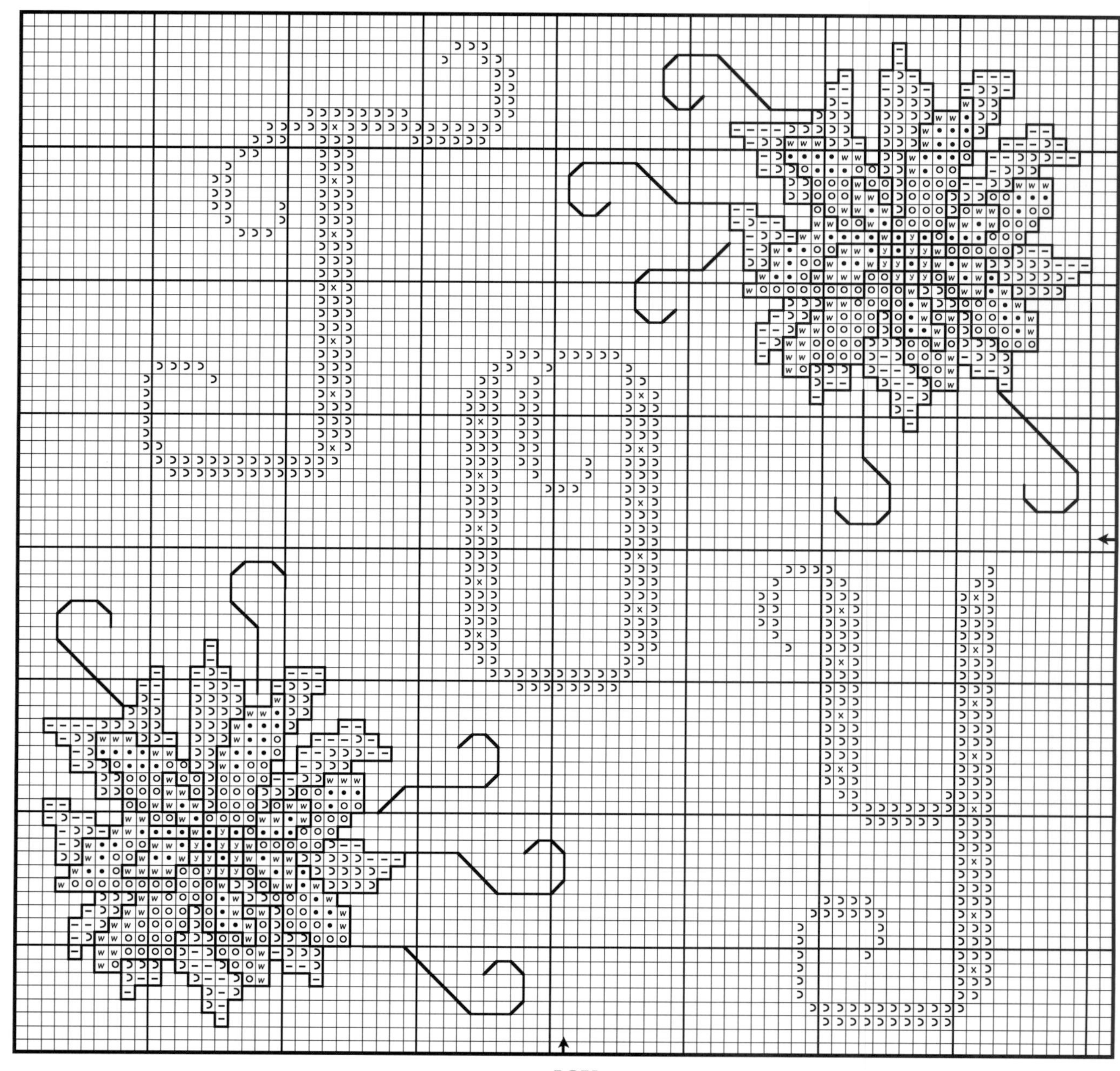
JOY

Joy and Noel Pillows

Joy Pillow

	DMC	Color
w	815	garnet, med.
○	304	red, med.
●	321	red
ɔ	699	green
–	700	green, bt.
y	727	topaz, vy. lt.
x	white	white
bs	783	gold

Fabric: 14-count white Aida
Stitch count: 74H x 78W
Design size:

14-count	5⅜" x 5⅝"
18-count	4⅛" x 4⅜"
20-count	3¾" x 4"
22-count	3⅜" x 3½"

Instructions: Cross stitch using two strands of floss. Backstitch using two strands of floss.

Backstitch (bs) instructions:

783	leaves, poinsettia petals, center of poinsettias
321	tendrils next to poinsettias

Noel Pillow

	DMC	Color
●	666	red
○	699	green
–	700	green, bt.
x	white	white
bs	783	gold

Fabric: 32-count white Jobelan from Wichelt Imports, Inc.
Stitch count: 81H x 77W
Design size:

12-count	6¾" x 6½"
14-count	5⅞" x 5½"
18-count	4½" x 4⅜"
32-count	5" x 4⅞"

Instructions: Cross stitch over two threads, using two strands of floss. Backstitch (bs) using one strand 783.

Materials:
¼ yd. 44/45"-wide red Christmas-print fabric (for *Noel* pillow)
⅓ yd. 44/45"-wide green Christmas-print fabric (for *Joy* pillow)
1 yd. ⅜"-wide white lace trim (for *Noel* pillow)
1 yd. ⅜"-wide white lace trim (for *Joy* pillow)
Thread to match fabrics
Polyester filling
Disappearing-ink fabric-marking pen
Measuring tape

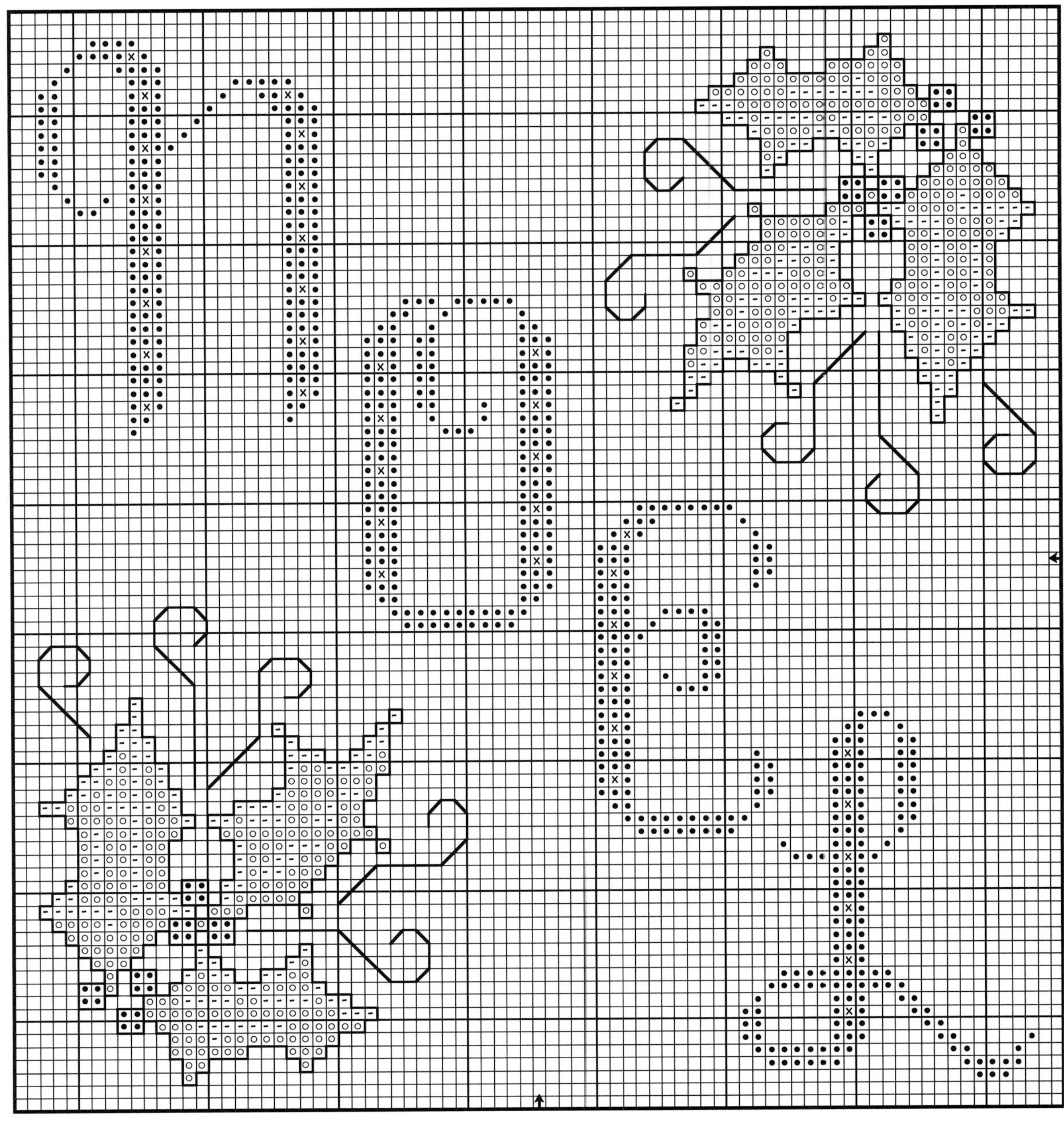

NOEL

Straight pins
Needle
Scissors
Sewing machine
Iron

1. Complete cross stitch following instructions given.
2. For *Noel Pillow*, cut one 6½" x 6¾" square from red print for pillow back. Cut 4"-wide strips from red print and piece together to make a 72"-long strip for ruffle. For *Joy Pillow*, cut one 7½" x 7" piece from green print for pillow back. Cut 4½"-wide strips from green print and piece together to make a 72"-long strip for ruffle. Set aside.
3. Mark perimeter of *Noel Pillow* front, using disappearing-ink fabric-marking pen and following "tracks" of fabric to achieve straight lines. Mark top and bottom ¼" away from upper and lowermost stitches of holly leaves, respectively. Mark sides ⅜" away from widest points of gold, backstitched tendrils. Repeat for *Joy Pillow*, marking top and bottom ⅜" away from upper and lowermost stitches of poinsettia leaves, respectively. Mark sides ½" away from widest points of red, backstitched tendrils. Trim each pillow front to ½" from perimeter lines.
4. For each pillow, baste lace trim around perimeter of pillow front, using perimeter lines as a placement guide and placing right sides of trim and fabric together and raw edge of trim toward raw edge of cross-stitch fabric. Set aside.
5. For each pillow, fold ruffle strip in half lengthwise and press. Sew one gathering thread along raw-edge side of strip ⅜" in from edge of fabric and another ¼" in from edge of fabric. Pull threads to gather ruffle and place ruffle around pillow, adjusting fullness as needed. Pin ruffle around perimeter of pillow front, placing right sides of fabric together and aligning raw edges. Sew ruffle to pillow front, using a ½" seam allowance and being careful not to catch trim.
6. To finish each pillow, pin pillow front to back, placing right sides of fabric together. Sew around perimeter along stitching line, leaving an opening at bottom of pillow for turning. Remove pins. Trim seams, clip corners, and turn. Stuff pillow with polyester filling. Whipstitch opening closed.
Option: Tack ribbon of your choice to back of pillow for hanging.

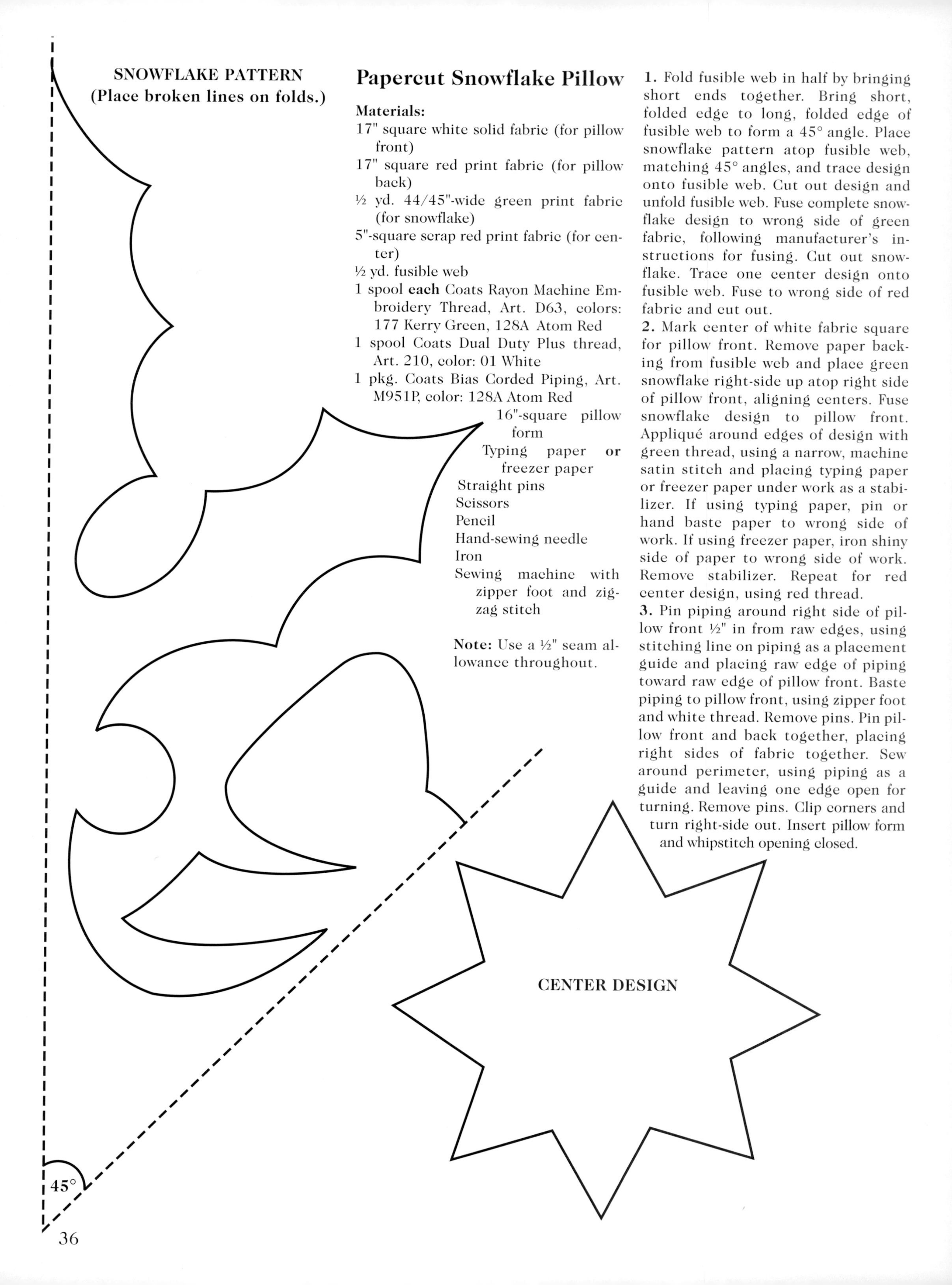

Papercut Snowflake Pillow

Materials:

17" square white solid fabric (for pillow front)
17" square red print fabric (for pillow back)
½ yd. 44/45"-wide green print fabric (for snowflake)
5"-square scrap red print fabric (for center)
½ yd. fusible web
1 spool **each** Coats Rayon Machine Embroidery Thread, Art. D63, colors: 177 Kerry Green, 128A Atom Red
1 spool Coats Dual Duty Plus thread, Art. 210, color: 01 White
1 pkg. Coats Bias Corded Piping, Art. M951P, color: 128A Atom Red
16"-square pillow form
Typing paper **or** freezer paper
Straight pins
Scissors
Pencil
Hand-sewing needle
Iron
Sewing machine with zipper foot and zigzag stitch

Note: Use a ½" seam allowance throughout.

1. Fold fusible web in half by bringing short ends together. Bring short, folded edge to long, folded edge of fusible web to form a 45° angle. Place snowflake pattern atop fusible web, matching 45° angles, and trace design onto fusible web. Cut out design and unfold fusible web. Fuse complete snowflake design to wrong side of green fabric, following manufacturer's instructions for fusing. Cut out snowflake. Trace one center design onto fusible web. Fuse to wrong side of red fabric and cut out.

2. Mark center of white fabric square for pillow front. Remove paper backing from fusible web and place green snowflake right-side up atop right side of pillow front, aligning centers. Fuse snowflake design to pillow front. Appliqué around edges of design with green thread, using a narrow, machine satin stitch and placing typing paper or freezer paper under work as a stabilizer. If using typing paper, pin or hand baste paper to wrong side of work. If using freezer paper, iron shiny side of paper to wrong side of work. Remove stabilizer. Repeat for red center design, using red thread.

3. Pin piping around right side of pillow front ½" in from raw edges, using stitching line on piping as a placement guide and placing raw edge of piping toward raw edge of pillow front. Baste piping to pillow front, using zipper foot and white thread. Remove pins. Pin pillow front and back together, placing right sides of fabric together. Sew around perimeter, using piping as a guide and leaving one edge open for turning. Remove pins. Clip corners and turn right-side out. Insert pillow form and whipstitch opening closed.

Christmas Tree Pillow

Materials:
9" x 12" scrap green felt
Two 13½" squares red felt
12"-square pillow form
4 green cotton tassels
Straight pins
Scissors
Thread, colors: white, metallic gold, green, red
Hand-sewing needle
20 small flowers cut from lace trim
1 pkg. pearl beads, assorted sizes
Sewing machine

1. Enlarge tree pattern as indicated. Trace tree pattern onto green felt and cut out. Center felt tree atop one red felt square. Pin. Hand-sew around tree ⅛" in from edge, using green thread. Pin flowers to tree, arranging as desired. Tack flowers to tree, using white thread. Remove pins.
2. Sew small and medium-sized pearl beads to tree between flowers, using white thread.
3. Trace outline of basket at bottom of tree. Fill in basket area with long and short horizontal satin stitches, using metallic gold thread. Work French knots in center of flowers and between flowers and pearls on tree, using a doubled strand of metallic gold thread. Referring to photo on page 20, sew an eight-pointed star at top of tree, using gold metallic thread, extending top, bottom, and side points, and making small, crisscross stitches between long stitches.
4. Sew medium-sized pearl to center of star, using white thread.
5. Place red felt squares with right sides together, aligning edges. Sew along three sides, using a ¼" seam allowance. Clip corners and turn right-side out. Insert pillow form and whip- stitch opening closed, turning felt edges under as you stitch. Tack a tassel at each corner of pillow, using red thread.

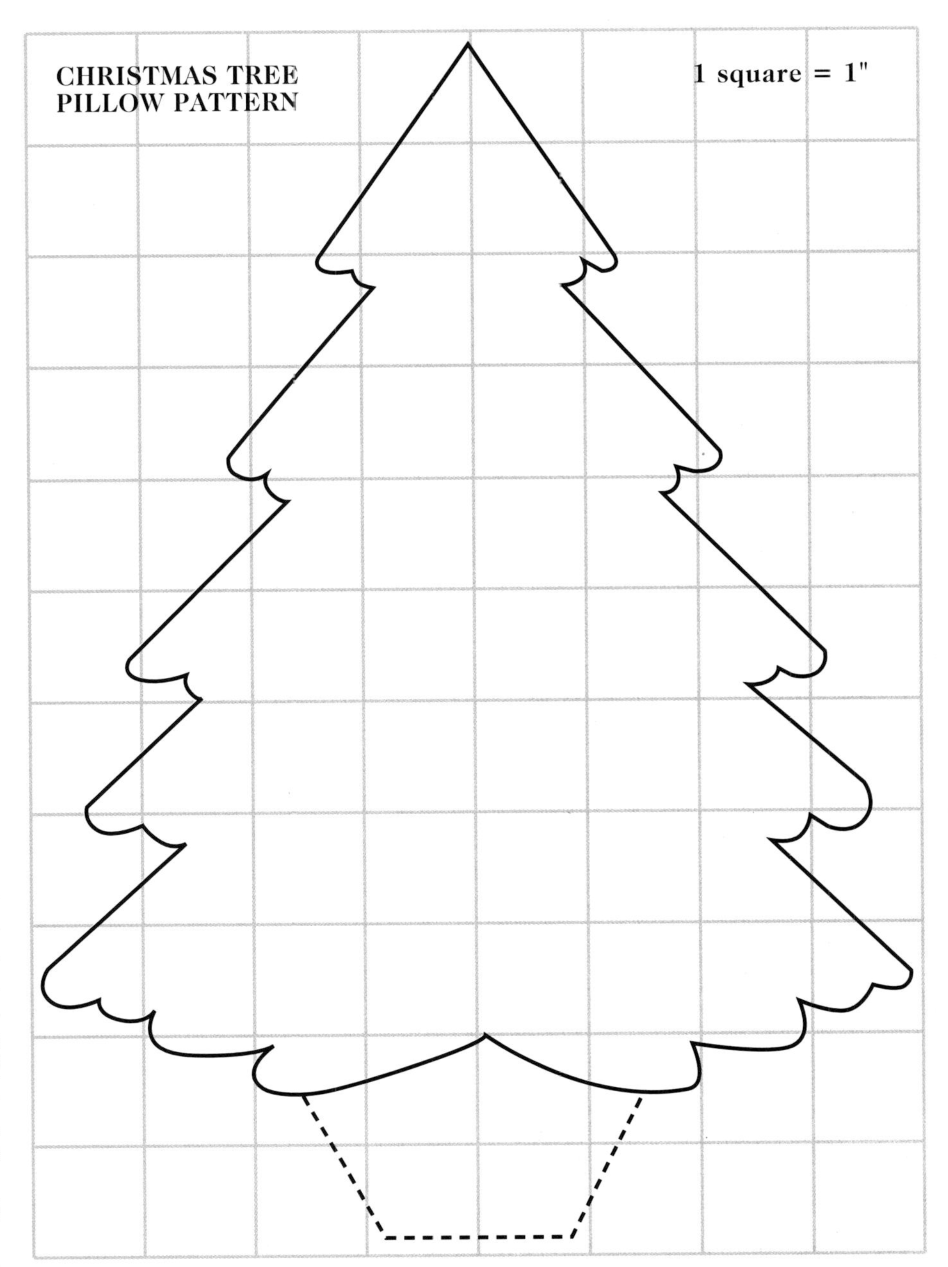

Golden Angels and Kings

Materials:

1 yd. 44/45"-wide unbleached muslin, washed, ironed, cut into four 16" squares (for pillow fronts and backs)
⅓ yd. 44/45"-wide gold lamé
DecoArt™ Americana metallic acrylic paint, color: glorious gold
Kreinik Japan Thread #1, color: gold
Two 12"-square pillow forms
Two 16" squares thin quilt batting
3½ yds. ⅝"-wide cording
Freezer paper (for stencils)
Stencil brush **or** sponge
Palette **or** old plate
Scissors: very fine paper-cutting, sewing
Paper towels
Straight pins
Hand-sewing needle
Iron
Sewing machine with zipper foot

Note: Materials listed will make one *Golden Angels* pillow and one *Golden Kings* pillow. These are intricate stencils to cut, and freezer paper is much easier to cut than stencil plastic. It adheres to muslin and works well for these designs. Americana glorious gold paint used is colorfast on muslin. To use another color or brand of acrylic paint, mix textile medium with color so that it will be permanent on fabric.

1. Enlarge patterns as indicated. Trace onto paper side of freezer paper.
2. Cut away shaded stencil shapes, leaving 2½" of freezer-paper border around all sides. Iron angel shapes on one muslin square and king shapes on another, placing freezer paper shiny-side down and leaving paper around edges as border.
Note: Angels and kings will not be stenciled; background will be stenciled gold.
3. Squeeze gold paint onto palette and spread out. Dip stencil brush or

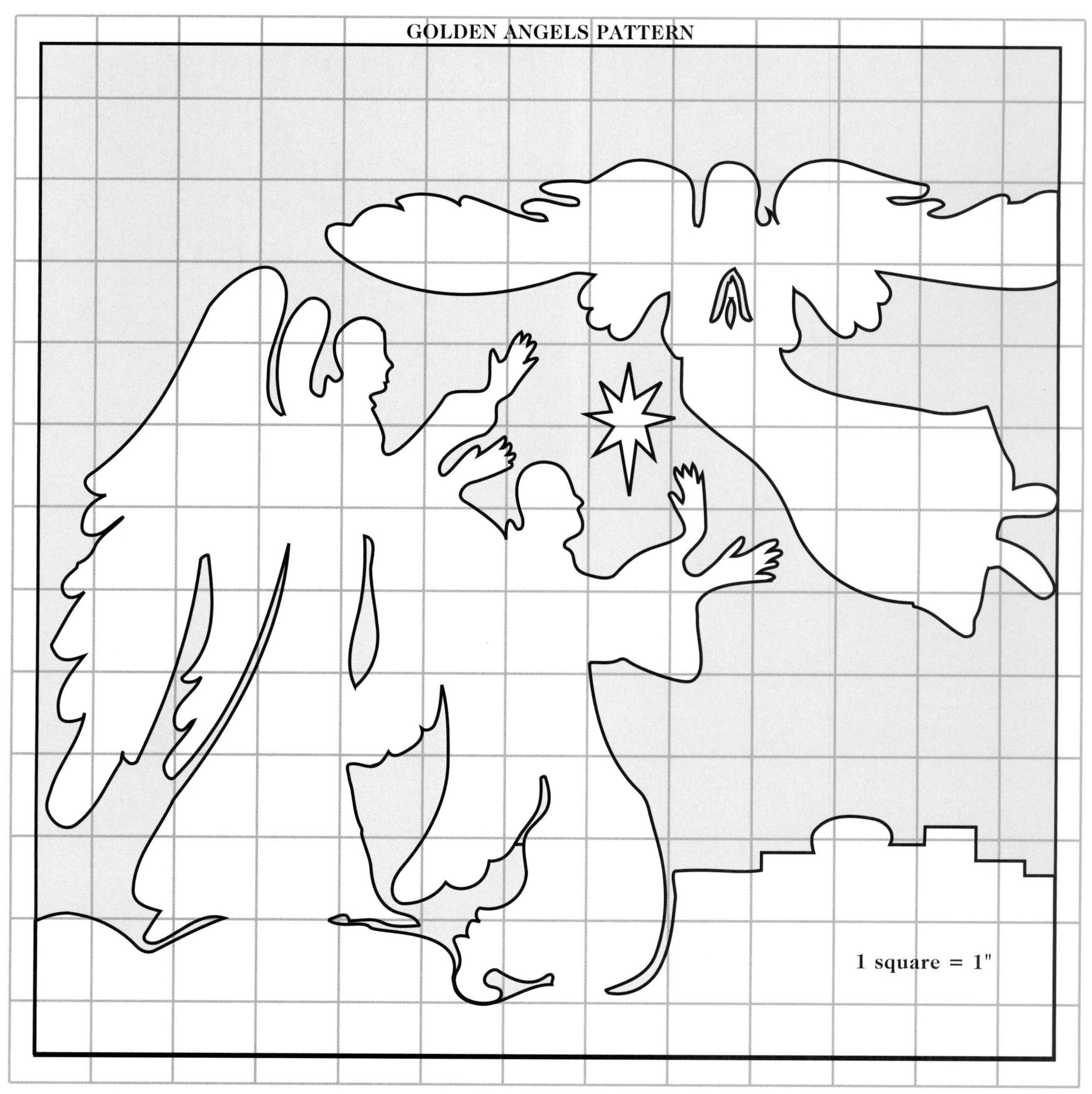

sponge in paint and blot excess on paper towel. Test on muslin scrap. (**Note:** Brush or sponge should be almost dry—two thin layers of color are better than one thick layer.) Stencil over cut area of pattern. Let dry.

4. Carefully peel off freezer paper. Iron stenciled muslin between paper towels to set paint.

5. Place stenciled muslin square right-side-up atop batting and pin or baste together. Hand or machine quilt around all stenciled areas, including perimeter lines, using gold thread. Remove pins or basting thread. Set aside.

6. Cut lamé crosswise into four 3" x 44" strips. Piece strips together to measure 4¾ yds. for covering cording. Sew one end of cord to one end of lamé strip, centering cord on wrong side of fabric. Fold fabric strip around cord, placing wrong sides of fabric together and aligning raw edges. Pin fabric as needed to begin. Place cording under zipper foot with raw edges to the right. Machine stitch close to cord, being careful not to crowd cord. As you near end of cord, remove work from sewing machine, hold loose end of cord firmly, and push gold lamé toward stitched end to create a shirred effect. Place work in machine again and continue to end of gold lamé.

7. Place cording around perimeter of design, with raw edge of cording toward raw edge of muslin. Align stitching line on cording and perimeter line on pillow and sew together along stitching line, using zipper foot on sewing machine.

8. Pin pillow front to back, placing right sides of fabric together. Sew around perimeter along stitching line, leaving open at bottom. Remove pins. Trim seams, clip corners, and turn. Insert pillow form and whipstitch opening closed.

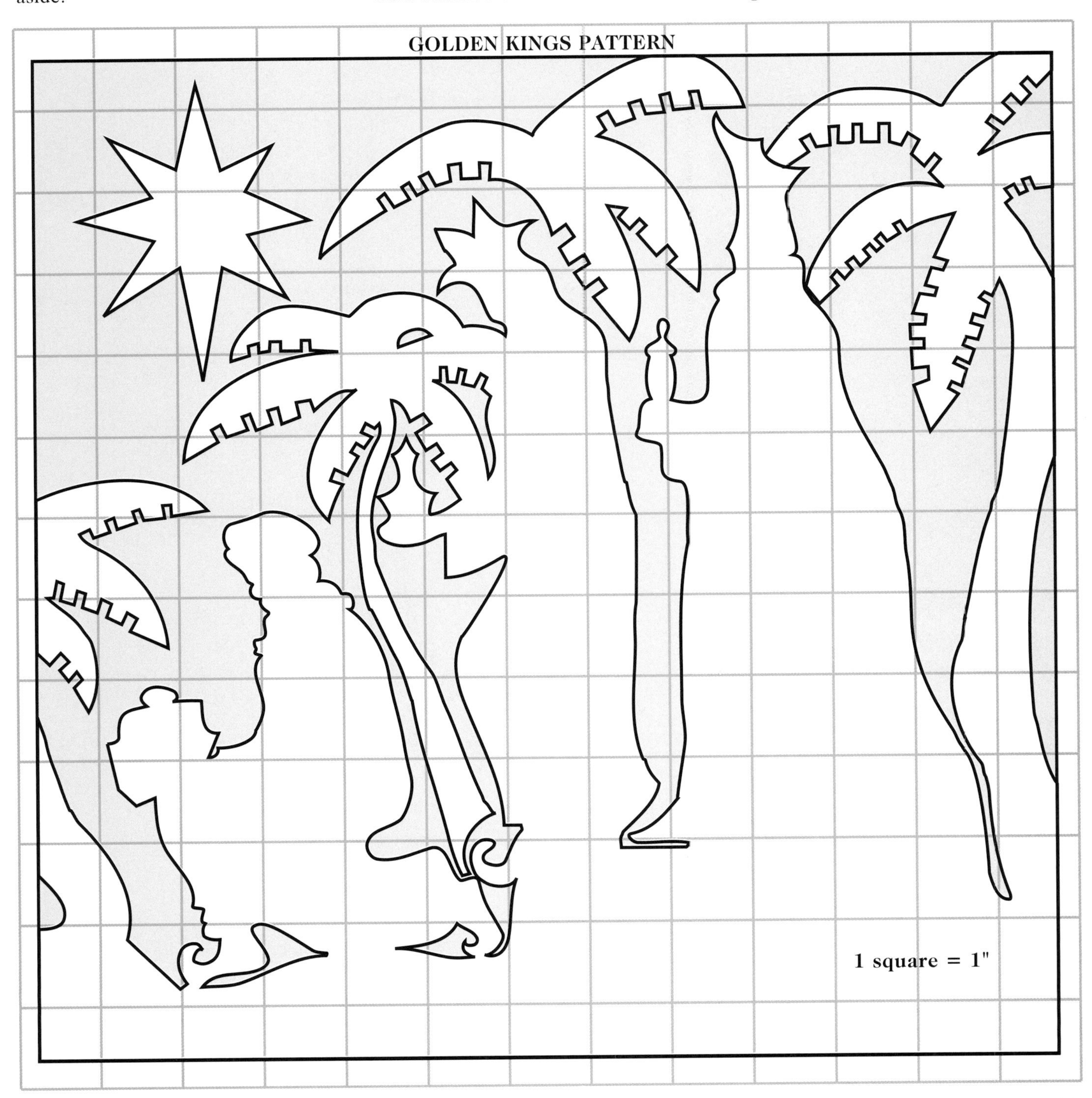

NEW!
Tough on Grease. Easy on Hands.
IVORY
FIMO
EBERHARD FABER
Delta
LIGHT CHOCOLATE
Glass Seed Beads
USA
Berol PRISMACOLOR
Magenta
PC 930
Magenta

CHRISTMAS FAVORITES

At a tender age, we learn the family Christmas rituals. We begin choosing treasured decorations and ornaments, which only we can hang upon the tree. Many of us also begin building holiday collections of favorite items such as teddy bears, music boxes, Santas, snowmen, or angels. Some collect seasonal china or crystal. Whatever your special collection is made of, you find pleasure each year searching for a wonderful new addition—especially one you can create with your own hands.

***Above**—Up on the housetop . . . that's where Santa has climbed, with a bag full of presents and a jolly expression, in this spirited design called* Down the Chimney. *Chart is on page 50.*

Sleighful of Santas

Hitch up the reindeer! We have a sleigh piled full of Santas, with something for every stitcher and crafter out there. You must know someone who collects unusual Santa Clauses and would love to add one of these delightful pieces to her treasure trove—or perhaps you have a fondness for Old Saint Nick yourself. Either way, this selection of four Kriss Kringles will bring Christmas joy to both the maker and the recipient of each project.

Every little girl or boy tries, at least once, to stay awake late enough to catch a glimpse of Santa Claus. But, little eyelids always droop in sleep before the jolly, white-bearded man appears. The cross-stitch design titled ***Down the Chimney***, shown at left, catches a traditionally dressed Santa just before he climbs into the chimney. The cross-stitch piece is wonderfully detailed, from the pretty border to the delicate snowflakes falling from the sky.

Remember the fun of playing with modeling clay in art class? The ***Clay Claus*** ornament, shown above right, is just as much fun to make. This whimsical ornament features candy-cane-striped trim on Santa's coat, pants, and hat; and white clay squiggles as his beard and mustache. This clay-crafted charmer will be certain to attract attention as it hangs from a tree branch or doorknob. And shaping and baking clay ornaments is fun for the whole family!

Our ***Wood-Burned Santa Egg***, shown on page 44, features an old-fashioned Saint Nicholas. The wood burning gives visual depth to the face of Santa and to the accents, a pine branch, a bag of toys, and the little sack of presents shown in the photos on page 53. Painted details—white beard, mustache, eyebrows, and fur trim of hat; red holly berries

Above*—Have fun molding and shaping* Clay Claus, *a whimsical ornament with cute details. Instructions are on page 51.*

and green holly leaves—add the finishing touches to this wonderful Father Christmas. Show off your creation by placing him on a mantel or coffee table, or with a display of other Santa Clauses.

Santa's blushing bride makes an appearance in the dynamic duo of ***Mr. & Mrs. Claus Ornaments***, shown below. Styrofoam® eggs serve as the foundation for this festive pair. Most of the necessary fabric for husband and wife can probably be found in your scrap basket, waiting to be put to good use. Mr. Claus' beard is made from white muslin that you fray to obtain a fuzzy look. The happy couple will add holiday cheer when suspended from the branches of your evergreen.

Above*—The lifelike* Wood-Burned Santa Egg *shows a traditional Saint Nicholas with painted details, plus a bag of toys and a pine branch (see photos on page 53). Instructions begin on page 52.*

Left*—With Styrofoam® eggs as their foundations, the* Mr. & Mrs. Claus Ornaments *make lightweight additions to your tree. Scraps of fabric will be enough for their faces and caps, and tidbits of assorted trims will complete their features. Instructions begin on page 51.*

Choir of Angels

Angels were present at the first Christmas, when they heralded the birth of the newborn King. Today they are a popular decorating motif during the holiday season. They can range from elegant to doll-like, but they always have happy, sweet faces and beautiful wings.

Our big-hearted ***Angel to Watch Over You***, shown below, hangs serenely above a mantel, with her calm, blue eyes and high forehead giving her a peaceful expression. Let her watch over your loved ones from above the fireplace or make her for a child's bedroom as a nighttime guardian angel. Chances are several folks on your gift list would love a quilted angel for Christmas.

Classic cross-stitch designs, ***Heirloom Christmas Angels***, shown on page 46, give pleasure twice—first as you stitch them and later when they grace the walls of your home. One angel is robed in blue and gold; the other in red and green with a lovely skirt-border pattern of bells. The angels' halos are golden and solid-looking, which is a style reminiscent of very early paintings of the heavenly creatures. These timeless designs are destined to be keepsakes that will be passed on to future generations.

Above—An Angel to Watch Over You *will be the perfect gift for almost anyone on your list. With her sweet face and her wings spread wide, she'll bring happiness and good thoughts to all. Instructions begin on page 57.*

Above—Heirloom Christmas Angels—*timeless cross-stitch designs—will add joy to your holiday decorating. Charts and color codes are on pages 54 and 55.*

This adorable *Recycled Bottle Angel*, shown with two of her friends, can be your decorative contribution to the recycling effort. Her dress, which will hide the empty dishwashing-detergent bottle beneath, is white, with gold-braid trim and lace edging. Use your sewing talents to make the dress; then get "crafty" to paint her pretty face on a wooden ball. Her angelic, strawberry-blonde curls are glued to her head, and her outstretched wings are cut from cardboard. Make certain your angel won't get "flighty," by placing sand in the bottom of the bottle.

Above*—Curly hair, painted features, and a white robe transform a dishwashing-detergent bottle into an adorable angel. Instructions for the* Recycled Bottle Angel *are on page 57.*

Animal Friends

Remember the animals at Christmastime. Scatter birdseed in the snow for the feathered friends who haven't flown south, purchase a special toy for a household pet, or adopt a lonely puppy or kitten from the local animal shelter. And while you're about it, take another step this year to remember our animal friends. Stitch and sew the projects featured on these pages, for yourself and as gifts.

The ***Folk-Art Bunnies Throw*** and ***Pillow***, shown below, serve a multitude of wintertime purposes. You can snuggle beneath the throw and prop your head on the pillow as you read a book, arrange them in a casually artistic manner on a wooden deacon's bench, or make them for a child's nap-time pillow and blanket. For the background of both pieces, choose a wool fabric that brings to mind cozy nights and cups of hot cocoa.

On the opposite page, a cross-stitched kitty shows her Christmas curiosity. The nosy tabby peers from her mantel perch into a stocking full of goodies. The bright-colored border of ***Christmas Curiosity***, with its pattern of trees and holly accented by beads, features the message, "Merry Christmas."

Opposite*—A curious, cross-stitched cat wears a red bow for a collar as she stares intently into a jam-packed stocking. Chart for* Christmas Curiosity *begins on page 60.*

Left*—Those who love the country look will undoubtedly "hop to it" and make the* Folk-Art Bunnies Throw *and* Pillow. *The rabbits, hearts, and leaves can be made from felt or Doe Suede™. Instructions begin on page 58.*

MERRY
CHRISTMAS

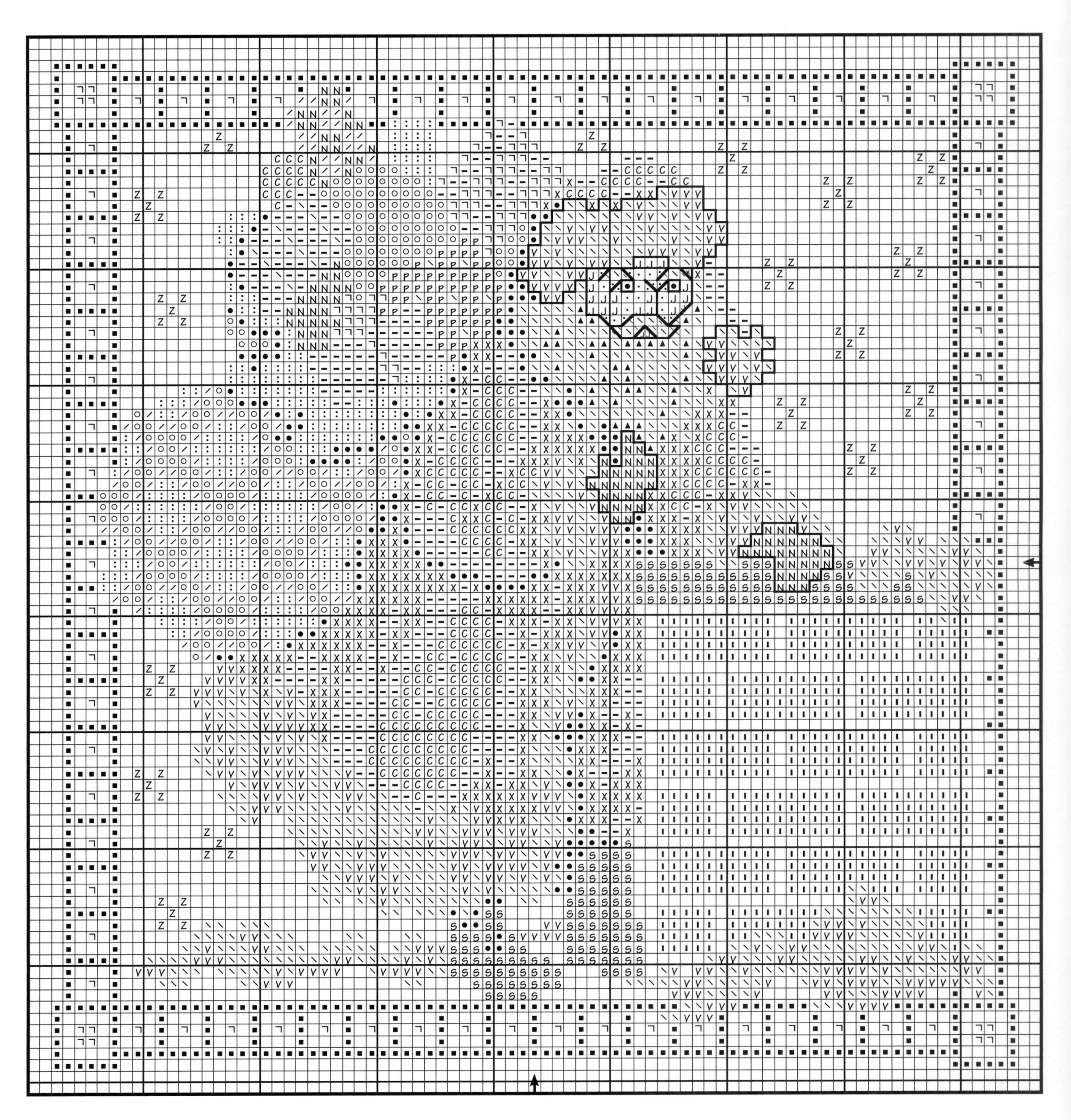

Down the Chimney

	DMC	Color
●	939	navy blue, vy. dk.
X	815	garnet, med.
−	321	red
C	3705	melon, dk.
·	754	peach flesh, lt.
J	352	coral, lt.
V	932	antique blue, lt.
▲	3024	brown gray, vy. lt.
\	white	white
S	414	steel gray, dk.
O	700	green, bt.
:	523	fern green, lt.
/	472	avocado green, ul lt.
¬	307	lemon
N	798	delft, dk.
P	807	peacock
Z	809	delft
▮	433	brown, med.
■	309	rose, dp.

Fabric: 14-count navy Aida from Zweigart®
Stitch count: 87H x 83W
Design size:

14-count	6¼" x 6"
16-count	5½" x 5⅛"
18-count	4⅞" x 4⅝"
22-count	4" x 3¾"

Instructions: Cross stitch using two strands of floss. Backstitch using two strands 939.

Clay Claus

Materials:

FIMO® polymer clay, colors: Carmine (1 oz.), flesh pink, turquoise, black, white (**each** less than 1 oz.) (**Note:** Clay is sold in 1- or 2-oz. pkgs.)
18" length DMC pearl cotton (coton perlé), color: 321
2 black seed beads (for eyes)
Aleene's Right-On gloss waterbase finish
Artist's paintbrush (for applying finish)
Old scissors **or** craft knife
Large needle
Cookie sheet
Rolling pin
Aluminum foil
Waxed paper

Note: Follow manufacturer's instructions when working with clay. Soften clay by warming it in your hands. Keep your hands clean, as clay attracts smudges. Clay will not dry out but should be stored away from sunlight.

1. Trace patterns onto waxed paper. Cut out. Cover a smooth surface with waxed paper. To roll out each clay color, place between two sheets of waxed paper and roll with rolling pin. (**Note:** Utensils and surfaces used for food preparation should not be allowed to come into contact with craft materials, including polymer clay.) Roll out Carmine clay to approximately 3/16" thick. Place body and leg patterns atop clay and cut out, using old scissors. Make pea-sized ball of flesh pink clay for face; pinch to flatten. Roll out turquoise clay to approximately 3/16" thick and cut out mittens. Roll out black clay to approximately 3/16" thick and cut out boots.

2. To make curlicues for trim, roll thin, white and Carmine clay ropes the size of a toothpick. Place one Carmine and one white rope side by side and twist together to form one striped rope for each cuff, each leg, hat, and top of ornament. To make curlicues for beard, roll out thin, white, clay ropes the size of a toothpick and shape into curls. Set aside.

3. Line cookie sheet with aluminum foil to prevent contact with clay. Place Claus' body atop aluminum foil and gently spread arms away from body. To assemble Claus, lightly press a mitten onto end of each arm and a boot onto straight end of each leg. Use needle to make holes in top of hat, in bottom of body, and in top (curved end) of each leg, referring to pattern pieces for placement. Set one beard curlicue aside. Place remaining beard curlicues atop body as indicated on pattern; then gently press on flesh pink face, letting chin overlap curls slightly. Place set-aside beard curlicue with rest of beard curlicues, using one end to form a mustache atop face. Press two seed beads into face for eyes. Press striped, curlique ropes on arms, legs, and body, as indicated on pattern pieces. Bake, following manufacturer's instructions, and let cool.

Note: Bake legs in two steps. Place curlicues on one side and bake, then repeat on other side. Generally, bake clay at 260–270°F for 20–30 minutes, having adequate ventilation to take away the "plastic" smell during baking. Clay must bake long enough for the minute grains of plastic to melt and fuse together. When cool, a properly baked piece will be hard and not pliable.

4. Coat Claus with three coats of gloss finish, using paintbrush and letting dry between each coat and after final coat. Thread a short length of pearl cotton (coton perlé) through hole in leg and hole in bottom of body. Tie a knot in thread ends to attach leg to body. Repeat for second leg. Thread a 10" length of pearl cotton (coton perlé) through holes at top of ornament and tie a knot in thread ends to form hanger.

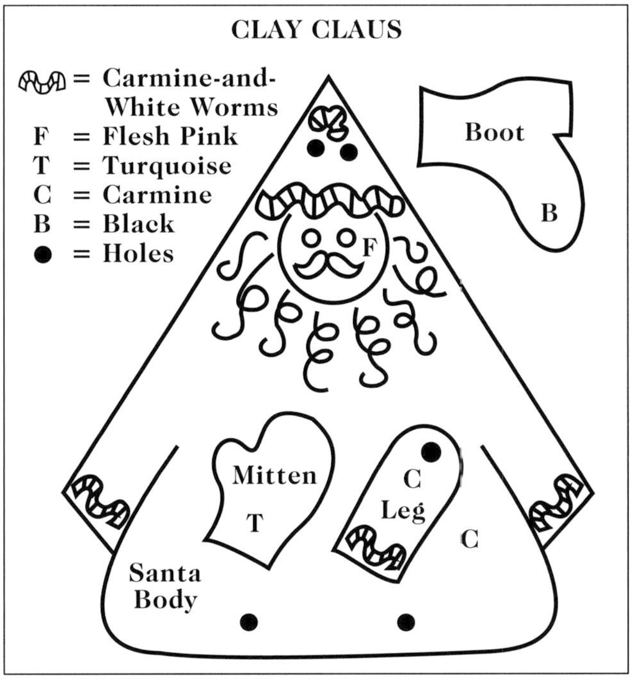

CLAY CLAUS

= **Carmine-and-White Worms**
F = Flesh Pink
T = Turquoise
C = Carmine
B = Black
● = Holes

Boot
B
F
Mitten
T
C
Leg
C
Santa Body

Mr. & Mrs. Claus Ornaments

Materials:

Two 2" x 2½" STYROFOAM brand plastic foam eggs
⅛ yd. 44/45"-wide pale pink cotton fabric
¼ yd. 44/45"-wide white cotton fabric
⅜" x 6¾" scrap white felt
6"-square red fabric (**Note:** Designer used knit velour fabric.)
Four 3mm black pom-poms
5mm red pom-pom
5mm pink pom-pom
½" white pom-pom
10"-length ¾"-wide white lace
17"-length ½"-wide white lace
6"-length ⅛"-wide red satin ribbon
18"-length green cotton crochet thread (for hangers)
Small, purchased holiday trim of your choice for Mrs. Claus' hat (**Note:** Designer use lacquered holly leaves with berries for model. If desired, leaves can be cut from a small scrap of green felt and 3mm red pom-poms can be used for berries.)
Darning needle
Aleene's Tacky Glue (for making glue-and-water mixture)
Aleene's Thick Designer Tacky Glue (for gluing parts of ornaments together)
Sewing thread, colors: red, white
Hand-sewing needle
Small handful of polyester filling
Toothpicks (for spreading glue)
Cup (for mixing glue and water)
Red fine-tip permanent marker
Pencil
Ruler
Scissors
Waxed paper
Powder blush
Cotton Swabs
Sewing machine (optional)

Note: Please read instructions carefully before beginning.

Covering the eggs:

1. Cut six ½"-wide strips from pale pink cotton fabric, cutting from selvage to selvage.

2. In cup, mix 1½ Tbsp. Aleene's Tacky Glue with 1½ Tbsp. water.

3. Soak pale pink fabric strips in glue-and-water mixture. Run strips between fingers to remove excess, letting excess drip back into cup.

4. Wrap three strips around one Styrofoam® egg, as if winding a ball of yarn. (**Note:** Hold egg with large end up and begin at top to wrap fabric strips vertically around egg.) Wrap remaining strips around second egg in same manner. Set wrapped eggs on waxed paper and let dry thoroughly before proceeding.

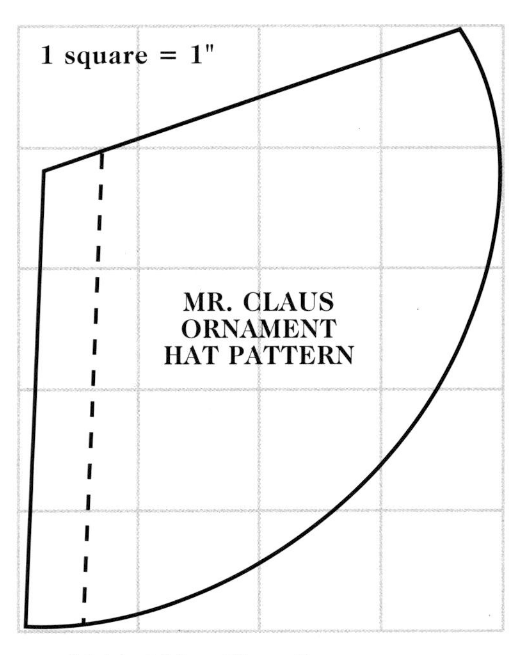

Making *Mrs. Claus Ornament*:
1. To make mobcap, cut one 5½"-diameter circle from white cotton fabric. Machine zigzag or hand-sew ½"-wide white lace around edge of cotton circle, using white thread. Hand gather approximately ¼" away from edge of lace, using doubled thread. Check cap for fit at top of egg, referring to photo on page 44 for placement. Adjust as needed and knot thread ends together to secure. Stuff mobcap with small handful of polyester filling.
2. Glue cap to large end of egg.
3. To make collar, gather 10" length of ¾"-wide white lace to measure 4½". Seam ends together and knot thread to secure. Glue to bottom of egg.
4. Tie red satin ribbon into a bow. Trim bow tails as desired and glue bow to center front of lace collar.
5. Glue two black pom-poms in place for eyes. Glue pink pom-pom in place for nose.
6. Glue holiday trim to mobcap, referring to photo for placement.

Making *Mr. Claus Ornament*:
1. To make beard, cut four 3" x 4½" rectangles from white cotton fabric. Place rectangles one atop the other, aligning edges, and machine- or hand-sew together along one 4½" edge, using white thread. Sew a second time for reinforcement. Cut at ¼" intervals to stitching line and roll between the palms of your hands to fray raw edges, or "frizz" beard. Glue beard to egg, referring to photo for placement.
2. To make Mr. Claus' hat, enlarge hat pattern as indicated. Cut out pattern. Lightly trace around pattern on wrong side of red fabric, using pencil. Cut out. Fold in half, placing right sides of fabric together, and sew, using a ½" seam allowance and red thread. Trim seam allowance to ⅛". Turn hat right-side out and glue to large end of egg, covering ends of beard. Glue white felt scrap around edge of hat for trim.
3. Glue two black pom-poms in place for eyes. Glue red pom-pom in place for nose.

Finishing the ornaments:
1. Freehand draw mouths on *Mr. & Mrs. Claus Ornaments*, using red permanent marker.
2. Apply powder blush to cheeks, using cotton swabs.
3. Cut cotton crochet thread in half and thread darning needle with one 9" length. Pass threaded needle through top of Mrs. Claus' mobcap. Remove needle from thread, bring thread ends together, and tie in a knot to form hanger. Thread darning needle with remaining length of cotton crochet thread and repeat for Mr. Claus, folding down tip of hat, and taking a stitch at top of hat through fold.
4. Glue folded-down tip of Mr. Claus' hat in place. Glue white pom-pom to tip of hat.

Wood-Burned Santa Egg

Materials:
3" x 5" wooden egg
Wood burner with cone point, shading point, and mini-flow point
¼ yd. 44/45"-wide very sheer organza fabric
Brown ultra-fine permanent marker **or** fabric marker
Berol Prismacolor pencils, colors: #938 white, #923 scarlet lake, #909 grass green
Acrylic sealer (**Note:** Designer used Illinois Bronze Simply Wonderful Wood Sealer and Finish.)
Paintbrush (for applying sealer)
Pencil sharpener
Masking tape
Scissors

Note: The three patterns are applied evenly around the surface of the egg to create a continuous design.

1. Trace patterns onto sheer organza, using brown marker and leaving at least 2" between each design. Cut designs apart.
2. Tape organza with pattern for Santa's face securely onto egg and trace over lines with brown marker. The ink will go through holes in weave of fabric onto surface of egg. Remove fabric from egg.
3. Insert cone point into wood burner, following manufacturer's instructions and safety precautions. Burn all lines of pattern (basic lines) into egg, using cone point. Wash egg to remove excess ink. Let dry completely. Change to shading point and, referring to photo on page 44, burn in shadows around face and under hair, beard, and lapels. Change to mini-flow point and burn in curving, detail lines of beard and hair. Reinforce, or darken, lines around holly and facial features by going over them again. Change to shading point and, using tip of point make short, diagonal and vertical lines along broken line to indicate fur on cap.
4. Tape organza with patterns for back of Santa's hat, side of Santa's beard, and tree branch onto egg securely, placing to the right of Santa's face (Santa's left side). Trace over lines with brown marker. Remove fabric from egg.
5. Burn all lines of pattern into egg, using cone point. Wash egg to remove ink. Let dry completely. Change to shading point and, referring to detail illustration of pine needles and photo on page 53, burn in pine needles, touching once with side of point tip for each needle. Note that some needles overlap slightly. Make short lines around ball on end of cap and continue with short, diagonal and vertical lines along broken line to indicate fur on cap, using tip of shading point and matching fur from one section to the next so that it continues around the egg. Burn in shadows along both sides of cap, continuing around to front of egg.
6. Tape organza with pattern for bag of toys onto egg securely, placing to the left of Santa's face (Santa's right side). Trace over lines with brown marker. Remove fabric from egg.
7. Burn all lines of pattern into egg, using cone point. Wash egg to remove ink. Let dry completely. Change to shading point and, referring to photo on page 53, burn in shadows on bag and strap. Make short, diagonal and vertical lines along broken line to indicate fur on cap. Change to mini-flow point and burn in details.
8. Compare design against photos to assure that all lines are wood burned. Darken any areas that look too light.
9. Using sharp, white pencil and medium-to-hard pressure, color in hair, beard, eyebrows, mustache, fur around cap, and ball on end of cap. Sharpen point and color in whites of eyes. Using sharp, scarlet lake pencil, color in holly berries. Using sharp, grass green pencil, color in holly leaves.

10. Seal egg with at least two coats of acrylic sealer, letting dry thoroughly between coats.

Note: If using a sealer other than that specified, pencil in an area on a scrap of wood and test the sealer to be sure it will not harm the color of the wood or the colors of the color pencils.

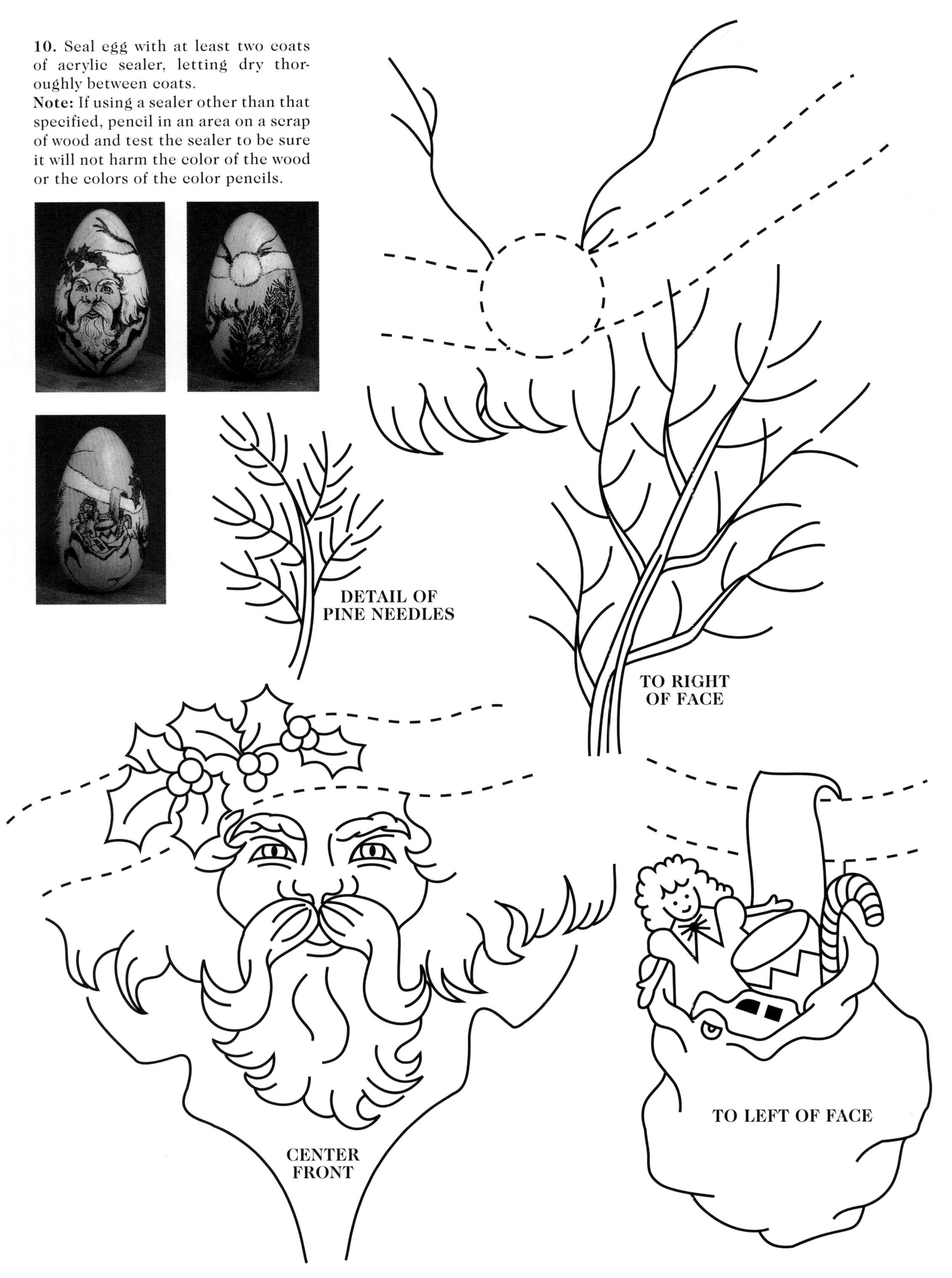

Primitive Angel with Candle

	DMC	Color
○	746	off white
/	727	topaz, vy. lt.
=	726	topaz, lt.
V	725	topaz
3	783	Christmas gold
Z	782	topaz, med.
+	407	sportsman flesh, dk.
II	950	sportsman flesh, lt.
-	948	peach flesh, vy. lt.
⊙	754	peach flesh, lt.
4	435	brown, vy. lt.
c	436	tan
L	437	tan, lt.
·	930	antique blue, dk.
6	931	antique blue, med.
X	932	antique blue, lt.

Fabric: 25-count dirty linen
Stitch count: 100H x 117W
Design size:

14-count	7⅛" x 8⅜"
18-count	5½" x 6½"
25-count	8⅞" x 9⅜"
27-count	7½" x 8⅝"

Instructions: Cross stitch over two threads, using two strands of floss. Backstitch eyes and nose using one strand 435.

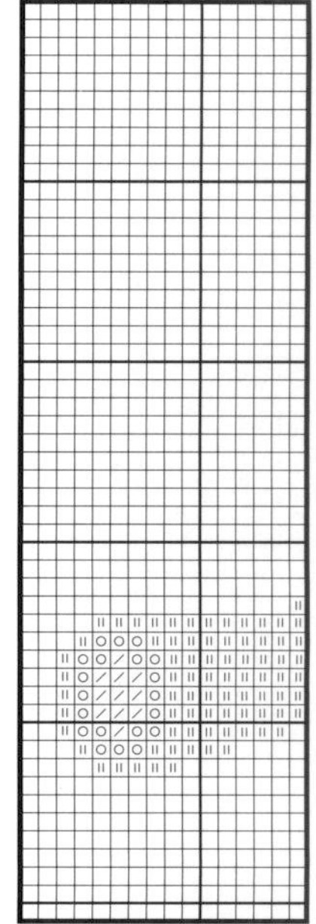

PRIMITIVE ANGEL WITH CANDLE

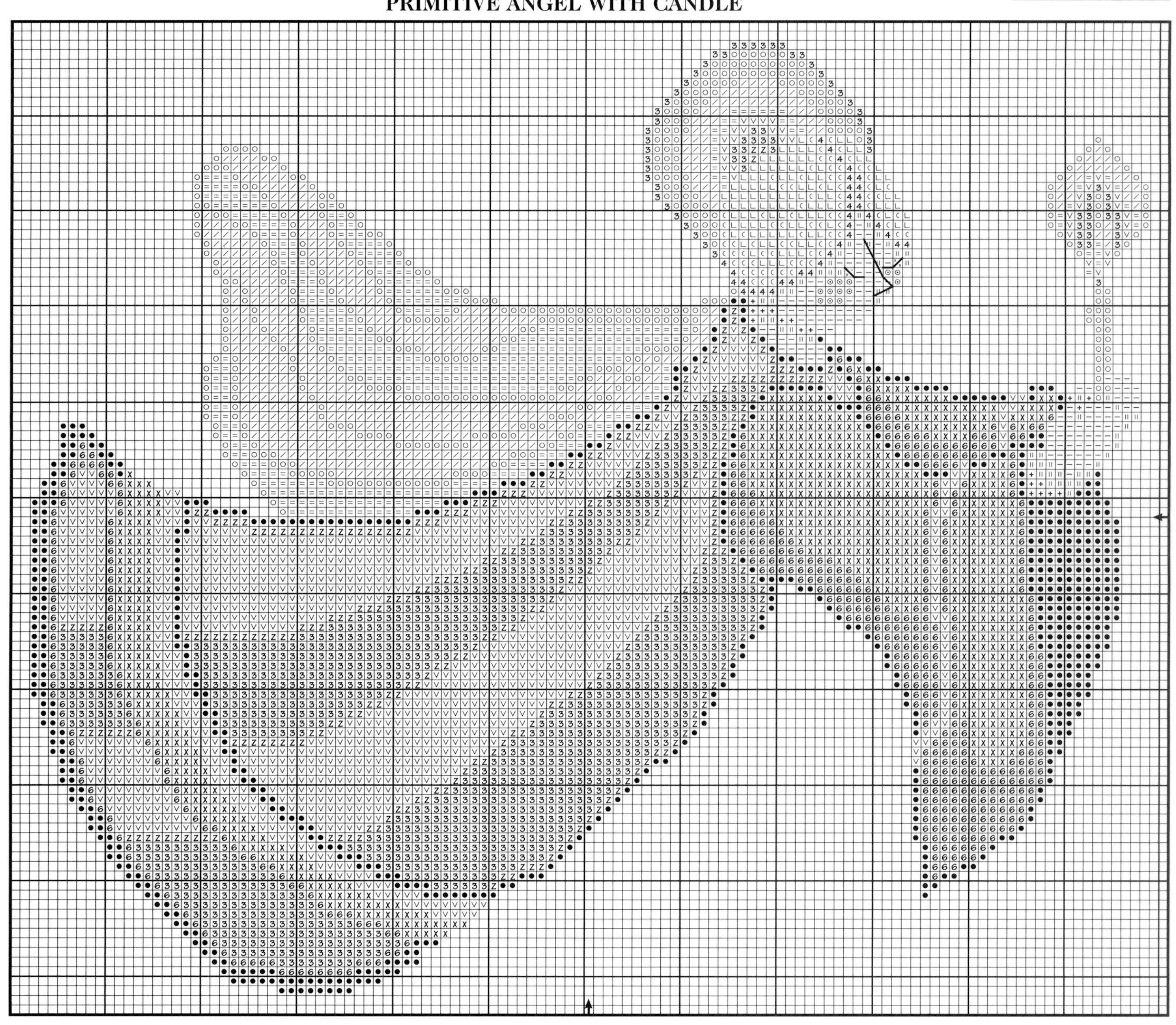

Shaded portion indicates overlap from previous page.

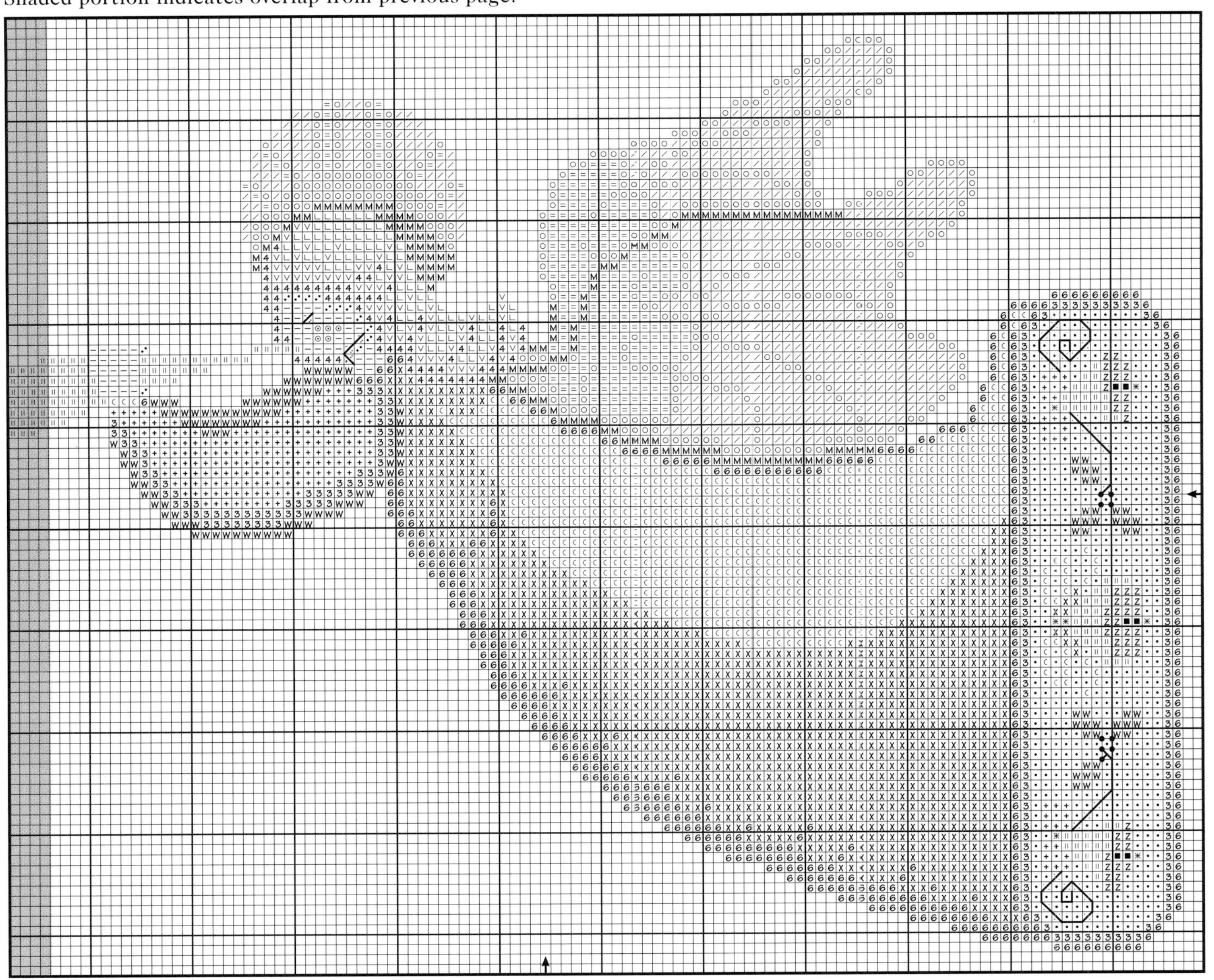

PRIMITIVE ANGEL WITH HORN

Primitive Angel with Horn

	DMC	Kreinik Metallics	Color
··	950		sportsman flesh, lt.
−	948		peach flesh, vy. lt.
⊙	754		peach flesh, lt.
4	435		brown, vy. lt.
V	436		tan
L	437		tan, lt.
ll [	415		pearl gray
		001HL	silver
Z [	414		steel gray, dk.
		019BF	pewter
M [	782		topaz, med.
		002HL	gold
O [	783		Christmas gold
		002HL	gold
= [	725		topaz
		028BF	citron
/ [	727		topaz, vy. lt.
		028BF	citron
C	304		Christmas red, med.
X	816		garnet
6	815		garnet, med.
W	890		pistachio green, ul. dk.
3	319		pistachio green, vy. dk.
+	367		pistachio green, dk.
·	725		topaz
■	413		pewter gray, dk.
✳		028BF	citron

Fabric: 25-count dirty linen
Stitch count: 90H x 125W
Design size:
14-count 6⅜" x 8⅞"
18-count 5" x 7"
25-count 7¼" x 10"
27-count 6⅝" x 9¼"

Instructions: Cross stitch over two threads, using two strands of floss. When floss and Kreinik Metallics are bracketed together, use one strand floss and two strands Kreinik Metallics. Backstitch using one strand of floss. Make French knots beside holly on garment design, using two strands 304 and wrapping floss around needle twice.

Backstitch instructions:
950 eye
304 design on garment

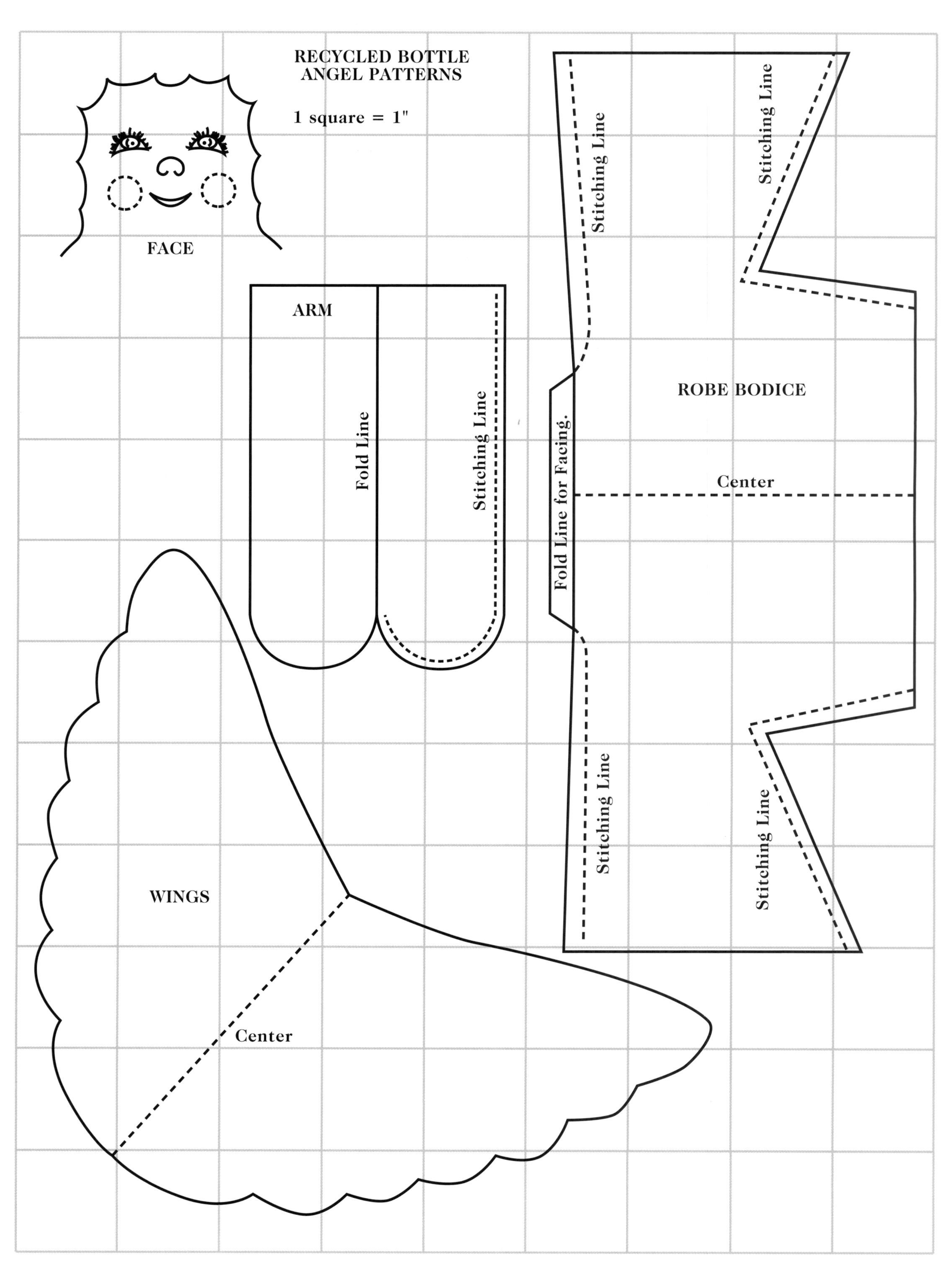
RECYCLED BOTTLE
ANGEL PATTERNS
1 square = 1"
FACE
ARM
Fold Line
Stitching Line
ROBE BODICE
Stitching Line
Stitching Line
Fold Line for Facing.
Center
Stitching Line
Stitching Line
WINGS
Center

Recycled Bottle Angel

Materials:

22-oz. Ivory® dishwashing liquid bottle, empty
⅓ yd. 44/45"-wide white cotton fabric
Thread to match
¾ yd. ⅓"-wide white flat lace
2 yds. ⅛"-wide gold braid
¾ cup sand
2¼" wooden ball
Curly Hair™, color: strawberry blonde
Delta Ceramcoat® acrylic paints, colors: light chocolate, fleshtone, adobe, white, black
Paintbrushes: liner, small **or** medium
Paper (for patterns)
6" x 8" scrap white cardboard
Small handful polyester filling
Scissors
Sharp knife
Fabric Glue Stick
Tacky glue
Graphite paper
Pencil
Hand-sewing needle
Sewing machine

Note: Materials listed will make one *Recycled Bottle Angel.*

1. Remove label from plastic bottle. Cut off neck of bottle at twist-off cap area, using sharp knife. Pour sand into bottle to add stability. Apply tacky glue to bottle neck, center wooden ball on top of bottle neck, and hold in place until glue sets. Let dry.

2. Trace all patterns onto paper. Transfer lines for hair onto ball, using graphite paper and pencil. Apply two coats light chocolate paint to hair area and two coats fleshtone to face area, letting dry between coats. Transfer facial features to wooden ball. Paint nose and mouth adobe. Mix small amount of water with adobe; paint cheeks. Paint whites of eyes white and irises black. Paint highlights in eyes white. Outline eyes using black. Thin black paint and draw eyelashes, using liner paintbrush.

3. Cut two arm pieces from white cotton. Fold right sides of fabric together along fold line and sew along raw edges, leaving straight edge open for turning. Turn right-side out and stuff lightly. For hands, paint curved ends with fleshtone, painting approximately 1" up. When dry, glue top of arm to side of bottle approximately ¾" down from bottle neck.

4. Cut two bodices for robe from white cotton. Place bodice pieces with right sides of fabric together and sew side seams and shoulder seams. Cut 8" x 20" rectangle from white cotton for skirt. Sew gathering thread along one long edge. Sew lace along opposite long edge of rectangle, sewing edge of right side of lace to edge of wrong side of fabric. Glue gold braid to right side of skirt hem to cover raw edges. Let dry. Join skirt to bodice, placing right sides of fabric together and gathering rectangle as you go to have 1" overlapping when completely around bodice. Turn right-side out. Cut a slit down back of bodice to dress angel. Place robe on angel, placing arms in sleeves. Tack overlapping fabric edges at back of skirt together to hold skirt together.

5. Cut two 8"-long pieces gold braid. Glue end of one piece to robe at waist. Cross braid over to opposite shoulder and glue other end to back of waist. Repeat procedure with second piece of gold braid, beginning at opposite side of waist, to form a crisscross pattern across bodice of angel's dress. Cut a third piece of gold braid 20" long. With center of braid at center back of waist, tie a knot in braid at center front of waist. Let remaining braid hang.

6. Cut hair into 4"-long pieces. Gently pull several pieces apart to make hair appear fuller. Glue hair pieces to head in hair area until area is covered.

7. Cut one set of wings from cardboard. Cut wings from two pieces white cotton, adding ⅓" allowance to fabric. Spread glue over one side of cardboard with glue stick. Press fabric right-side up onto cardboard wing. Let dry. Repeat procedure for opposite side of cardboard. Let dry. When cardboard is completely dry, cut excess fabric from wings. Apply a line of tacky glue down center of wings. Overlap fabric to hide slit in back of robe and press wings to overlapped fabric. Hold in place until glue sets. Let dry.

Angel to Watch Over You

Materials:

⅔ yd. 44/45"-wide unbleached muslin, washed and ironed
Thread to match
1 yd. Pellon® Fleece
Large handful of Poly-fil® stuffing
12" x 36" piece heavyweight interfacing
21 yds. medium brown Persian wool yarn (for hair)
DecoArt™ Americana™ acrylic paint, color: crimson tide
Americana Fabric-Painting Medium
DecoArt™ So-Soft Fabric Acrylics, colors: Williamsburg blue, black
Small paintbrush
Pigma 01 very-fine-line permanent marker, color: brown (**Note:** Brown Pigma 01 pen was used for model.)
Berol Prismacolor colored pencil, color: magenta
Disappearing-ink fabric-marking pen
Hand-sewing needle
9" square freezer paper (for heart stencil)
Stencil brush **or** soft sponge
Aluminum foil (for paint)
Paper (for pattern)
Paper towels
Pencil
Lipstick case (for making hair)
Scissors
Sewing machine
Iron

1. Enlarge pattern as indicated. (**Note:** Angel is symmetrical. Half of pattern is given on page 58.) Trace around half-pattern on paper, flip half-pattern, align along center line, and trace around second half. Cut out complete pattern. Cut two angel shapes from muslin, three from fleece, and one from heavyweight interfacing. Trace facial features, heart, and quilting lines onto one piece of muslin, using disappearing-ink fabric-marking pen.

2. Paint face as follows. Paint irises of eyes Williamsburg blue. Let dry. Paint pupils black, leaving a small spot of muslin unpainted for highlight in each eye. Let dry. Outline eyes and nose, using brown, permanent marker. Make soft, short strokes for eyebrows, using brown permanent marker. Outline and color lips, using magenta pencil.

3. To stencil heart shape, trace shape in center on papery side of freezer paper. Cut shape from paper, leaving a cut-out heart shape in center of paper. Iron freezer-paper heart stencil, shiny-side down, onto muslin. Mix crimson tide paint with fabric-painting medium on foil. Dab brush into paint and blot excess on paper towel. Test on scrap muslin. On angel front, lightly brush color from paper toward center of heart shape. Let dry. Add dotted line around perimeter of heart, approximately ¼" away from edge of heart, using brown, permanent marker.

4. To assemble angel, layer one piece fleece, one piece interfacing, two pieces fleece, painted angel front right-side up, and unpainted, muslin angel back right-side down atop a flat surface. With sewing machine stitch length set on approximately eighteen stitches per inch, sew around perimeter of angel, using a ¼" seam allowance and leaving an opening along top of one wing, as indicated on pattern, for turning. Clip all seams. Turn angel right-side out, having muslin showing on front and back and all fleece and interfacing inside.

5. Machine- or hand-quilt lines in the wing without opening for turning. Quilt line from shoulder down on that side only. Lightly stuff angel head and center of angel behind stenciled heart with poly-fil® stuffing. Quilt line from remaining shoulder down. Whipstitch opening closed. Quilt lines in remaining wing.

6. To make hair, braid nine 36"-long strands of yarn (3-ply) into a braid approximately 10" long. Hand sew braid to front of head around seam, tucking loose ends of braid under. To make each curl, lay one short piece of yarn (1-ply) along lipstick case. Make ten wraps around the case and over the single ply with one strand (three plies) of yarn 36" long. Pull 3-ply wraps together tightly and secure by tying a knot around them, using the single ply of yarn. Slip off case. Repeat to make ten curls. Sew curls around head just behind braid, spacing evenly.

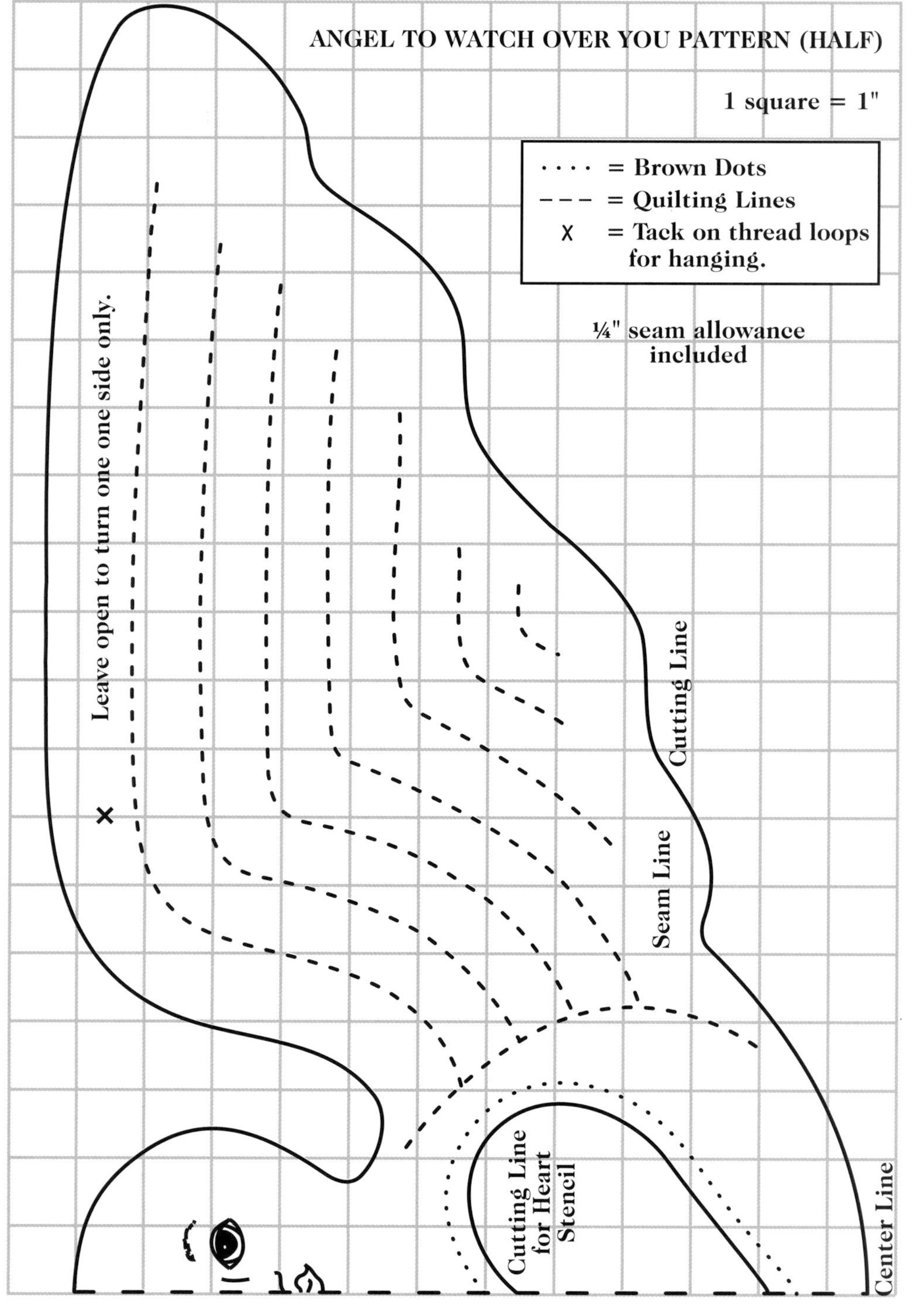

7. To hang for display, cut two pieces thread to twice the desired hanging length, bring ends together, and tie a knot in thread ends to form hanging loops. Tack a thread hanging loop at each of the two *X*s on the wings.

Folk-Art Bunnies

Note: For these projects, a general materials list has been given. Specific materials for each project have been listed separately.

General materials:

One spool very fine (size .004) invisible thread
Tracing paper and pencil
Straight pins
Measuring tape
Scissors
Iron
Sewing machine with zigzag stitch and blind hem stitch

Folk-Art Bunny Throw
Materials:

1⅔ yds. 60"-wide wool fabric to complement Doe Suede™
Thread to match
10" x 14" scrap tan Doe Suede™ **or** felt
9" square red Doe Suede™ **or** felt
6" x 9" scrap green Doe Suede™ **or** felt
½ yd. Pellon® Wonder-Under® Transfer Web

Finished size: 60" x 60", including fringe.

1. Enlarge pattern as indicated. (**Note:** Half of pattern is shown.) Place tracing paper dull-side up atop a flat surface. Lightly trace half of pattern onto tracing paper. Flip pattern, align along center line, and lightly trace second half of pattern onto tracing paper. Place Wonder-Under® paper-side up atop a flat surface. Place tracing-paper pattern atop Wonder-Under® and transfer pattern onto paper side of Wonder-Under®. Cut out pattern pieces. Fuse rabbits to wrong side of tan Doe Suede™, heart to wrong side of red Doe Suede™, and "comma" shapes to wrong side of green Doe Suede™, following manufacturer's instructions for fusing. Cut out shapes.

2. To prepare wool fabric, zigzag approximately 1¼" in from edge along top and bottom. Fringe by pulling threads from edges to machine stitching.

Note: Selvage edges of fabric used for model had a finished appearance without actually having been finished. Depending on the fabric you choose for your throw, you may want to narrowly hem the side edges, or fringe them as for the top and bottom edges.

3. Center middle "comma" shape 1" above fringe along one edge of throw. Place remaining shapes, referring to pattern for placement, and fuse in place.

4. To work invisible appliqué, set sewing machine for a blind hem stitch. Model was appliquéd invisibly using machine's blind hem stitch, a very short stitch length, fine, invisible thread in the needle, and thread to match fabric in the bobbin. Sew along beside the appliqués, having straight stitches in the ditch at edge of appliqué. Zigzag part of blind hem stitch going over into the appliqué.

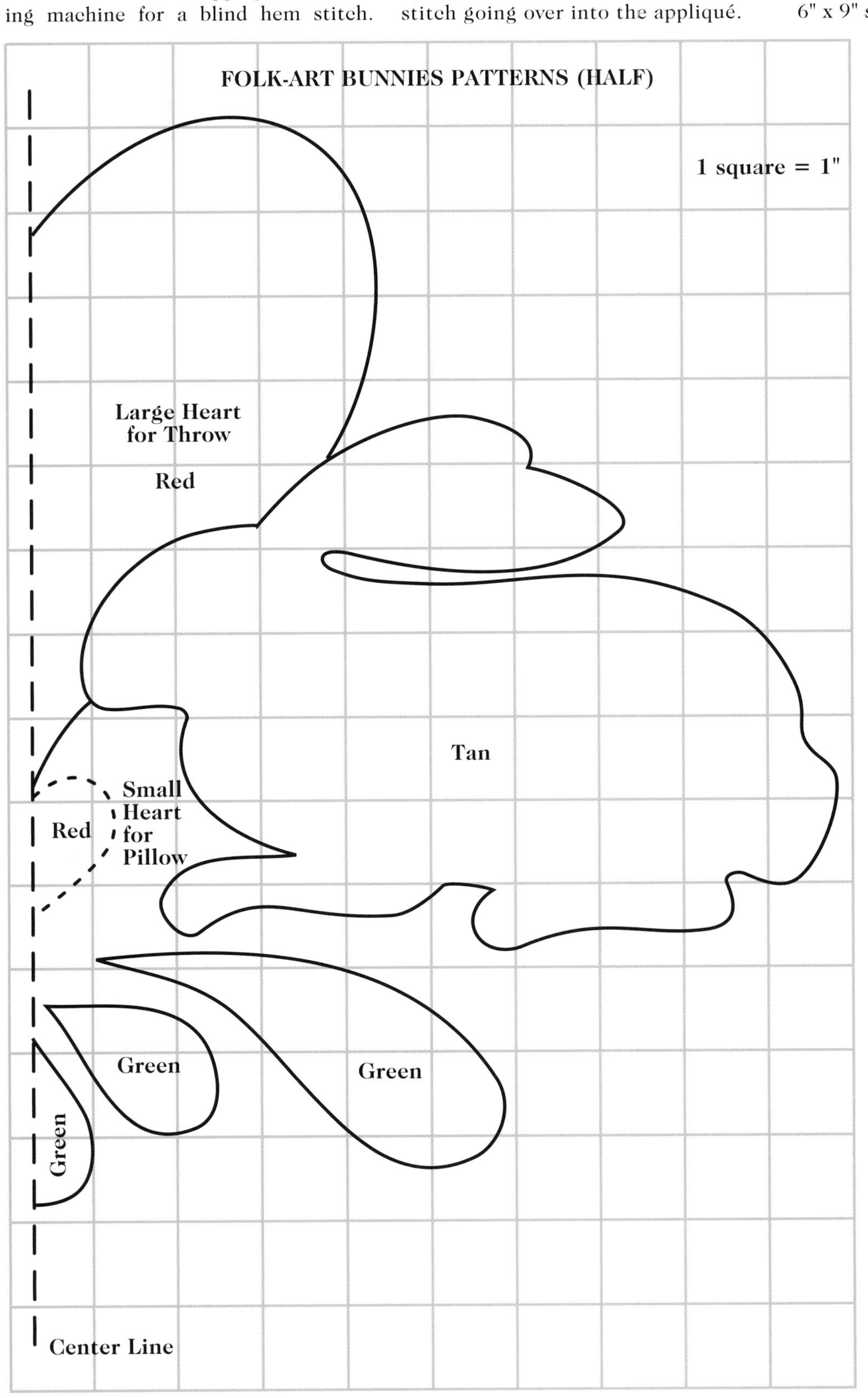

Folk-Art Bunny Pillow

Materials:

½ yd. 54–60"-wide wool fabric to complement Doe Suede™
Thread to match
10" x 14" scrap tan Doe Suede™ **or** felt
2½" square red Doe Suede™ **or** felt
6" x 9" scrap green Doe Suede™ **or** felt
½ yd. Pellon® Wonder-Under® Transfer Web
Poly-fil® stuffing

Finished size: 16½" x 27", including fringe.

1. Cut fabric into two 16½" x 27" pieces. Zigzag approximately 1¼" in from edge on **each** side of **each** piece. Fringe by pulling threads from edges to machine stitching. Set aside.
2. Prepare appliqué pieces as for *Folk-Art Bunny Throw*, noting difference in heart used. (See pattern.) Center appliqué pieces on right side of one piece of fabric, referring to pattern for placement. Fuse pieces to fabric and machine appliqué as for *Folk-Art Bunny Throw*.
3. Place appliquéd front right-side up atop wrong side of unappliquéd backing piece, aligning edges. Pin or baste front and backing pieces together and machine-sew pieces together at zigzagged edge of fringe, leaving a 6" opening along bottom of pillow for stuffing. Remove pins or basting thread. Stuff pillow with Poly-fil® stuffing. Sew opening closed.

Christmas Curiosity

	DMC	Kreinik Metallics	Color
●	319		pistachio, vy. dk.
▼	367		pistachio, dk.
o	369		pistachio, vy. lt.
//	368		pistachio, lt.
▲	320		pistachio, med.
◐	815		garnet, med.
6	498		red, dk.
+	321		red
♥[	741		tangerine, med.
		002BF	gold
∧[	742		tangerine, lt.
		002BF	gold
W[	725		topaz
		002BF	gold
T[	726		topaz, lt.
		002BF	gold
⁚[	727		topaz, vy. lt.
		002BF	gold
e[	415		pearl gray
		001BF	silver
◣	783		gold
◤	304		red, med.
>	726		topaz, lt.
∖	727		topaz, vy. lt.
·	white		white
V	762		pearl gray, vy. lt.
◢	415		pearl gray
8	414		steel gray, dk.
◣	801		coffee, dk.
M	433		brown, med.
3	434		brown, lt.
⌐	435		brown, vy. lt.
⊙	738		tan, vy. lt.
/[	712		cream
	white		white
ll[	738		tan, vy. lt.
	712		cream
U	436		tan
Z[	3021		brown-gray, dk.
	436		tan
✳[	434		brown, lt.
	3021		brown-gray, dk.
■	3371		black-brown
5[	355		terra cotta, dk.
	3371		black-brown
X[	355		terra cotta, dk.
	356		terra cotta, med.
=	355		terra cotta, dk.
⅃[	758		terra cotta, lt.
	356		terra cotta, med.
a	725		topaz

Mill Hill Glass Seed Beads

x	00165	Christmas red
★	02011	Victorian gold
●	00165	Christmas red

Fabric: 25-count moss green Lugana® from Zwiegart®

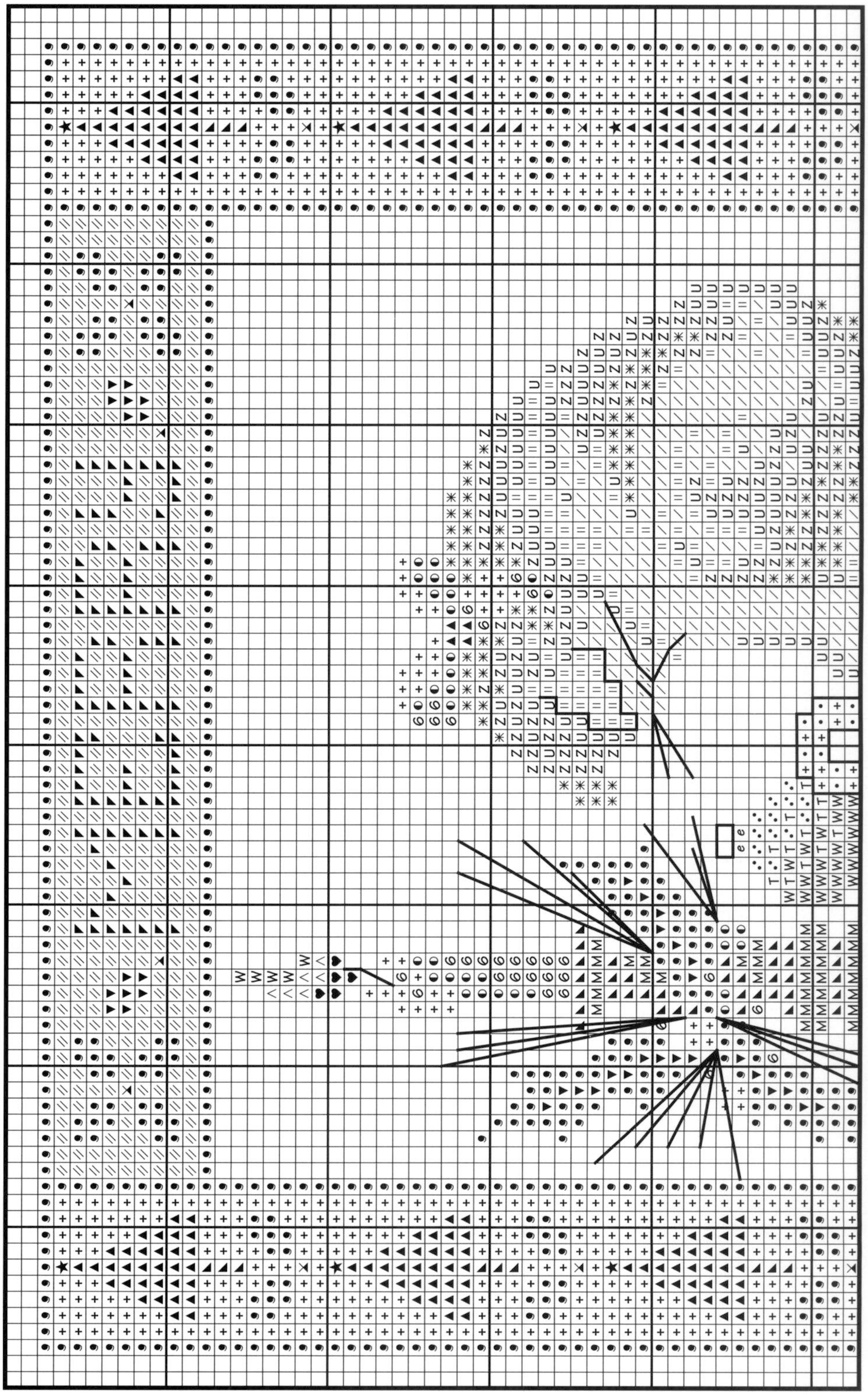

Stitch count: 126H x 82W

Design size:

14-count	9" x 5⅞"
18-count	7" x 4½"
25-count	10" x 6½"
27-count	9⅓" x 6"

Instructions: Cross stitch over two threads, using two strands of floss. Backstitch using one strand of floss unless otherwise indicated. Make straight stitches using one strand of floss. Attach Mill Hill Glass Seed Beads using a single strand of matching floss. **Note:** Where

Shaded portion indicates overlap from previous page.

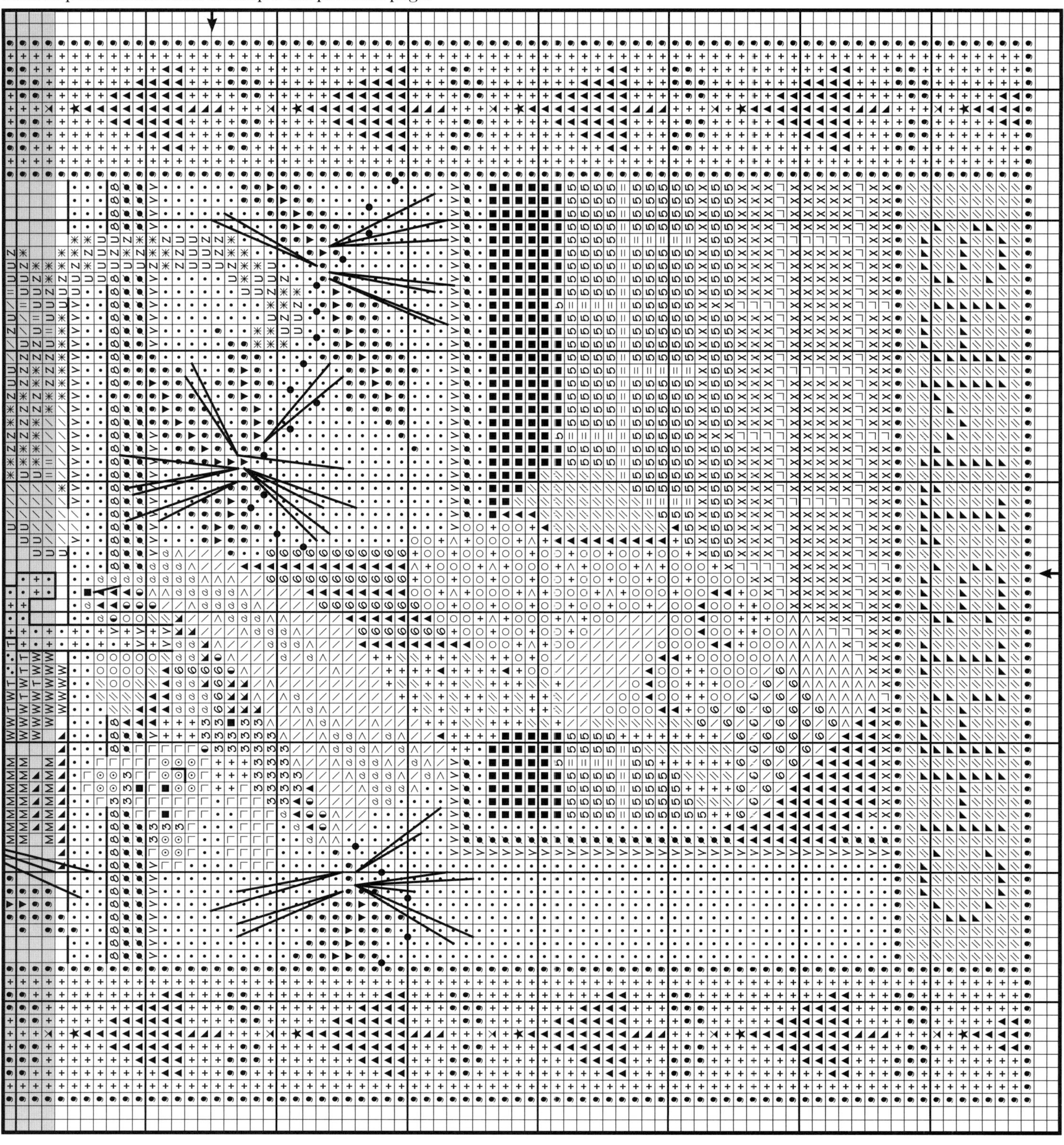

symbol ⧗ appears place three red seed beads per symbol and where symbol ★ appears place two gold beads per symbol. When two colors are bracketed together, use one strand of each. When combining floss and Kreinik Metallics, use one strand floss and two strands Kreinik Blending Filament.

Backstitch instructions:

3021	cat's eye and ear
3371	teddy bear's mouth, nail holding stocking
414	candy cane, mantel's edge
815	candlewick
[414 001BF	hanger on gold ornament

Straight stitch instructions:

319	pine needles
white	cat's whiskers

A MEMORABLE TREE

Each year we painstakingly select a tree from the dozens we see, carefully transport it to its holiday home, and begin the task that will transform it into the glimmering, shining centerpiece of the Christmas season. First the sparkling lights and colorful garland are twined about the tree. Then we hang the precious ornaments we gather throughout our lives. Finally the tree topper—angel, star, or another Yuletide symbol—crowns the evergreen. The choice of ornaments may vary, but the annual thrill of decorating the tree remains constant. It often represents the true beginning of the celebrations that lead to Christmas.

The delights of handcrafted ornaments are twofold—the joy of making them, and the pleasure of giving them to friends or hanging them on your tree. Shown on the tree at right are Christmas Ball Ornaments *(also shown in detail),* Holiday Bells, Victorian Lace Eggs, *and* Cone Ornaments. *Instructions are on pages 70–71.*

Handmade Treasures

As families open boxes of ornaments, brought from attics and basements to the prominently displayed Christmas tree, they remember holiday seasons past. Many ornaments carry special memories. As each ornament is carefully unwrapped and then hung from the branches, family members smile, recalling its history. Many are gifts from very special people or treasures a loved one has made by hand. On the following pages, you'll find lovely and unusual ornaments to craft for your own tree or to give to family members and friends.

Not one but four examples of our handcrafted delights hang from the branches of the evergreen shown at left. The ***Christmas Ball Ornaments***, also shown in detail far left and below, shine with bright-colored taffeta and varied trims, such as ribbon flowers, lace, and braid.

Glue colorful fabric scraps to Styrofoam® bells to make the quick-to-finish ***Holiday Bells***. Trim them with satin ribbon and silk flowers and add metallic gold thread for hangers. You can vary the fabric to convey old-world charm, contemporary appeal, or classic, country flavor.

The ***Victorian Lace Eggs***, shown on the tree, are a vision of rose taffeta, creamy lace, and burgundy ribbon. Pearl beads make an elegant border around the eggs. Also hanging from the branches of the tree are the frilly ***Cone Ornaments***, which are made from lace-covered teal taffeta and filled with silk flowers.

Making "roll-and-cut" sugar cookies is a regular holiday event for many families. Many of us recall fondly the time spent with our mothers and grandmothers in the warmth of a Christmas kitchen, rolling out, baking, decorating, and sampling these tasty, sweet treats.

Above—Clay Ornaments, *painted in Williamsburg blue and white, and* Copper Ornaments *of colonial-inspired design will give your tree Early-American charm. Use cookie cutters to create the clay shapes; then bake and decorate with paint to personalize each ornament. It's a fun family project!* Copper Ornaments *designs include a pineapple, a dove, and a heart-in-hand motif.* *Instructions are on pages 73 and 74.*

The cookie-cutter ***Clay Ornaments***, shown at left, provide a wonderful way to expand on a favorite tradition. Create the colonial blue designs pictured or let the members of your family decorate the baked shapes any way they choose. This "cookie baking" is so much fun that you may decide you want to make it an annual, Christmastime event at your home. Also on page 66, the ***Copper Ornaments*** will add a subtle glow to the beauty of your holidays. Suspend the colonial-inspired ornaments, in the shapes of pineapple, dove, and heart-in-hand, from brightly colored embroidery floss.

Above—*The* Victorian Egg Ornaments *feature cross-stitch designs of a nutcracker, a rose, and Santa, formed to real egg shells and accented with assorted trims. Charts and instructions are on pages 72–73.*

Left—*Crochet an entire choir of* Angels with Rosebuds *for your holiday evergreen—they'll become a treasured part of your seasonal celebration. Instructions begin on page 74.*

Above—Choose scraps from your sewing basket to craft the festive Fan Ornaments. *Instructions are on page 76.*

The ***Victorian Egg Ornaments***, shown on page 67, are a combination of cross stitch and crafting. Made using real egg shells, the ornaments are very fragile. We suggest storing them, carefully wrapped, in butter bowls or in egg cartons.

The hand-made, crocheted ***Angels with Rosebuds***, shown on page 67, contrast prettily with the green tree branches. Remove the hanging loops and the angels can serve as place-card holders at a holiday dinner party.

Use your favorite seasonal fabric scraps and assorted trims to make the eye-catching ***Fan Ornaments***, shown above. Craft your fans with calico prints for a country Christmas or, if you prefer Victorian charm, mix soft pastels with delicate laces and trims.

Cute little ***Calico Angels***, shown on page 69, dressed with varied floral prints in shades of red and blue, will give your tree a down-home look. Their robes boast lace-trimmed petticoats,

and they have embroidery-floss hair and French-knot eyes. Blanket-stitched wings add to their homespun appeal.

Bring Yuletide cheer to the kitchen, a room sometimes neglected when the house is bedecked for Christmas. Ask your children to "lend a hand" in making the ***Handprint Ornaments*** on the kitchen tree shown at right. They'll enjoy playing with paint, and you'll have precious keepsakes to cherish once your little ones have grown up.

Christmas Ball Ornaments

Materials:

Three ½-yd. pieces 44/45"-wide taffeta in contrasting colors
Nine 3"-diameter STYROFOAM brand plastic foam balls
Four 450-ct. boxes of straight pins
Assorted ribbons and braids (for hangers)
Assorted ribbons, braids, laces, and satin-ribbon roses of your choice (for trim)
Ruler **or** tape measure
Straight pins
Scissors
Hot glue gun

Note: Materials listed will make nine *Christmas Ball Ornaments.*

1. Cut fabric into 1½" squares.
2. Fold one square of fabric diagonally, placing wrong sides of fabric together. (See Illustration 1).
3. Place triangle on Styrofoam® ball and pin at top, center of triangle, leaving a space the size of the pin head between pin and top of fabric. (See Illustration 2).
4. Fold sides of fabric inward to form a diamond, making sure head of pin does not show. (See Illustration 3).
5. Pin through each unpinned corner of the two, newly-formed triangles. (See Illustration 4).
6. Repeat with second square of same color fabric so that second diamond touches top point of first diamond. (See Illustration 5).
7. Repeat with third and fourth squares, covering top of ball completely. (See Illustration 6).
8. Find opposite point of Styrofoam® ball and repeat Steps 2–7. (See Illustration 7).
9. Choose another color square and repeat process by placing top point of diamond on each line or fold of existing diamonds. Be sure to cover raw edges of fabric of existing diamonds completely. Work completely around top end of ball, adding eight additional diamonds. (See Illustration 8). Repeat on bottom of ball.
10. Return to top of ball and repeat process of covering all diamonds by working around top again with sixteen additional squares.
11. Repeat process on bottom of ball. On last row of diamonds, trim bottom of each diamond in half so that pins will form a straight line in middle of ball.
12. Cover all pins with ribbon and lace, pinning or gluing ribbon and lace to ball.
Note: Only pins on last top and bottom rows should be showing.
13. Form ribbon loop for hanging and secure at top of ball with pins or glue. Glue silk-ribbon roses and trims to ball, as desired, to finish.
14. Repeat Steps 2–13 for remaining balls.
Options: Attach loop to middle of first four diamonds to change look of ball. Changing colors and types of fabric will also change look.

Holiday Bells

Materials:

3" STYROFOAM brand plastic foam bell
9"-square scrap fabric of your choice
8" length gold metallic thread (for hanger)
8" length ¼"-wide ribbon in color of your choice
Assorted small silk flowers
Tacky glue
Mod Podge®
½"-wide paintbrush
Straight pins
Scissors

Note: Materials listed will make one *Holiday Bell.*

1. Cut ½"-wide bias strips of fabric in varying lengths. Apply glue to wrong side of fabric and cover bell completely with fabric, overlapping strips slightly. Let dry.
2. Apply at least five coats of Mod Podge® to bell, letting dry between coats.
3. Glue ribbon and silk flowers to bell as desired, referring to photo on page 64 for placement.
4. Form a loop with gold thread, aligning ends. Insert pin through thread ends and into bell at center top to form hanger. Glue to secure.

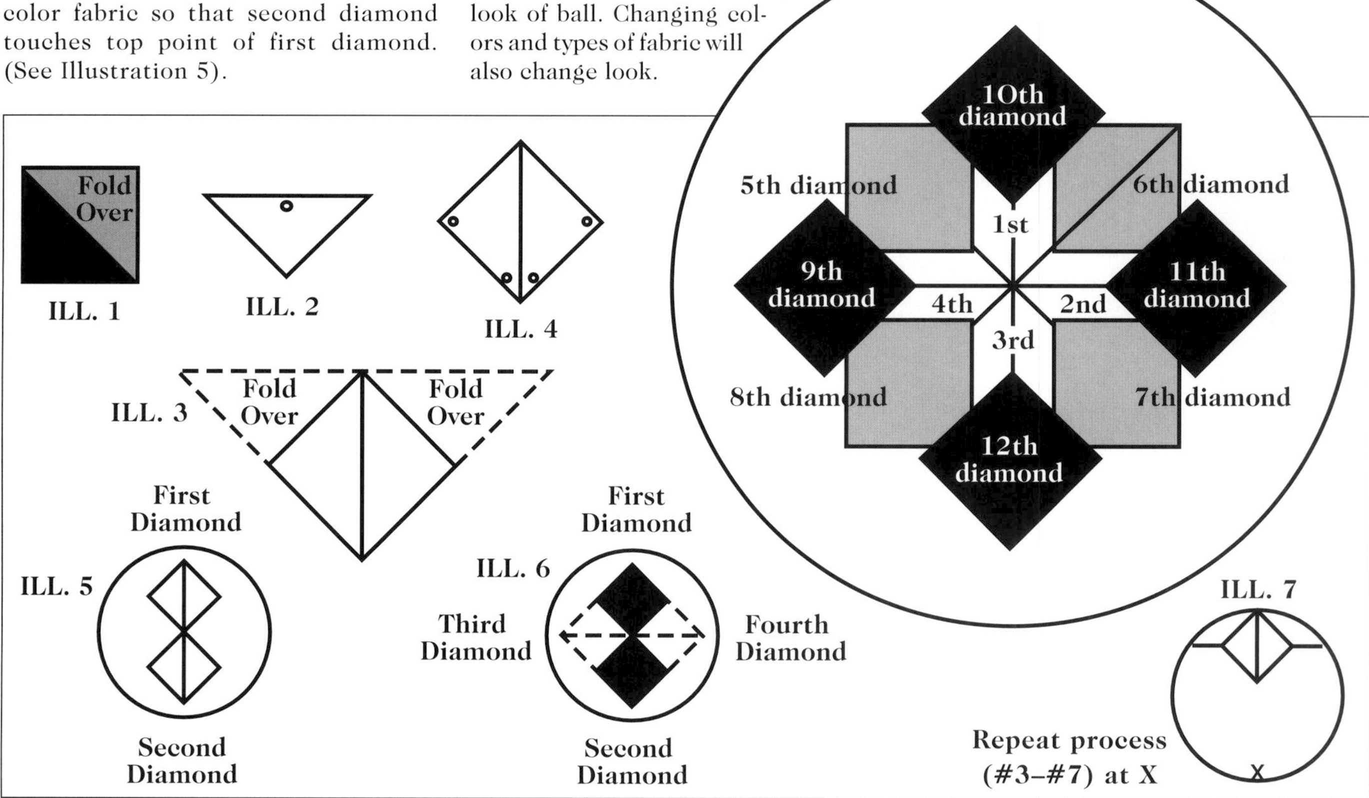

Cone Ornaments

Materials:
6" x 8" scrap teal taffeta
6" x 8" scrap cream lace
Thread to match taffeta
8¼" length ¾"-wide cream lace trim
8¼" length ¼"-wide teal satin ribbon
6" x 8" piece Pellon® Wonder-Under® Transfer Web
10" length gold metallic thread (for hanger)
Spanish moss
12 small teal silk roses
Baby's breath
Glue gun **or** tacky glue
Paper (for pattern)
Pencil
Sewing machine
Scissors

Note: Materials listed will make one *Cone Ornament.*

1. Enlarge pattern as indicated. Trace pattern onto paper and cut out.
2. Fuse taffeta to lace, using Wonder-Under® Transfer Web and following manufacturer's instructions for fusing.
3. Place pattern atop fabric and cut out. Fold fabric in half with taffeta to outside. Sew edges together along stitching line as indicated on pattern, reinforcing point of cone by back-stitching. Turn right-side out.
4. Apply glue around top, outside edge of cone and press on lace trim. Glue on ribbon atop lace trim.
5. Stuff cone with Spanish moss.
6. Apply glue to rosebud stems and insert stems into moss. Glue ends of gold metallic thread on opposite sides of cone to form hanger. Fill in spaces between rosebuds with baby's breath, dipping stem ends in glue as for rosebuds.

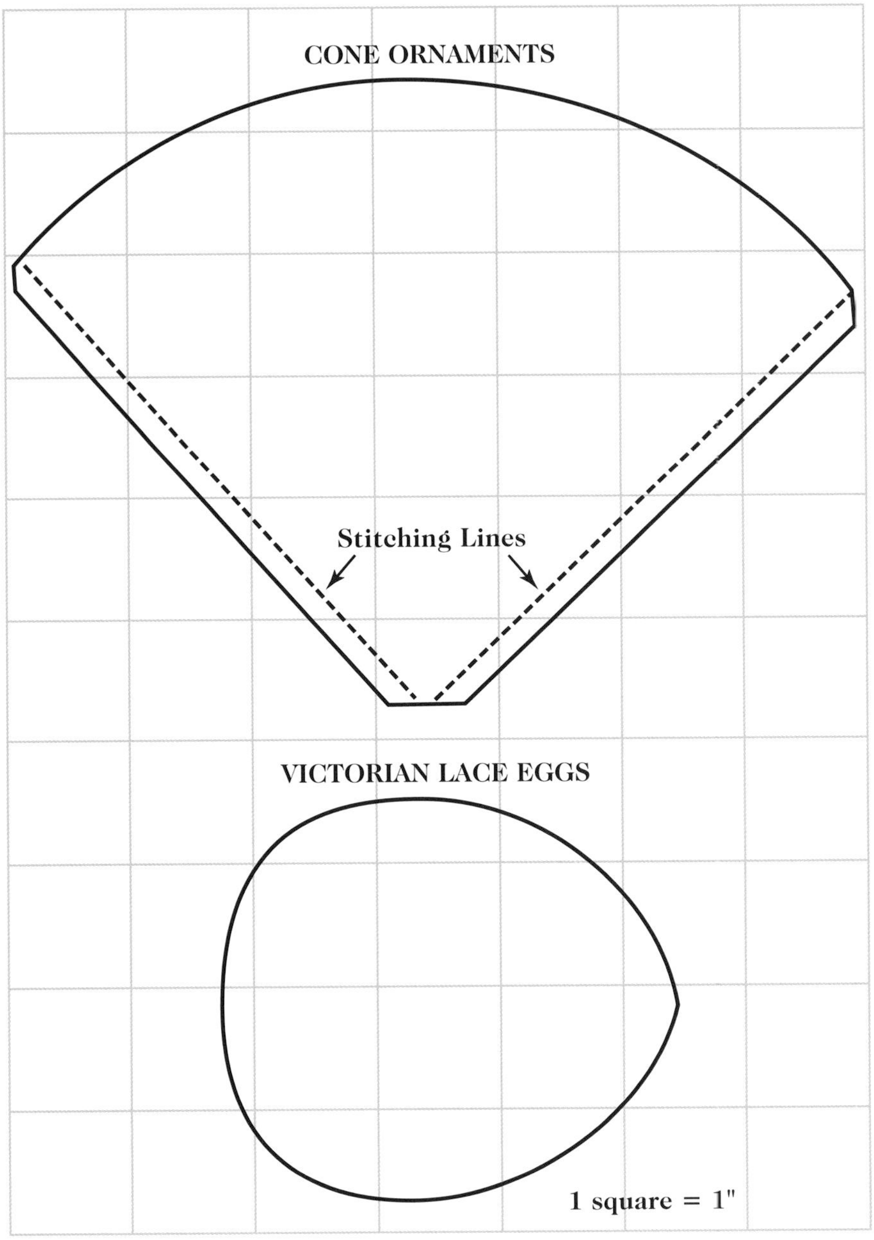

CONE ORNAMENTS

Stitching Lines

VICTORIAN LACE EGGS

1 square = 1"

Victorian Lace Eggs

Materials:
2½" STYROFOAM brand plastic foam egg
4" x 8" scrap cream lace
4" x 8" scrap rose-colored taffeta
8½" length ¾"-wide cream lace
8½" length pearls by the yard
1 yd. ⅛"-wide burgundy ribbon
3¼ yds. cream-colored crochet thread
Five ¾" rose-colored satin-ribbon roses
7" length gold metallic thread (for hanger)
Thread to match lace
3" length flexible wire
2" square cardboard
Straight pins
Tacky glue
Toothpicks
Hand-sewing needle
Scissors
Paper (for pattern)
Pencil
Sewing machine (optional)

Note: Materials listed will make one *Victorian Egg.*

1. Enlarge pattern as indicated. Trace pattern onto paper and cut out.
2. Fold 4" x 8" piece of lace in half. Place pattern atop lace at an angle and cut out. Repeat for taffeta.
3. Layer one piece each of taffeta and lace with right sides up. Machine- or hand-sew gathering lines ¼" and ⅛" from edge. Pin top of fabric to center top of large end of egg. Pull threads to gather slightly. Apply glue around edge of fabric with toothpick and press fabric in place. Half of egg will be covered. Repeat for second half of egg, overlapping fabric edges. Let dry.
4. Glue ¾"-wide lace around egg, covering overlapping fabric edges.Glue ribbon atop lace. Let dry. Glue on pearls.
5. To make tassel, cut 3 yds. crochet thread and wrap around cardboard. Cut short piece of thread and tie all threads together at top. Cut threads along bottom to make fringed end. Remove from cardboard and tie again ½" from top. Trim thread. Glue tassel to bottom of egg.
6. Tie remaining ribbon into a bow and secure center with wire. Glue bow to top of egg.
7. Glue three roses at top of egg and one on either side at bottom of egg.
8. Thread needle with gold thread, pass needle through rose at center top of egg, and tie a knot in thread ends to form hanger.

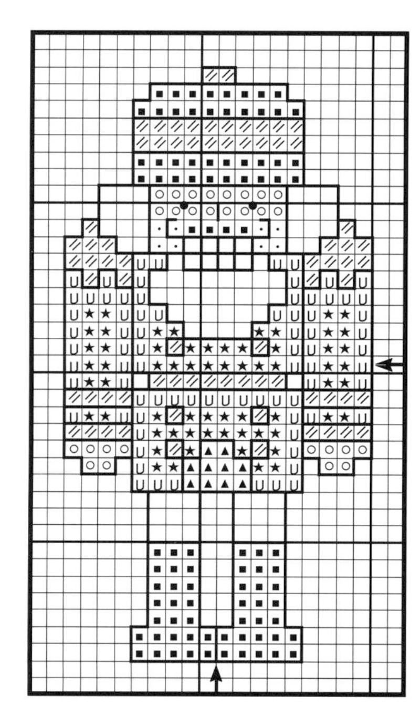

NUTCRACKER

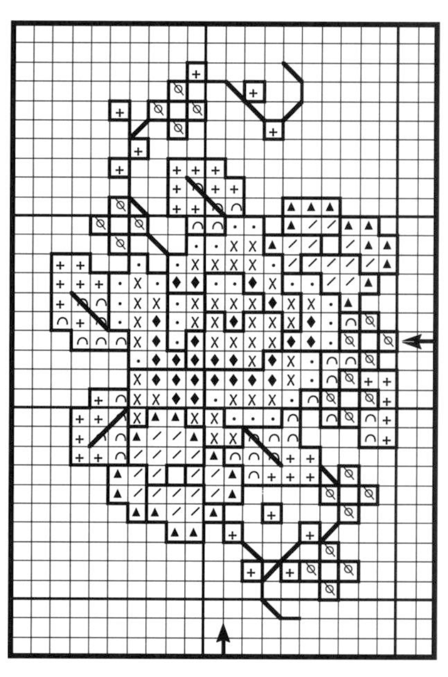

ROSE

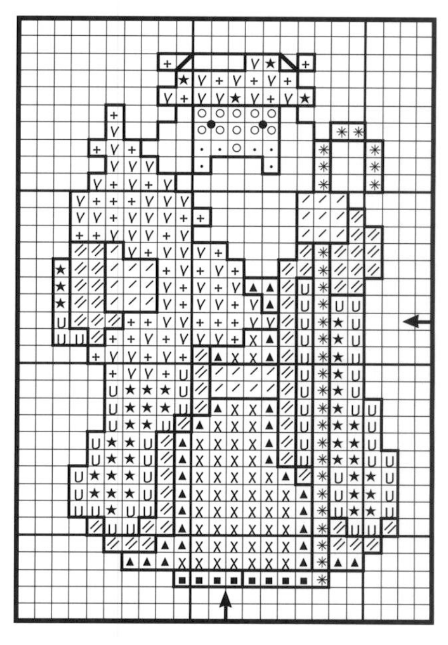

SANTA

Victorian Egg Ornaments

Nutcracker

DMC	Kreinik Metallics	Color
○ 754		peach flesh, lt.
• 353		peach flesh
★ 309		rose, dp.
U 815		garnet, med.
▲ 930		antique blue, dk.
■ 3799		pewter-gray, dk.
⁄⁄ [	002BF	gold
676		old gold, lt.

Fabric: 22-count white Hardanger from Zweigart®
Stitch count: 35H x 18W
Design size:

14-count	2½" x 1¼"
18-count	2" x 1"
22-count	1⅝" x ⅞"
25-count	2⅞" x 1½"

Instructions: Cross stitch over one thread, using one strand of floss. Backstitch using one strand 3799. Make French knots for eyes where ● appears at intersecting grid lines, using one strand 3799 and wrapping floss around needle once. When DMC and Kreinik Metallics are bracketed together, use one strand of floss and two strands of Kreinik Blending Filament

Rose

DMC	Color
⊘ 3326	rose, lt.
♦ 3607	plum, lt.
X 3608	plum, vy. lt.
• 3609	plum, ul. lt.
+ 471	avocado, vy. lt.
∩ 470	avocado, lt.
⁄ 208	lavender, vy. dk.
▲ 341	blue-violet, lt.
bs 801	coffee, dk.

Fabric: 22-count white Hardanger from Zweigart®
Stitch count: 29H x 18W
Design size:

14-count	2⅛" x 1¼"
18-count	1⅝" x 1"
22-count	1⅜" x ⅞"
25-count	2⅜" x 1½"

Instructions: Cross stitch over one thread, using one strand of floss. Backstitch using one strand of floss.
Backstitch (bs) instructions:

470	tendrils
801	remainder of backstitching

Santa

DMC	Kreinik Metallics	Color
○ 754		peach flesh, lt.
• 353		peach flesh
V 320		pistachio, med.
+ 319		pistachio, vy. dk.
⁄ 208		lavender, vy. dk.
■ 433		brown, med.
✳ 434		brown, lt.
▲ 930		antique blue, dk.
X 932		antique blue, lt.
★ 309		rose, dp.
U 815		garnet, med.
⁄⁄ [	002BF	gold
676		old gold, lt.

Fabric: 22-count white Hardanger from Zweigart®
Stitch count: 31H x 20W
Design size:

14-count	2¼" x 1½"
18-count	1¾" x 1⅛"
22-count	1⅜" x 1"
25-count	2½" x 1⅝"

Instructions: Cross stitch over one thread, using one strand of floss. Backstitch Santa's hair, using one strand 930. Make French knots for Santa's eyes where ● appears at intersecting grid lines, using one strand 801 and wrapping floss around needle once. When floss and Kreinik Metallics are bracketed together, use one strand of floss and two strands of Kreinik Blending Filament.

Finishing instructions
Materials:
3 jumbo eggs
All-purpose white glue
Acrylic paint, colors: red, lavender
Assorted 6" lengths of metallic gold trim, pearls-by-the-yard (cannot be unstrung) and gold, strung sequins (Refer to photo for trimming ideas.)
1 small pkg. gold sequins
1 small pkg. 2mm pearl beads
6" length gold embroidery thread (for each hanger)
Water-base varnish
Straight pin
Paintbrush
Scissors
Hair dryer(optional)

Note: Materials listed will make three *Victorian Egg Ornaments*. As you work with eggs, remember they are fragile!
1. Complete cross stitch following instructions given.

2. Carefully make a small hole in each end of egg, using straight pin. Blow out yoke and white.
3. Paint egg and let dry. Varnish egg and let dry.
4. Cut around perimeter of stitched design in an oval shape, cutting approximately ¼"–⅜" away from edge of design. Neatly glue stitched design to egg, centering vertically. (**Note:** Smallest end of egg will be top of ornament; largest end will be bottom.) Apply one coat of glue over entire piece of cross-stitch fabric, including stitching, and let dry.
Note: Glue dries clear and will protect stitching. A hair dryer may be used to speed drying.
5. Glue 6" lengths of gold trim, sequins, or pearls-by-the-yard around edge of cross-stitch fabric.
Note: 6" lengths will be ample for going around edges of cross-stitch fabric. Trim excess as needed for a neat finish.
6. Glue loose sequins and beads over hole in bottom of egg.
Note: Approximately six to seven sequins and six to seven beads will be sufficient for covering hole completely while forming a decorative finish.
7. Bring ends of gold embroidery thread together, forming a loop, and tie ends in a knot to secure. Insert knot into hole in top of egg and glue to secure.
8. Glue loose sequins and beads around hanging loop and over hole in top of egg.
9. Repeat for remaining ornaments.

Clay Ornaments

Materials:
Two 2-oz. pkgs. Sculpey clay, color: #001 white (makes 4–5 ornaments)
Blue permanent markers with fine and extra-fine points
Bell, bird, heart, and candle cookie cutters **or** cutters of your choice (**Note:** Dimensions of cookie cutters used are: bell, 2¾" x 2¾"; bird, 4½" x 2"; large heart, 3⅛" x 3"; small heart, 2⅝" x 2⅛"; candle, 3⅛" x 3¾".)
2"-length 24-gauge floral wire (for **each** hanger)
Plastic wrap (for storing clay)
Utility scissors **or** wire cutters
Rolling pin
Waxed paper
Cookie sheet
Aluminum foil
Pencil
Ruler
Heavy paper (optional)
Craft knife (optional)

Option: If desired, make patterns from heavy paper and use craft knife to cut shapes from clay.
Note: Follow manufacturer's instructions when working with clay. Soften clay by warming it in your hands. Keep your hands clean, as clay attracts smudges. Wrap leftover clay tightly in plastic wrap and store away from sunlight.

1. Knead clay. Cover a smooth surface with waxed paper. To roll out clay, place between two sheets of waxed paper and roll with rolling pin. (**Note:** Utensils and surfaces used for food preparation should not be allowed to come into contact with craft materials, including polymer clay.) Roll out clay to 3/16" thick. Cut out shapes with cookie cutters, or use patterns to trace shapes onto clay, and cut out using craft knife. Re-roll leftover clay and cut additional shapes.
Note: If using cookie cutters that are not used solely for crafting purposes, be sure to wash them thoroughly in hot water and dishwashing liquid to remove all traces of clay before using them to make cookies.
2. Form **each** 2" length of wire into a "U" shape around pencil. Carefully insert ends of wire in 3/16" edge at top center of **each** ornament. Line cookie sheet with aluminum foil to prevent contact with clay. Place ornaments on cookie sheet and bake at 275°F for fifteen minutes. Remove from oven and let cool. Remove from cookie sheet.
3. Decorate ornaments as desired, using felt-tip markers and referring to photo on page 66 for decorating ideas.
Note: If you choose to seal the ornaments, be sure to test a small area first. Some clear varnish or acrylic sprays will react with the marker and cause it to bleed, ruining the ornament. You may wish to bake and decorate a small piece of leftover clay for testing purposes.

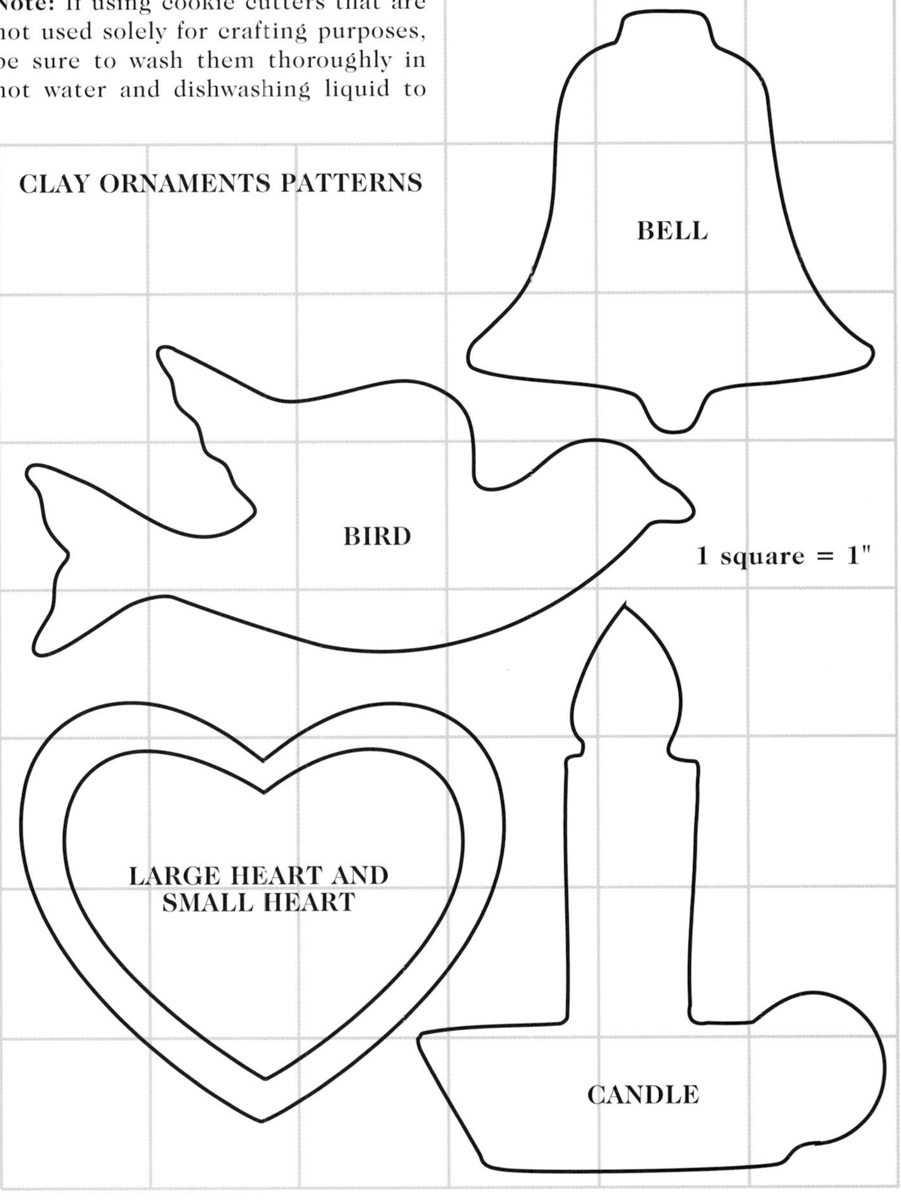

Copper Ornaments

Materials:

1 square foot 36-gauge copper tooling foil
Partial skein red embroidery floss, cut into 5" lengths (for hangers)
Copper cleaner **and** old, soft cloth
High-gloss spray varnish
Paper (for patterns)
Scissors: utility, sewing

Old magazine	Masking tape
Craft stick	Needle
Pencil	Awl **or** ice pick

Note: Materials listed will make six *Copper Ornaments,* two **each:** dove, pineapple, and heart-in-hand.

1. Enlarge patterns as indicated. Trace onto paper and cut out.
2. Place desired pattern atop copper and tape in place. Place copper atop old magazine and trace over all pattern lines with pencil, applying firm pressure. **Note:** Magazine will provide a somewhat soft working surface, which will aid in marking copper.
3. Remove pattern and cut out ornament, using utility scissors. Carefully smooth edges of ornament and flatten as needed, using craft stick. Go over pattern lines again, if needed, to make more distinct. (For heart-in-hand ornament, turn ornament wrong-side up and carefully press inside area of heart with craft stick, making heart slightly raised on front of ornament.) Punch a hole at top of ornament, using awl or ice pick.
4. Clean copper with copper cleaner and dry thoroughly. Spray one side of ornament with varnish and let dry. Repeat for remaining side.
5. Thread needle with 5"-length embroidery floss, run through hole, remove needle from floss, and tie a knot in floss ends to form hanger.
6. Repeat Steps 2–5 for each ornament.

Angels with Rosebuds

Crochet Abbreviations and Terms:
beg—begin(ning)
bet—between
ch—chain stitch
dc(s)—double crochet(s)
dec—decrease
lp(s)—loop(s)
nxt—next
rem—remaining
rep—repeat * to * number of times indicated
rnd—around
sc(s)—single crochet(s)
sk—skip
sl st—slip stitch
sp(s)—space(s)
st(s)—stitch(es)
tr—treble crochet
yo—yarn over
=—equal to or counts as
"V" sp—dc, ch and dc all in the same sp.
To decrease: Insert hook in st (= 2 lp on hook), insert hook in nxt st, yo, pull lp through st (= 3 lp on hook), yo, pull thread through all 3 lp.

Materials:
36 yds. size 10 crochet thread, color: white (**Note:** DMC Baroque was used for model.)
40" length variegated pink crochet thread
24" length green crochet thread
2 cotton balls (for stuffing head)
10" length clear nylon monofilament (for hanger)

Size 8 crochet hook	Index card
Fabric Stiffener	Tacky glue
Rustproof pins	Toothpick
Stretching board	Plastic wrap

Finished size: 3½" tall
Note: Materials listed will make one *Angel with Rosebud* ornament.

Angel
Head—Leave a 2" tail to use as marker. Ch 5, sl st in 1st ch to form ring.
Rnd A: Ch 3, 11 dc in ring (= 12 dc). **Do not** join rows. Mark rows by weaving beg tail up bet last st at the end of each row and first st of nxt row.
Rnd B: Make 2 sc in 3rd ch and in each dc (= 24 sc).
Rnds C–G: Sc in each sc (= 24 sc; count **as** you work).
Rnd H: (1 sc in nxt sc, dec nxt sc) rnd (= 16 sc).

Rnd I: Insert cotton ball. Dec in each sc (= 8 sc).
Rnd J: Sc in each sc (= 8 sc). Trim tail.
Rnd K: (Sc in nxt sc, 2 sc in nxt sc) rnd (= 12 sc).
Bodice—Row 1: Ch 4. *Dc in nxt sc, ch 1.* Rep * 10 times, sl st in 3rd ch and sp at beg of row (= 12 sp).
Row 2: Ch 5. *Dc in nxt sp; ch 2.* Rep * rnd, sl st in 3rd ch and sp (= 12 sp). Use blunt end of hook to fill head and neck.
Row 3: Ch 5, dc in same sp, ch 1. *In nxt sp make dc, ch 2, dc (= "V" sp), ch 1.* Rep * rnd, sl st in 3rd ch and sp (= 12 "V" sp).
Row 4: Ch 5, dc in same sp, ch 2, sk ch-1 sp. *In nxt "V" sp make dc, ch 2, dc, ch 2, sk ch-1 sp.* Rep * rnd, sl st in 3rd ch and sp (= 12 "V" sp).
Row 5: In same sp make ch 4, dc, ch 1, dc, ch 2, sk ch-2 sp (= mark hole in back for adding wings later). *In nxt "V" sp make dc, ch 1, dc, ch 1, dc; ch 2, sc in nxt sp, ch 2.* Rep * 10 times, sl st in 3rd ch.
Row 6: Sc in ch 1. *Ch 3, sc in nxt ch-1 sp.* Rep * 2 times. Ch 1, fold right-side out, sk 8 ch-1 sps, sc in nxt ch-1 sp. *Ch 3, sc in nxt ch-1 sp.* Rep * 2 times, ch 1, sk 8 ch-1 sps. Sl st in 1st sc and ch (= 8 sp including ch-1 sp under arms).
Skirt—Row 7: In same sp make sl st, ch 4, dc, ch 1, dc, ch 2. *Sk 1 sp, in nxt sp make dc, ch 1, dc, ch 1, dc, ch 2.* Rep * 2 times, sl st in 3rd ch and sp (= beg of 4 panels).
Row 8: Ch 4, dc in same sp; ch 1, in nxt ch-1 sp make dc, ch 1, dc (= 2 "V" sp per panel). *Ch 2, sk ch-2 sp, in each of nxt two ch-1 sps make dc, ch 1, dc, with ch 1 bet "V" sp.* Rep * 2 times, ch 2, sl st in 3rd ch and sp.
Row 9: Ch 4, dc in same sp, in nxt 2 ch-1 sp make dc, ch 1, dc (= 3 "V" sp per panel). *Ch 2, in each of nxt three ch-1 sp make dc, ch 1, dc.* Rep * 2 times, ch 2 sl st in 3rd ch and sp.
Rows 10–11: Ch 4, dc in same sp; in nxt "V" sp make dc, ch 2, dc; in nxt "V" sp make dc, ch 1, dc (= 3 "V" sp per panel). *Ch 2, in nxt "V" sp make dc, ch 1, dc; in nxt "V" sp make dc, ch 2, dc; in nxt "V" sp make dc, ch 1, dc.* Rep * 2 times, ch 2, sl st in 3rd ch and sp.
Rows 12–13: Ch 5, dc in same sp. *In each "V" sp make dc, ch 2, dc, with ch 2 bet four panels.* Rep * rnd, sl st in 3rd ch and sp.
Rows 14–15: Rep rows 12–13 except beg with ch 6 and make ch 3 in "V" sp instead of ch 2 each time; make ch 2 bet panels. Fasten off.
Right Wing—Attach thread on back of bodice at row 5 in ch-2 sp.
Row 1: Ch 3, sc in ch-2 sp above on row 4; ch 3, sc in ch-1 sp to right on row 3; ch 3, sc in ch-2 sp on row 2 to right; ch 3, sc in ch-1 sp on row 1 to right (= 4 sp).
Row 2: Ch 6, turn. *In each sp make sc, ch 3.* Rep * across, in last sp also make dc (= 5 sp).
Rows 3–4: Rep row 2 (= 6 & 7 sp).
Row 5: Ch 6, turn. *In each sp make sc, ch 3.* Rep * across except in nxt-to-last sp make sc, ch 2, dc in last sp (= 7 sp).
Row 6: Ch 3, turn, sk ch-2 sp. *In nxt sp make sc, ch 3.* Rep * across, in last sp also make dc (= 7 sp). Fasten off right wing. Make left wing to correspond but **do not** cut thread after row 6 of left wing.
Edging—Row 7: Ch 6, turn, sc in sp just made, ch 3, sc in nxt sp. *Ch 2, in nxt sp make dc, ch 1, dc, ch 1 dc; ch 2, sc in nxt sp.* Rep * 3 times, ch 2, sc in nxt sp, sl st in sc in row 1 at neck (= 4 scallops). Sl st over to and in 1st sc on right wing, sc in sp, ch 2, sc in nxt sp. *Ch 2, in nxt sp make dc, ch 1, dc, ch 1, dc; ch 2, sc in nxt sp.* Rep * 3 times, ch 3, sc in nxt sp, ch 6, sc in same sp. Fasten off.

To Stiffen:
Make cone of index card or thin cardboard and cover with plastic wrap. Saturate all but head of angel in fabric stiffener or a two-to-one solution of fresh white glue and water. Gently squeeze out excess. Insert cone in skirt and shape skirt, shoulders, and wings. Lay angel on back on plastic-covered stretching board. Use **rustproof** pins to hold wings in shape until almost dry. (**Note:** Use fan or hair dryer to speed drying.) Remove pins. Shape wings up and out with fingers and remove cone. Adjust skirt so angel stands. Curve wings and shape head. Let dry completely. Add rosebud as follows. To finish as an ornament, knot monofilament ends together. Use crochet hook to loop hanger through top of head, forming a lark's-head knot.

Rosebud
Note: Make dcs and scs under 1 strand of thread in chain. Bud will curl naturally.
Rose—With pink thread, ch 10, make 3 dc in 5th ch from hook, 3 dc in nxt 4 chains (= 15 dc); sc in base of rose. Cut thread and knot ends.
Leaves—Leave 3" tails on both ends for tying rose to ornament. With green thread, make a lp on hook and sc in base of rose. (Ch 6, sc in 4th ch and each rem ch and 1st sc; sc in base) 2 times. Cut thread 3" long and knot ends. Dab knots with glue and let dry. Trim pink thread only. In front of bodice, row 4, use crochet hook to pull green tails to back through center sp and again to front sps to left and right of center. Tie knots in front under rosebud and secure with dab of glue on toothpick. Dab glue on green ends, twist together to form stem, curve, and press to shape. When dry, trim bottom of stem to desired length.

Handprint Ornaments

Materials:
- Two 8" squares muslin, washed and ironed
- 1¼"-square scrap red felt
- 1¼" square Pellon® Wonder-Under® Transfer Web
- 8" square Pellon® fleece
- Brayer (printer's hand-inking roller) **or** small paintbrush
- Aluminum foil **or** disposable pie plate
- Non-toxic fabric paint, color: kelly green
- 6"-length ⅛"-wide red satin ribbon
- Sewing thread, color: red
- Disappearing-ink fabric-marking pen
- Red permanent fine-tip marker
- Pinking shears
- Plastic cover (for table)
- Old plate **or** aluminum foil
- Sewing machine with zigzag or decorative stitches
- Scissors
- Pencil
- Iron

HANDPRINT ORNAMENTS PATTERN

Note: Materials listed will make one *Handprint Ornament.*

1. Place muslin atop plastic-covered table. Squeeze paint onto plate or foil. Roll brayer in paint, coating roller evenly. Roll brayer over child's hand, coating it evenly with paint. Press child's hand on muslin, gently pushing down on back of hand. Have child lift hand straight up. If using one large piece of muslin when making several ornaments, leave 3" between handprints for cutting and sewing. Follow manufacturer's instructions for heat-setting paint.
2. Trace heart shape onto paper side of Wonder-Under®. Fuse to back of red felt, following manufacturer's instructions for fusing. Cut out heart shape and fuse to palm of handprint.
3. Layer plain backing muslin, fleece, and muslin with handprint right-side up. Pin layers together. Draw mitten shape around handprint with disappearing-ink fabric-marking pen, leaving approximately ¼" between ink line and fingers. Fold ribbon in half and insert ends between muslin layers at top of ornament to form hanging loop. Zigzag, sew decorative machine stitches

of your choice, or hand quilt along line around perimeter of ornament, using red thread and securing ribbon ends in seam. Remove pins.
Note: Raw edges of muslin will show.
4. Trim around perimeter of ornament, approximately ¼" away from stitched edge, using pinking shears.
5. Have child sign and date back of ornament with red, permanent, fine-tip marker.

Fan Ornaments

Note: Please read instructions carefully before beginning. For these projects, a general materials list and instructions have been given. Specific materials and instructions for each ornament have been listed separately. Materials listed will make three *Fan Ornaments*.

Materials:
Three 4" squares ½"-thick STYROFOAM brand plastic foam
⅛ yd. 44/45"-wide red fabric of your choice
⅛ yd. 44/45"-wide green fabric of your choice
⅛ yd. 44/45"-wide white fabric of your choice
¾ yd. ⅛"-wide green satin ribbon, cut into 9" lengths (for hangers)
Artists's palette knife **or** serrated steak knife
Fine-tip permanent marker
Tacky glue
Ruler
Tracing paper
Sharp pencil
Straight pins
Scissors
¾" putty knife
Toothpicks

Ornament #1
½ yd. ⅜"-wide green grosgrain ribbon
7" length ⅛"-wide white satin ribbon
3" green baby rickrack
½ yd. red baby rickrack

Ornament #2
25" twisted silk cord
⅜ yd. metallic green pearls-by-the-yard

Ornament #3
½ yd. ⅜"-wide green grosgrain ribbon
⅝ yd. white soutache braid
10" length ⅛"-wide white satin ribbon
2 small brass bells

Helpful Hints: A serrated knife will cut easily through plastic foam. For easier, smoother cuts, wax the knife blade before cutting. For smooth, round edges, "sand" the foam with another piece of plastic foam. For large pieces, cut first and then sand to final shape.
1. Trace pattern onto tracing paper three times and cut out.
2. Place fan pattern atop Styrofoam® square, aligning straight edges of pattern with edges of foam square. Mark top curve of fan shape on foam square, using permanent marker. Carefully cut curve, using serrated steak knife and a sawing motion. Gently "sand" rough edges with a scrap of Styrofoam®.
3. Mark bottom curve and fan blades using permanent marker. Score these lines using a sharp pencil.
4. Cut paper pattern apart. Pin pattern pieces right-side up atop right side of fabric of your choice. Trace around pattern pieces and cut out, adding ¼" seam allowances to all sides.
5. Working atop a flat surface, center fabric atop middle blade of fan. Position putty knife over fabric and scored lines. Push seam allowances into Styrofoam® at scored lines, using tip of knife and being careful not to push through Styrofoam®. (**Note:** For a clean, crisp seam, hold putty knife straight up and down while working.) Trim excess fabric with scissors. Tuck in stray edges with putty knife. Repeat for each blade, working to outside edge of fan. Leave top edges loose. Tuck curved seam at crescent of fan, using putty knife.
6. Clip fabric at top of fan at ½" intervals. Wrap fabric around edge of ornament, and glue in place.
7. Place fan atop wrong side of backing fabric. Trace around fan. Cut out, adding ¼" seam allowance to all sides. Clip top curve at ½" intervals to traced line. Place fabric on back of fan and glue seam allowances to edge of fan.
8. Repeat Steps 2–7 for remaining ornaments.
9. ***Ornament #1:*** Cut red rickrack to fit seams between fan blades and top edge. Apply a fine line of glue in blade seams, at top edge, and at crescent curve, using toothpick. Glue red rickrack over seams to cover, and along top edge of fan. Glue green rickrack along crescent curve, wrapping ends at edge of ornament. Tie white satin ribbon into a bow and glue to fan, referring to photo on page 68 for placement. Glue green grosgrain ribbon around edge of ornament, covering all seams and loose ends.
10. ***Ornament #2:*** Cut pearls-by-the-yard to fit seams between fan blades and crescent curve. Apply a fine line of glue in blade seams and along crescent curve, using toothpick. Glue pearls along straight seams first; then along crescent curve. Center twisted silk cord at top of fan and glue around edges, covering all seams and loose ends. Tie cord ends in a square knot at bottom point of fan. Tie a knot approximately 1" from each cord end. Dip cord ends in glue and twist to prevent cord from unraveling. Let dry and trim as desired.
11. ***Ornament #3:*** Cut soutache braid to fit seams between fan blades, top edge, and crescent curve. Apply a fine line of glue in blade seams,using toothpick, and gently press braid in place. Repeat for top edge and crescent curve, wrapping ends at edge of ornament. Tie white satin ribbon into a bow and tie a brass bell 1" from each ribbon end. Glue in place, referring to photo for placement. Glue green grosgrain ribbon around edge of ornament, covering all seams and loose ends.
12. To make hangers, fold each 9" length of green satin ribbon in half to form loop and knot ends together 1" from cut ends. Glue to back of each ornament at top center.

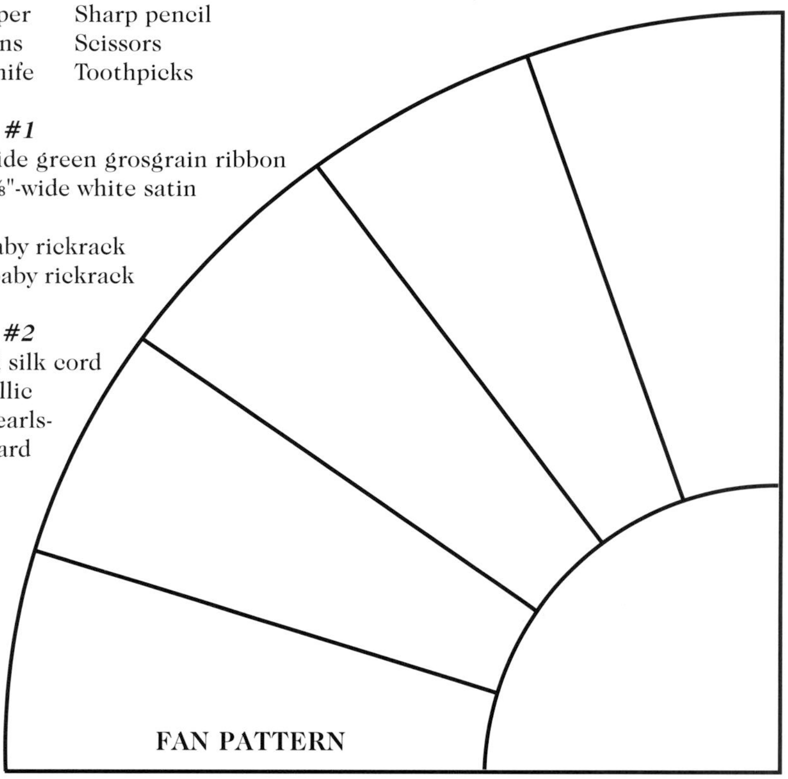

FAN PATTERN

Calico Angels

Materials:
Assorted scraps calico-print fabrics
Thread to match fabric scraps
2" square flesh-colored felt
¼ yd. Pellon® Wonder-Under® Transfer Web
1 skein **each** of DMC 6-strand embroidery floss, colors: #3773 (flesh, medium), #823 (navy, dark), color to match calicoes
6" length ¼"–⅜"-wide lace edging
Polyester filling
Straight pins
Scissors
Hand-sewing needle
Paper and pencil
Tacky glue
Sewing machine

Note: Materials listed will make one *Calico Angel* ornament.

1. Enlarge patterns as indicated. Trace angel body pattern onto paper and cut out. Cut two 7" squares from one fabric scrap for angel body. Lay pattern atop wrong side of one fabric scrap and mark. Pin fabric squares with right sides together and sew around three sides along pattern lines, leaving bottom open for turning. Trim seams and clip curves. Remove pins. Turn right-side out and press, turning bottom edges to inside.
2. Trace remaining pattern pieces, excluding face and hands, onto paper side of Wonder-Under®. Fuse to wrong side of fabric pieces, following manufacturer's instructions for fusing. Cut out all pieces and remove paper backing. Arrange pieces in their proper places on one side of angel, referring to photo on page 69 for placement, and fuse in place. Stuff lightly with polyester filling and whipstitch opening closed.
3. Cut face and hands from felt. Make French knots for eyes, using navy embroidery floss. Glue face in place, referring to photo for placement. Glue hands in place at ends of arms, holding until glue begins to set and then letting dry thoroughly. Work blanket stitch around wings and halo, referring to blanket stitch illustration and using floss color to match calico. Make hanger from 3" length floss, pulling threaded needle through top center of angel, removing needle from floss, and tying floss ends in a knot to form hanger.
4. Cut two 24"-long pieces from flesh floss. Fold in half. Hold one end securely in each hand and twist floss length in opposite directions until tightly twisted. Fold twisted floss in half, holding securely; then release one end and let floss twist. Tie a knot in raw-edge end to hold twist and trim ends close to knot. Glue knot at one side of face and let glue set. Loop and glue floss in place, referring to illustration and tucking second end under curls. Let dry.
5. Glue lace edging where skirt and petticoat meet, referring to photo for placement. Trim away excess edging. Let dry.

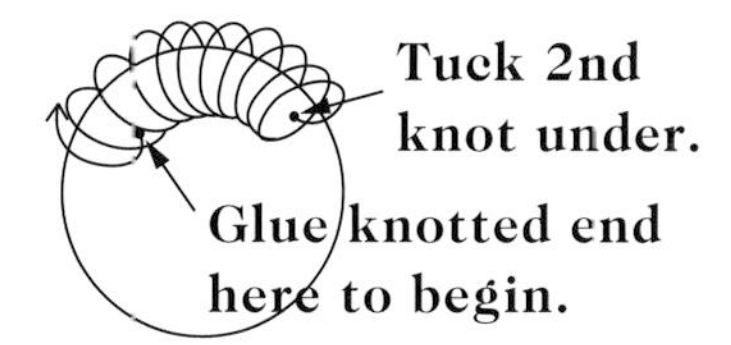

ANGEL HAIR ILLUSTRATION

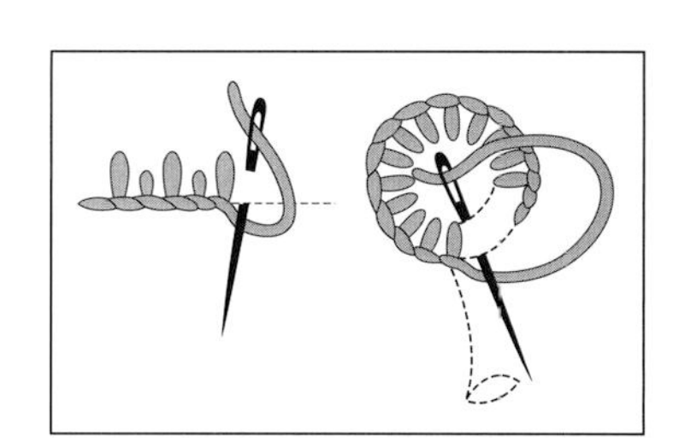
BLANKET STITCH

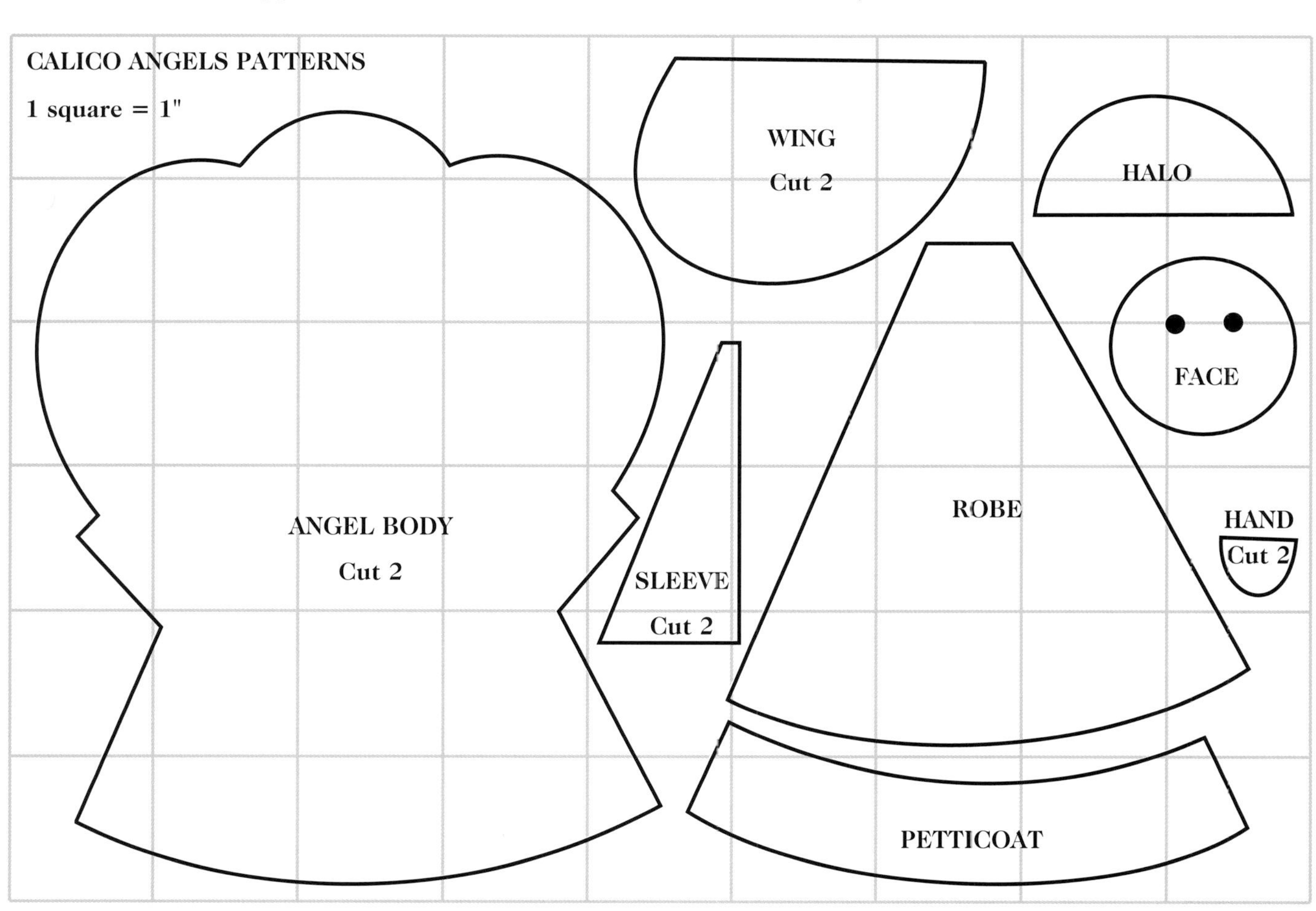

Staff SEEDLESS
RAISINS
100% NATURAL-NO PRESERVATIVES
Staff SEEDLESS
RAISINS
100% NATURAL-NO PRESERVATIVES
Jif
FISKARS
Aleene's
ORIGINAL
"TACKY"
GLUE
25% More
FREE

YULETIDE TABLES

The Yuletide season is filled with special events, but perhaps none is as popular and widely observed as the Christmas dinner. Family members gather from near and far to visit and exchange gifts, and a gala meal is always part of that celebration. Whether the meal takes place on Christmas Eve or Christmas Day the repast is always awe-inspiring—a giant, mouth-watering turkey with stuffing; a colorful assortment of vegetables and casseroles; warm, buttery bread; and a myriad of pies, cakes, and other tasty desserts. Handmade table accessories and centerpieces add an air of whimsy or elegance.

Decorative Dining

When family members and guests gather around the dining table for a holiday meal, the food satisfies their palates. But why not create a feast for the eyes, as well? Set a festive table this Christmas, and for years to come, with the collection of table runners, place mats, napkins, centerpieces, and more featured in this chapter.

The pineapple has, since Colonial days, been seen as a symbol of hospitality in this country. Appropriately, it is commonly used in centerpieces during the holidays, when guests are welcomed into every home. The ***Pineapple Centerpiece***, shown below, has the benefit of being assembled just once and used season after season, unlike one that contains fresh fruit. The entire pineapple, the red apples that surround it, and the green leaves that cover the wooden base are made from easy-to-work-with paper cord. We think this attention-getter is definitely one of a kind!

A pair of ***Plaid Table Trimmers***, shown at right, made from bright, red-and-green Christmas fabric with metallic gold threads woven through it, makes an appealing table covering. The metallic threads look wonderful with gold-trimmed crystal or china. Crisscrossed in the center, these runners allow the beauty of the table's surface to show. Choose an eye-catching plaid in traditional or non-traditional colors for your Yuletide table decor. Or use a fabric that complements your Christmas china for your table trimmers.

Sparkling metallic threads light up the muslin ensemble shown on page 82. Adorn a table with these natural-colored ***Muslin Place Mats and Napkins*** and their golden trees. The metallic trees on the fringed place mats are surrounded by free-form "meander quilting," also sewn with gold thread. The napkins feature a simple golden outline of a tree. This ensemble can be used for a fancy dinner or a simple breakfast with the family.

Opposite*—The* Plaid Table Trimmers *make an especially pleasing beginning to a colorfully set, seasonal table. The instructions, which include tips for accommodating different table sizes, are on page 88.*

Left*—It's a tropical fruit like you've never seen before—our* Pineapple Centerpiece *is crafted from paper cord. Instructions are on page 88.*

Above—Enchanting place settings will complement elegant china and crystal, or everyday dishes. Instructions for the Muslin Place Mats and Napkins ***are on page 89.***

The ***Poinsettia Runner and Trivet Set***, shown above right, is a pretty and practical table ensemble. Everyone loves the beauty of poinsettias, those brilliant, red flowers so representative of the Christmas season. Made from easy-care fabrics and assembled by following simple instructions, this machine-appliquéd runner and matching trivet will brighten winter days just as real poinsettias do. Place them on your table with a live poinsettia as a centerpiece.

Doily Place Mats and ***Rosebud Trees***, shown on page 84, will turn a table into a Victorian-look delight. Create the dainty place mats by weaving ribbon through purchased, round crochet doilies that have been treated with fabric stiffener. They look wonderfully romantic against a rich, wooden table. You can also make place mats using rectangular doilies; just remember to adjust the ribbon yardage before purchasing. The impressive rosebud table decorations are surprisingly simple to assemble. Just wrap the base

of a silk tree with fuchsia ribbon, then glue a garden of miniature or dried rosebuds onto the branches.

Above—The Poinsettia Runner and Trivet Set *will become a favorite table decoration—it's easy to make, as well as bright and festive. Instructions begin on page 89.*

***Above—**Give your table a touch of Victoriana with these* Doily Place Mats *and* Rosebud Napkin Rings and Trees. *You can craft these simple projects in your spare minutes, and you will certainly enjoy the impressive results. Instructions are on page 89.*

The ***Snowy Evergreens Place Mats and Napkin Rings***, and the ***Ho Ho Ho Place Mat***, shown at right, feature bright, Christmas colors and quick cross stitching. White lace and a ruffled, dotted-swiss edging trim the ***Snowy Evergreens*** set, and candy-cane-striped cording rims the ho-ho-ho design. The red fabric used for the snowy evergreens contrasts nicely with the green trees and white snowflakes. We show a clear plate and cup with our set, but plain white china would also look super with it.

You can stitch the ***Ho Ho Ho Place Mat*** in your spare minutes when the children are napping or while you are waiting at a doctor's office. Jingle bells at the tip of each Santa's hat are certain to amuse dinner guests.

***Above right**—Cross-stitched green trees and white snowflakes contrast beautifully with the red background of this table setting. Charts and instructions for the* Snowy Evergreens Place Mats and Napkin Rings *are on page 92.*

***Right**—Santa Claus in cross stitch, surrounded by snowflakes, stars, and a jolly "ho ho ho"—what a fun beginning to a Christmas meal! Instructions for the* Ho Ho Ho Place Mat *begin on page 92.*

Rudolph inspired the edibles and table decor shown above. The ***Reindeer Sandwiches*** are peanut-butter-and-jelly, cut diagonally and decorated with pretzel antlers, raisin eyes, and cherry noses. The ***Marshmallow Reindeer***, with their red, candy noses and plastic eyes, are not for consumption, but make whimsical decorations that kids can help create for their own table. The ***Sugarplum Tree*** is easy to make from twigs and soft candies, such as gumdrops.

Perhaps our most unusual centerpiece is the ***Holiday Aviary***, shown at right. The cheery house is painted with *trompe l'oeil* garlands, wreath, door, and windows, complete with painted curtains and candles. When placed in the center of the breakfast table, this delightful project will bring early-morning smiles to all.

Above*—Turn the kids' table into a party, with* Reindeer Sandwiches *and* Marshmallow Reindeer. *You probably already have everything you need to make these holiday charmers! Instructions are on page 94.*

Right*—These feathered friends didn't fly south for the winter—they're right at home in the* Holiday Aviary, *a whimsical centerpiece to delight family and friends. Instructions begin on page 94.*

Plaid Table Trimmers

Materials:
2 yds. 44/45"-wide plaid fabric of your choice
Thread to match
Hand-sewing needle
Scissors
Measuring Tape
Iron
Sewing machine

Note: Materials listed will make two runners and four napkins. Runners were made to be crisscrossed on table measuring 42" x 54". (See photo on page 81.) To make runners for a different size table, measure width and length of table and add 18" to each measurement. (This will give you a 9" drop on each side of table.)

1. Cut one 14½" x 72" piece from plaid fabric for runner. Cut one 14½" x 60" piece from plaid fabric for runner. Cut four 16" squares from plaid fabric for napkins.
2. To finish each runner, press raw edges under 1" along lengthwise edges and hem by hand. Turn raw-edge ends under narrowly and hem by hand. To make point at each end, fold runner lengthwise, placing right sides of fabric together, and machine-sew across ends. Turn right-side out. Fold seam just sewn toward center on wrong side of fabric, forming a point. Press. Tack down loose edge.
3. To finish each napkin, press raw edges under ¼". Turn raw edges under narrowly and hem by hand. Press.

Pineapple Centerpiece

Materials:
10¾"-diameter circle of ⅜"-thick wood
6" STYROFOAM brand plastic foam ball
Two 5½" squares 2"-thick STYROFOAM brand plastic foam
10 yds. paper cord (2½" wide when untwisted), color: natural (**Note:** Plaid Paper Capers™ was used for model.)
20 yds. paper cord, color: green
5 yds. paper cord, color: red
Ten 2" x 2" plastic apples
Twenty-five 8" lengths 22-gauge wire (for pineapple leaves)
Ten 3" lengths 22-gauge wire (for apple leaves)
Spackling (available at hardware stores)
Tracing paper
Wire cutters
Craft knife
Tacky glue
Scissors
Ruler

Making the pineapple:
1. Cut off 1½" from bottom of Styrofoam® ball and 1" from top. Glue two squares of Styrofoam® together and glue them to top of ball. Cut form into pineapple shape. (**Note:** Pineapple will be approximately 7½" tall.) Fill in space where Styrofoam® pieces join, using spackling. Let dry.
2. Untwist green and natural paper cords. Cut a circle from green to fit top, flat surface of pineapple. Apply glue along edge and press in place. Cover bottom of pineapple, using natural paper cord.
3. Cut natural paper cord into 2" squares (approximately 180 squares). Fold each square diagonally twice, forming a triangle with a 2" base. (**Note:** Each side of triangle will have a different design—one horizontal, the other vertical, because of grain, or texture, of paper.) Glue all triangles with design going same direction.
4. Begin first row at top of pineapple. Apply glue to wrong side of base of first triangle and press triangle as close to edge of green circle as possible. Apply glue to base of second triangle and overlap base of first triangle approximately ½", referring to Illustration 1. Continue around top of pineapple until first row is complete, overlapping each triangle as indicated. (**Note:** First row will stand up above the top, flat surface.) Continue with second row, overlapping first row as shown in Illustration 2. Continue rows until pineapple is covered.
Note: The triangle points on the last few rows may need to be glued down, as they may tend to stick out.
5. Trace pineapple leaf pattern onto tracing paper and cut out. Cut fifty leaves from green paper cord. Apply glue down center of one leaf, beginning 1" from top, and around edges. Place wire atop glue line in center of leaf and place another leaf atop wire. Press together and let dry. Repeat for remaining leaves. Insert leaves into top of pineapple and bend into desired shape, referring to photo on page 80.

Making the apples:
1. Untwist red paper cord and set aside. Measure apples from top center to bottom center and cut ¾"-wide strips of red paper cord this length. Apply glue to edges of paper cord and press onto apple, crimping top and bottom ends. Continue gluing on strips, overlapping previous strip slightly, until apple is covered.
2. Trace apple leaf pattern onto tracing paper and cut out. Cut twenty leaves from green paper cord. Follow instructions for pineapple leaves to assemble apple leaves. Insert wire into apple at stem and bend leaf into desired shape, referring to photo.

Assembling the centerpiece:
1. Cut leaves from green paper cord, using pattern for pineapple leaves. Place leaves in circle around base, with pointed ends extending approximately 1" beyond outer edge of wood base.
Note: These leaves do not require wires in center, since they will lay flat on base.
2. Place pineapple in center of base and arrange apples around it, referring to photo for placement. Glue to secure.

ILLUSTRATION 1

ILLUSTRATION 2

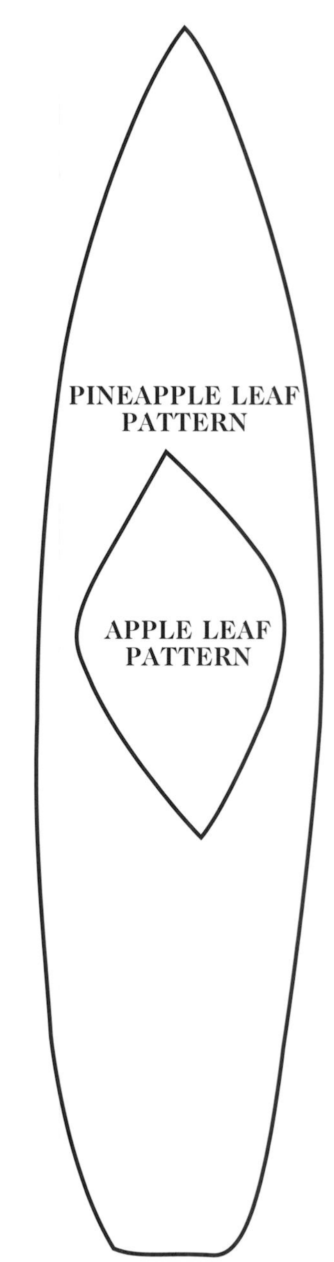

Muslin Place Mats and Napkins

Materials:
3½ yds. 44/45"-wide muslin
Thread to match
1 yd. Pellon® Fleece
One spool Kreinik Japan Gold #1
Freezer paper
White thread
Scissors
Iron
Sewing machine with darning foot and size 16 needle
Serger (optional)

Note: Materials listed will make six sets of *Muslin Place Mats and Napkins*. Darning foot does not put hard pressure on fabric being sewn, enabling you to sew in free-motion "squiggles" rather than in a straight line. Metallic thread is easy to use in machine when large machine needle with no snags or rough spots is used.

1. Enlarge tree pattern as indicated. Trace onto papery side of freezer paper and cut out. For mats, cut twelve 12" x 17" pieces from muslin and six 12" x 17" pieces from fleece. For napkins, cut six 18" squares from muslin.
2. To assemble each place mat, layer muslin pieces with wrong sides together and with fleece in between. Sew around perimeter ⅝" in from edges, using Japan Gold #1 in needle and white thread in bobbin. Iron tree pattern to upper-left corner of mat. Sew around pattern. Peel off freezer-paper pattern and reuse on another place mat.
3. Sew squiggles around tree in upper-left corner of each place mat, sewing as follows. Lower feed dogs on machine and attach quilting foot. Lower presser foot. Place both hands on place mat (as if placing them on a keyboard) and move place mat in small circles, forming squiggles and loops in random pattern. Keep loops inside seam line and outside design area.
4. Carefully open ⅝" seam allowance outside seam line and cut away excess fleece. Clip into muslin seam allowance every ⅛"–¼" to fringe.
5. For napkins, use serger to form rolled hem or use sewing machine to hem, or fringe edges. Iron tree pattern onto one corner of each napkin. Sew around tree with Japan Gold #1.

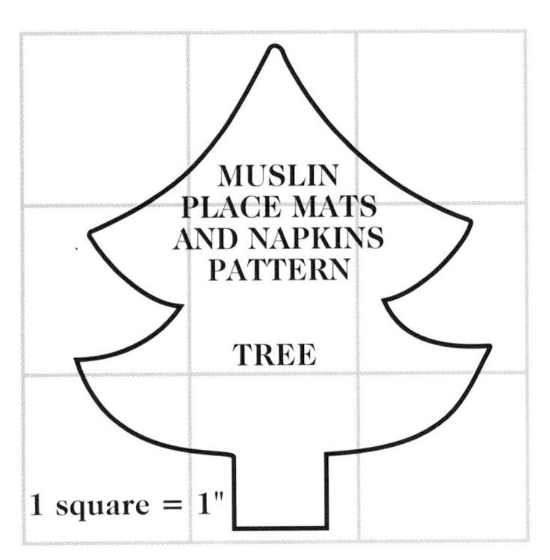

Crafting Fun with Roses

Doily Place Mats
Materials:
Four 12" crocheted doilies
6 yds. ¼"-wide burgundy satin ribbon
Corrugated cardboard **or** corkboard
Long straight pins
Plastic wrap
Craft glue
Fabric stiffener

Note: Materials listed will make four *Doily Place Mats*.

1. Cover corrugated cardboard or corkboard with plastic wrap.
2. Wet each doily thoroughly with fabric stiffener.
3. Place doilies on plastic-covered board and block into shape, securing with pins around edge. Let dry overnight.
4. Remove from board and weave ribbon through threads near edge of each doily. Overlap ribbon ends on back side and glue to secure. Cut remaining ribbon into four equal lengths and tie each length into a bow. Glue one bow to front of each doily to cover overlap of ribbon ends.

Rosebud Napkin Rings
Materials:
Cardboard paper-towel tube
6 yds. ¼"-wide satin ribbon
20 dried **or** silk miniature rosebuds
German statice
Measuring tape
Craft glue
Sharp knife
Scissors

Note: Materials listed will make four *Rosebud Napkin Rings*.

1. Cut four 1"-wide rings from tube.
2. Cut ribbon into 1½-yd. lengths. For each napkin ring, glue one end of ribbon to inside of cardboard ring. Wrap ribbon around ring, overlapping slightly and covering both inside and outside of cardboard ring. Glue ribbon end in place on inside of ring.
3. Glue statice and five rosebuds to each napkin ring as desired, referring to photo on page 84.

Rosebud Trees
Materials:
9"-tall green silk tree
130–150 pink and red dried **or** silk miniature rosebuds
5½" length 1⅜"-wide fuchsia ribbon
German statice
Hot glue gun

Note: Materials listed will make one *Rosebud Tree*.

1. Glue statice in spaces between branches.
2. Glue rosebuds on tree, spacing evenly.
3. Wrap ribbon around base of tree, overlapping ends and gluing to secure.

Poinsettia Runner and Trivet Set

Materials:
1 yd. 44/45"-wide white print fabric
1 yd. 44/45"-wide green print fabric (for poinsettia centers and backing)
½ yd. 44/45"-wide red print fabric
Small scrap hunter green solid fabric
2 pkgs. Coats Extra Wide Double Fold Bias Tape, Art. M. 890, color: 61A forest green
1 spool **each** Coats Rayon Machine Embroidery Thread, Art. D. 63, colors: 01 white, 177 kerry green
1 spool **each** Coats Dual Duty Plus All-Purpose Thread, Art.210, colors: 01 white (for construction), 61A hunter green (for binding)
Coats Clear Nylon Monofilament (for quilting)
1 yd. fleece (thin quilt batting)
½ yd. fusible web
Measuring tape
Straight pins
Scissors
Pencil
Paper
Iron
Sewing machine with zigzag stitch

Note: Use a ¼" seam allowance throughout for construction. Appliqué pieces do not have seam allowances. Trace patterns onto paper and cut out. Trace around paper pattern pieces as indicated on wrong side of fabric.
1. Cut two runner ends and one trivet front from red print. Cut one 18" x 14" rectangle from white print. Cut one 36" x

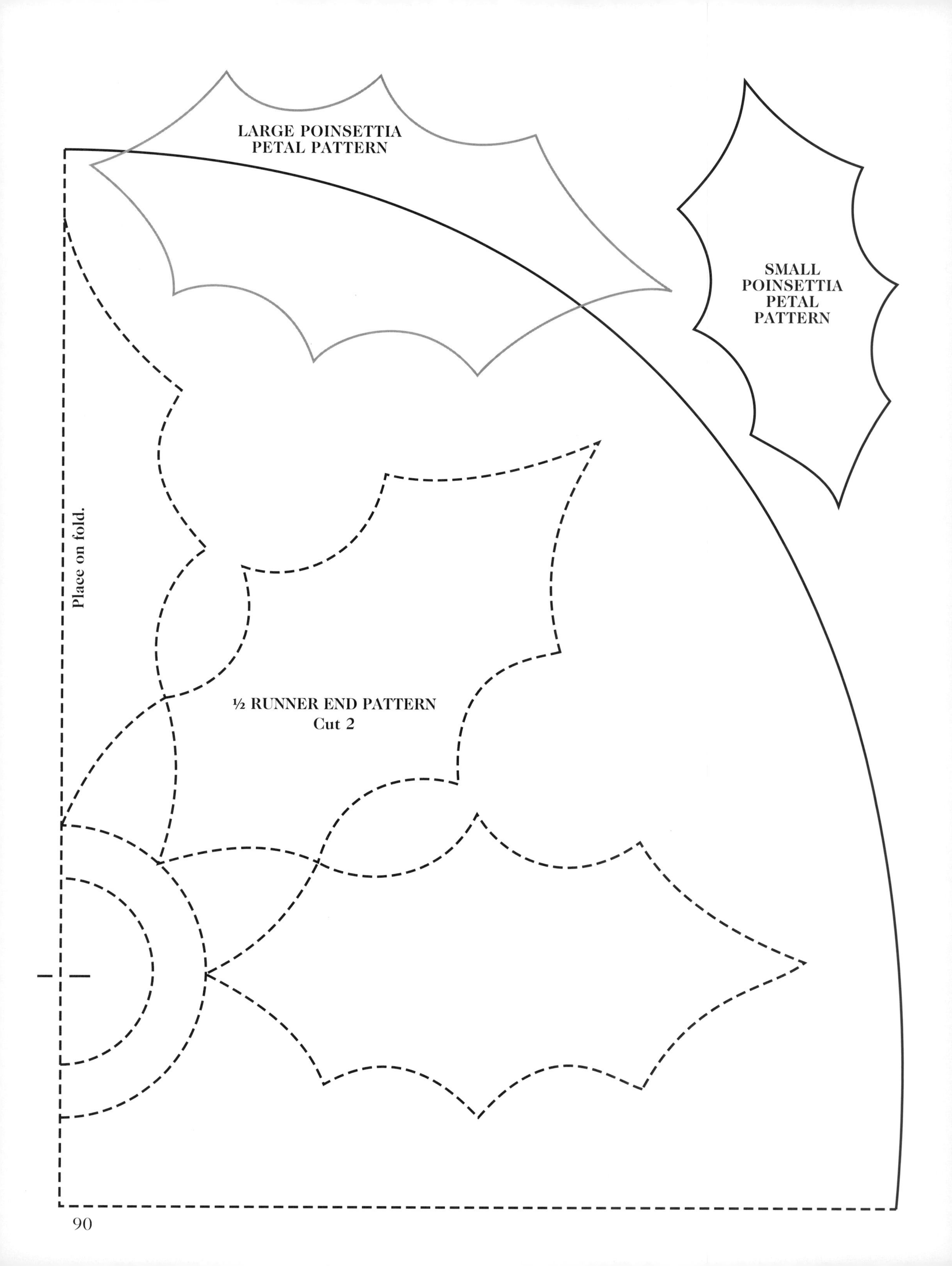
LARGE POINSETTIA
PETAL PATTERN
SMALL
POINSETTIA
PETAL
PATTERN
Place on fold.
½ RUNNER END PATTERN
Cut 2

14" rectangle for runner backing and one trivet back from green print.

2. Trace ten large and eight small poinsettia petals onto paper side of fusible web. Fuse petals to white print, following manufacturer's instructions for fusing. Trace two large circles, three medium circles, and one small circle onto fusible web. Fuse two large and one medium circle to green print. Fuse remaining three circles to hunter green solid. Cut out.

3. Fuse appliqué shapes in place on runner ends and trivet front, following dotted lines on patterns as a guide for placement. Machine appliqué pieces with rayon thread in machine and bobbin, using white for petals and green for circles.

4. Cut two 14" strips of bias tape. Open each tape length on center fold and press open, leaving outer folds intact. Sew one strip to each 14" end of white rectangle, using outer folds as a seam guide. Sew one appliquéd runner end to opposite side of each bias strip. Press.

5. Cut one 18" x 40" fleece strip for table runner and one fleece circle for trivet, using trivet pattern.

6. For both runner and trivet, layer backing right-side down, fleece, and assembled front right-side up. Pin or baste layers together.

7. Machine quilt around all appliqué pieces, using green thread in bobbin and monofilament in top of machine. Quilt white area of runner diagonally in both directions, spacing lines 2" apart. Quilt along seam lines. Remove pins or basting.

8. Trim fleece and backing on runner even with raw edges of runner front. Replace monofilament with green thread. Bind raw edges of runner and trivet with remaining bias tape.

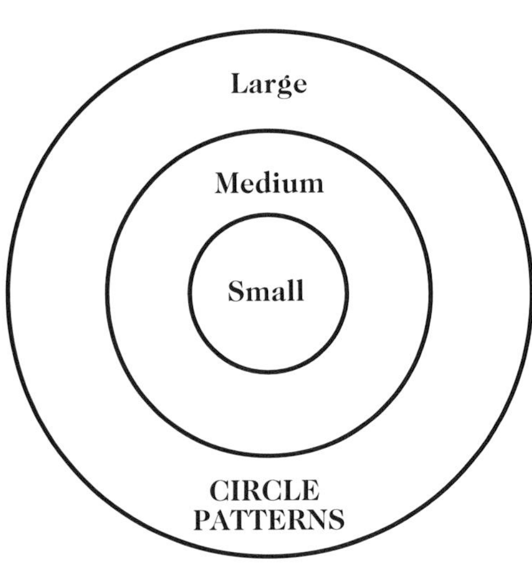

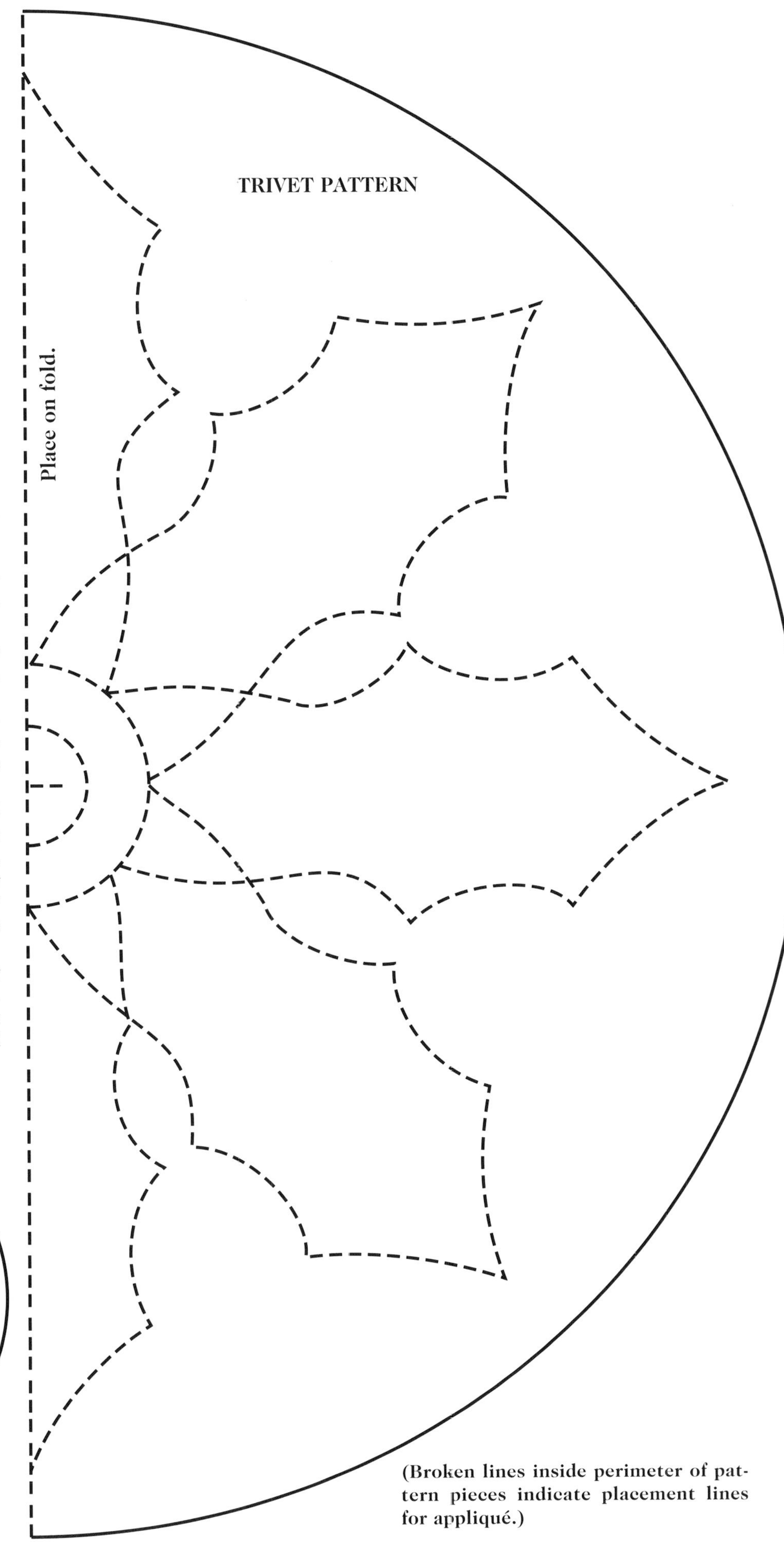

(Broken lines inside perimeter of pattern pieces indicate placement lines for appliqué.)

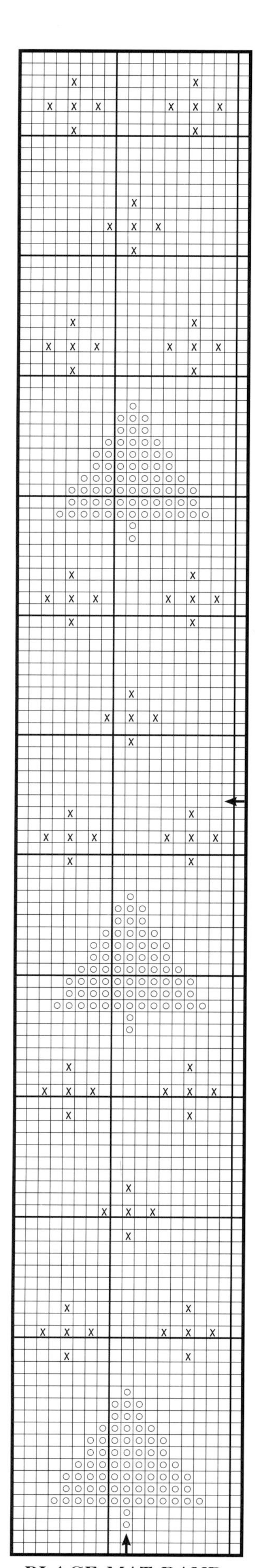
PLACE MAT BAND

Snowy Evergreens

DMC	Color
○ 909	emerald, vy. dk.
X white	white

Fabric: 14-count Aida from Charles Craft, Inc.
Stitch count:
Place Mat Band 121H x 15W
Napkin Ring 25H x 30W
Design Size:
Place Mat Band 8¾" x 1⅛"
Napkin Ring 1⅞" x 2¼"

Note: Cut one 17¼" x 12¾" piece cranberry Aida for front of place mat. Cut one 2¾" x 8¼" piece cranberry Aida for napkin ring. Begin stitching design on place mat 1" in from left and right edges, and 1⅜" in from top and bottom edges. Center design on napking ring.
Instructions: Cross stitch using two strands of floss.

Finishing instructions
Materials:
17¼" x 12¾" piece pre-quilted fabric (for place mat backing)
2¾" x 8¼" piece pre-quilted fabric (for napkin ring backing)
½ yd. 44/45"-wide complementary fabric (for ruffle)
2 yds. 1"-wide pre-gathered white lace trim (for place mat and napkin ring)
15" square complementary fabric (for napkin)
Sewing thread, color: red
1"-long strip red Velcro® Scissors
Hand-sewing needle Straight pins
Sewing machine Iron

Note: Materials listed will make one place mat, one napkin ring, and one napkin. Use a ½" seam allowance throughout.

Place Mat
1. Complete cross stitch following instructions given.

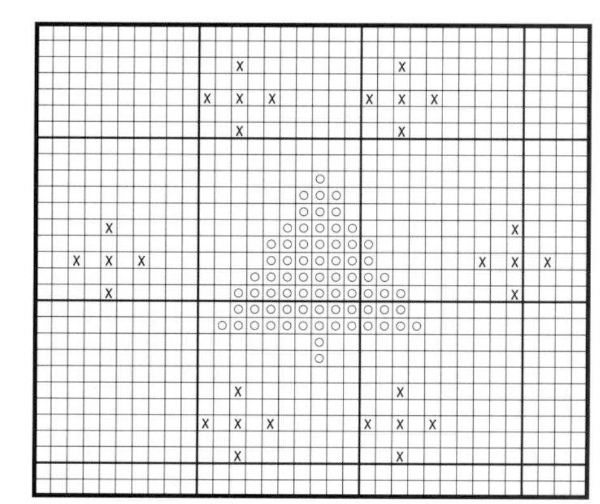
NAPKIN RING

2. Cut ruffle fabric into 6"-wide strips and piece to 130" length. Fold strip in half lengthwise, placing wrong sides to fabric together, and press. Run gathering thread close to edge along raw-edge side. Pull threads to gather ruffle.
3. Sew pre-gathered lace trim to ruffle, aligning raw edges.
4. Sew assembled ruffle and trim to place mat, placing trim side against right side of cross-stitch fabric and having raw edge of ruffle toward edge of cross-stitch fabric. Ease at corners, being careful not to catch trim.
5. Pin quilted backing and place mat together, placing right sides of fabric together and making sure ruffle and trim lay toward center of place mat. Sew together, being careful not to catch trim and leaving a 6" opening for turning. Remove pins. Trim seams, turn, and press. Whipstitch opening closed.

Napkin Ring
1. Complete cross stitch following instructions given.
2. Sew a 7½" length of pre-gathered lace trim to each long edge of cross-stitch fabric ⅛" from top and bottom edges of design, placing raw edge of trim toward raw edge of cross-stitch fabric.
3. Sew quilted backing to napkin ring, placing right sides of fabric together and making sure trim lays toward center of napkin ring. Leave one short end open for turning. Trim seams, turn, and press. Whipstitch opening closed.
4. Tack Velcro® on cross-stitch fabric side at one end of napkin ring and on quilted backing side at the other end. Overlap ends to use.

Napkin
1. To hem napkin, turn edges under ¼" around perimeter of fabric and press. Turn under ¼" again, press, and topstitch in place.

Ho Ho Ho Place Mat

DMC	Color
X 666	red, bt. (two skeins)
▮ 700	green, bt.
○ white	white
· 819	baby pink, lt.
bs 806	peacock, dk.

Fabric: 16-count white Aida from Charles Craft, Inc.
Stitch count: 175H x 228W
Design size:

11-count	16" x 20¾"
14-count	12½" x 16¼"
16-count	11" x 14¼"
18-count	9¾" x 12¾"

HO HO HO PLACE MAT

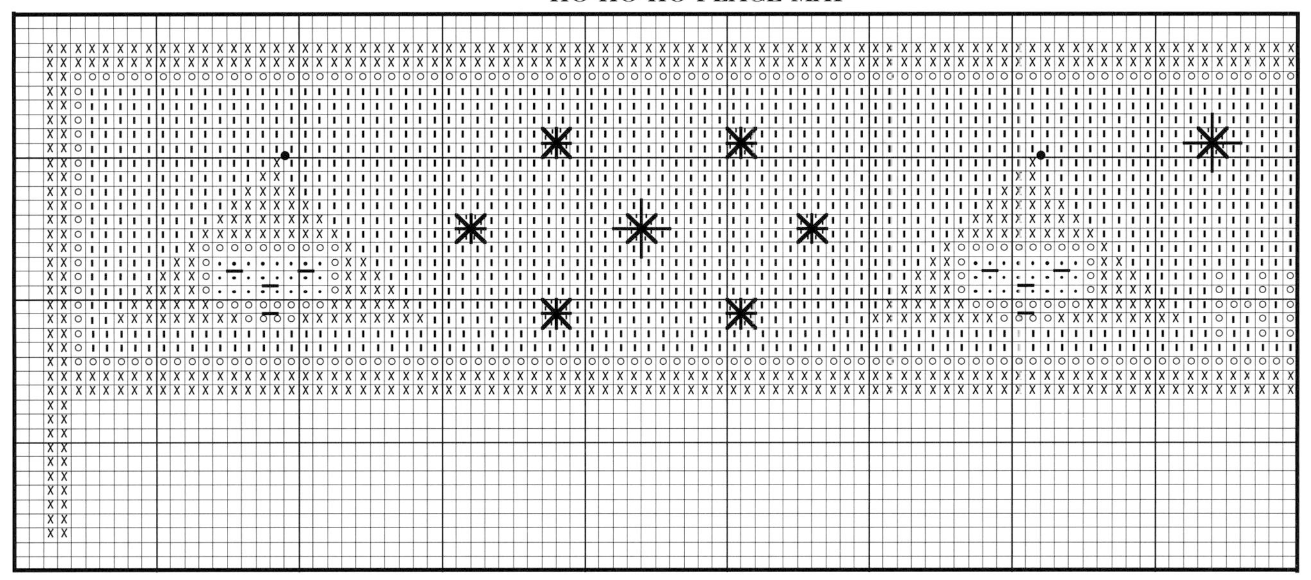

Shaded portion indicates overlap from the chart above.

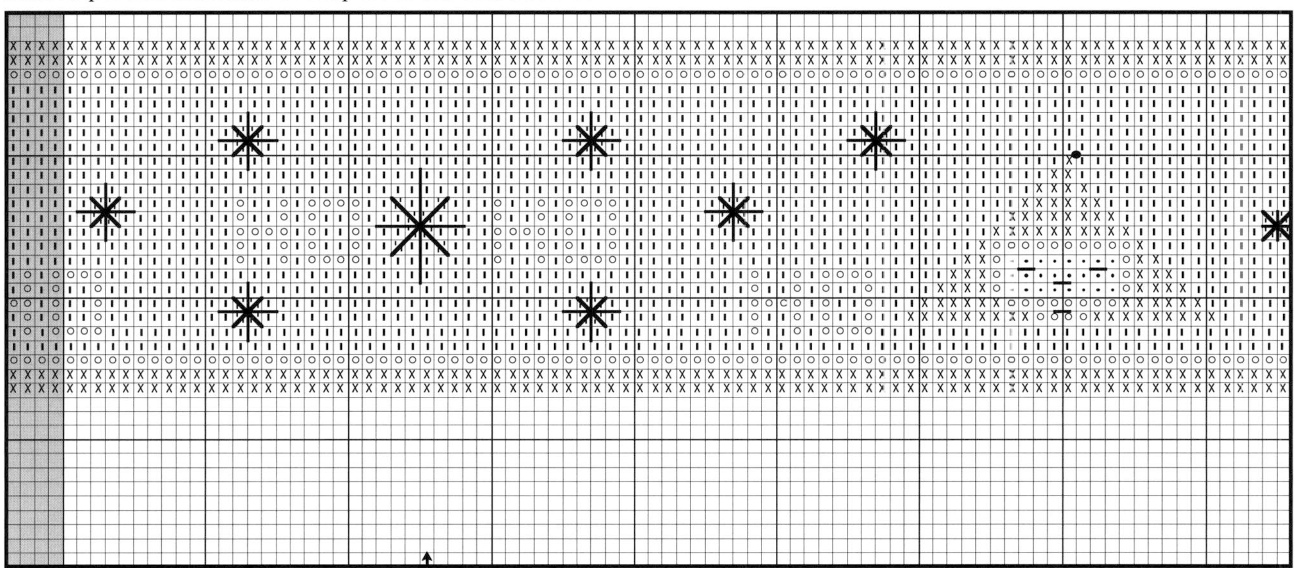

Note: Cut fabric 17¼" x 14".

Instructions: Cross stitch using two strands of floss. Backstitch using one strand of floss. Tack small jingle bell where • appears.

Backstitch (bs) instructions:

666 Santa's mouth and nose
806 Santa's eyes
white snowflakes

Materials:

17¼" x 14" piece white fabric (for backing)
1 yd. 44/45"-wide red-and-white striped fabric
2 yds. ¾" cording
4 small gold jingle bells
Hand-sewing needle
Straight pins
Sewing machine with zipper front
Red thread
Scissors
Iron

Note: Materials listed will make one *Ho Ho Ho Place Mat.*

Shaded portion indicates overlap from the chart above.

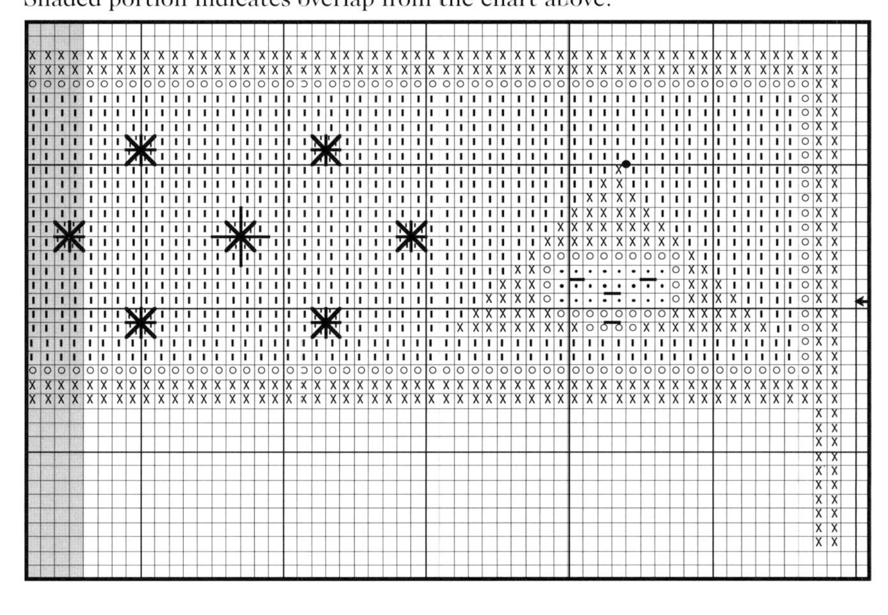

1. Complete cross stitch following instructions given.
2. To make cording, cut striped fabric into 3"-wide bias strips and piece together to a length of 72". Center cording on wrong side of fabric strip and sew one end of cord to one end of fabric strip. Fold cording strip around cord, placing wrong sides of fabric together and aligning raw edges. Pin as needed to get started. Place cording under zipper foot with raw edges to the right. Machine-sew close to cord, being careful not to crowd cord. Remove pins.
3. Pin cording to right side of cross-stitch fabric around perimeter of design, placing raw edge of cording toward raw edge of fabric and aligning stitching line on cording with edge of design. Machine-sew together, using zipper foot and overlapping cording ends at one corner. Remove pins.
4. Pin stitched front and backing with right sides together, aligning edges. Machine-sew together, leaving a 4" opening in one side for turning. Remove pins. Trim seams, clip corners, and turn. Press. Whipstitch opening closed.

Fun for the Kids Projects

Reindeer Sandwiches
Ingredients:
Peanut-butter-and-jelly sandwiches
Maraschino cherries
Pretzels
Raisins

1. Cut each sandwich in half diagonally.
2. Insert pretzels between bread slices to make antlers, referring to photo on page 86 for placement.
3. Press raisin eyes and cherry nose into bread.

Marshmallow Reindeer
Materials:
3 large marshmallows
2 chenille stems, color: brown
1 red hard candy (for nose)
4 miniature marshmallows
Toothpicks
2 plastic eyes
Tacky glue

Note: Materials listed will make one *Marshmallow Reindeer.* Keep *Marshmallow Reindeer* out of reach of small children and animals, as they are not intended for consumption.

1. For each reindeer, attach two marshmallows with flat sides together to make body, using toothpick. Attach remaining marshmallow to top of body, using toothpick and referring to photo on page 86 for placement.
2. Cut chenille stems into four pieces in desired length for legs, two pieces in desired length for antlers, and one short length for tail. Insert one end of each leg into bottom of marshmallow body. Place one miniature marshmallow on end of each leg. Bend antler pieces as desired, and insert into top of marshmallow head. Insert tail into marshmallow body, referring to photo for placement.
3. Glue plastic eyes and red candy nose onto head.

Sugarplum Tree
Materials:
STYROFOAM brand plastic foam (to fit in pot)
Gumdrops **or** other soft candy of your choice
½ yd. paper twist cord
Spray paint, color: white
3½" clay pot
Spanish moss
Hot glue gun
Tree twigs

1. Glue Styrofoam® into pot. Insert twig ends into foam to form tree.
2. Spray entire piece with white paint. Let dry.
3. Untwist paper cord and cut two 1"-wide strips. Twist one strip and glue around top of pot. Tie remaining strip into a bow. Glue bow to twisted strip at top of pot.
4. Glue Spanish moss atop Styrofoam® to cover.
5. Place gum drops on ends of twigs.

Holiday Aviary

Materials:
15" x 48" piece ¼"-thick Birch plywood (for birdhouse and roof)
12" x 22" piece ¾"-thick plywood (for base)
12" length ¼"-diameter wooden dowel
Thirty-six 5¾" x ¾" craft sticks
Acrylic paints, colors: red, white, light blue, light yellow, light green, medium green, dark green
Paintbrushes, sizes: small, medium, large
Spray paint, color: white
2 small red basket containers
Assortment of small and medium-size craft birds (**Note:** 18 birds were used for model: 15 small, 3 medium.)
Purchased snowman (**Note:** Snowman used for model is approximately 4" tall.)
Small amount Spanish moss
28–30 small nails **or** brads
2 small branches (for trees)
1 can spray snow
Cotton batting (for snow in yard)
Drill with 1¼" and ¼" bits
4 small scraps STYROFOAM brand plastic foam (for anchoring trees and bushes)
Jigsaw **or** scroll saw
Sandpaper
Graphite paper
Hammer
Hot glue gun
Pencil

Note: Materials listed will make one *Holiday Aviary.*

1. Enlarge patterns as indicated. Trace outlines of birdhouse front and back on ¼"-thick plywood. Cut out, using saw. On front piece, drill ¼" and 1¼" holes as indicated on pattern. Cut two 5⅞" x 9⅞" pieces for sides, one 7" x 6" piece for bottom, and two 5½" x 8¼" pieces for roof. Place side pieces between back and front pieces. Nail edges together. Nail on bottom piece. Center roof on top of birdhouse and nail in place. Cut 8¼" length from dowel and glue at top where edges of roof meet. Cut two 1½"-long pieces from remaining dowel. Glue dowels in small holes for perches.
2. Sand entire birdhouse. Paint house, using two coats of white paint and letting paint dry between coats. Paint roof green. Let dry.
3. Transfer patterns onto birdhouse, using graphite paper and pencil. (**Note:** Broken lines indicate placement of greenery.) Paint greenery, painting dark green leaves first, then medium green leaves, and then light green leaves, using small paintbrush. Paint number of leaves desired, referring to photo on page 87. Paint small red dots in greenery for berries.
4. Paint door, front window frames, all bows, and all candles red. (**Note:** To avoid smearing paint, let each color dry thoroughly before continuing with the next.) Mix small amount of red and yellow paint, and paint all candle flames. Paint curtains light blue. Add white accents. Paint remainder of inside of window yellow. Paint doorknob yellow. Paint door frame green. Paint trim along inside of frame white. Paint side and back window frames and shutters dark green. Outline inside of side and back windows, using red paint. Paint greenery at base of all candles. Paint wreath on door and at top front of birdhouse as for garland in Step 3. Let dry.
5. Spray roof lightly with snow. Set birdhouse aside.
6. Cut craft sticks in half and glue around plywood base approximately ¼" apart. Spray base and fence white. Cut branches approximately 12" long and spray white.

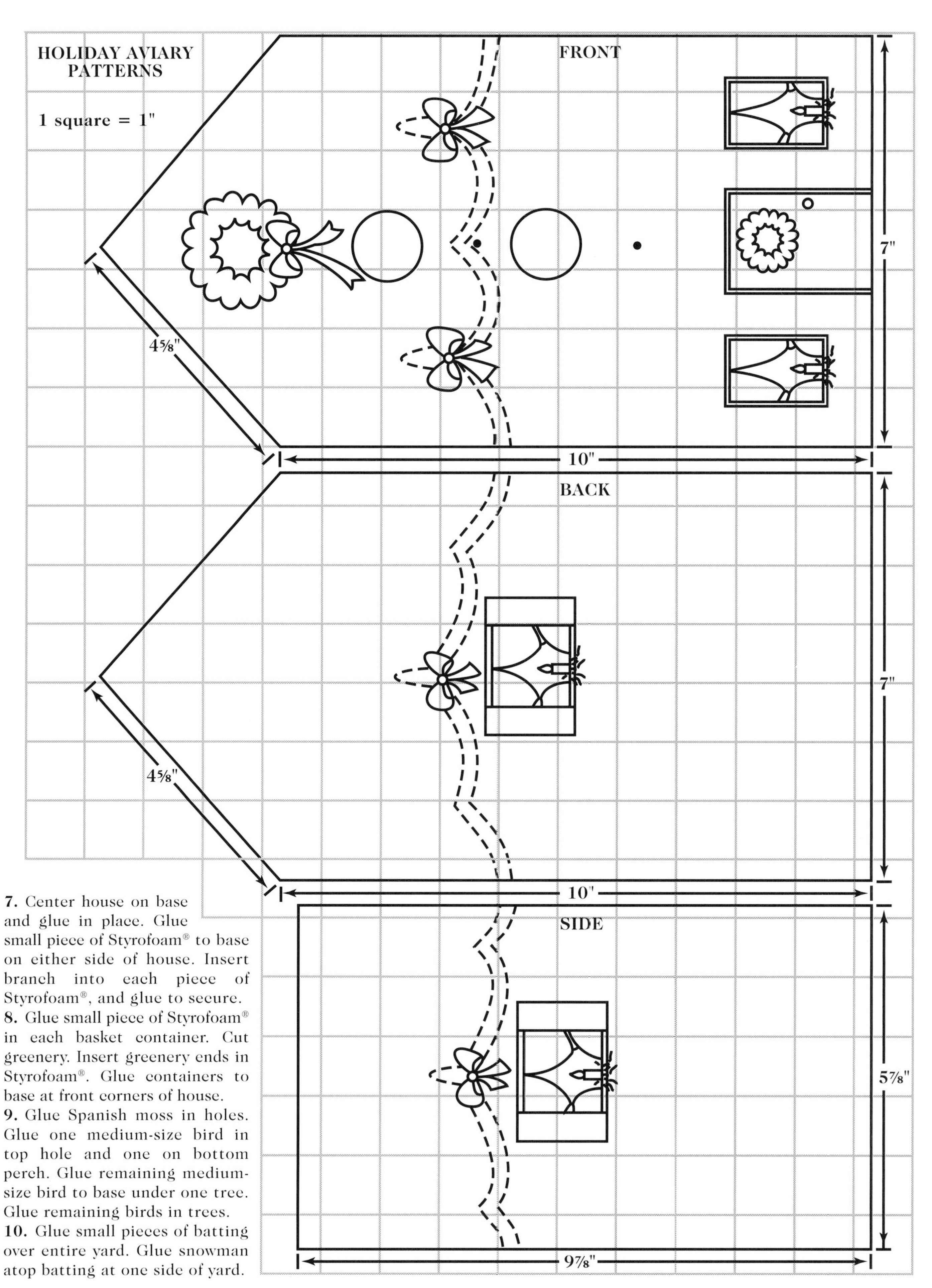

7. Center house on base and glue in place. Glue small piece of Styrofoam® to base on either side of house. Insert branch into each piece of Styrofoam®, and glue to secure.
8. Glue small piece of Styrofoam® in each basket container. Cut greenery. Insert greenery ends in Styrofoam®. Glue containers to base at front corners of house.
9. Glue Spanish moss in holes. Glue one medium-size bird in top hole and one on bottom perch. Glue remaining medium-size bird to base under one tree. Glue remaining birds in trees.
10. Glue small pieces of batting over entire yard. Glue snowman atop batting at one side of yard.

WT
WESTRIM CRAFTS
SNOWFLAKES
WT
WESTRIM CRAFTS
BEADS
WT
WESTRIM CRAFTS
LEAF SEQUINS
WT
WESTRIM CRAFTS
BLACK&DECKER
3/8" Cordless Drill/Screwdriver
15074
BLACK&DECKER
High-Speed Steel
Drill Bit Set
Metal/Wood
5-Piece
Drills in metal, wood and plastic
The ideal general-purpose drill bit
Easily resharpened
For all drills and drill presses
RIM CRAFTS
BEADS
METAL
WT
WESTRIM CRAFTS
N

QUICK & EASY

The tempo of the days leading up to Christmas always increases until the hustle and bustle of the holidays has become a fast-paced but fun-filled frenzy. Inevitably, we find we have neglected to purchase or make a gift for someone—perhaps the host of the neighborhood Christmas party, or a niece or nephew—but definitely someone who should not be forgotten. Or we discover a glaringly bare spot on a wall or table that needs a new decoration. There's still time for something that comes from the hands and the heart—a simple, quick-to-make project. The amount of time, even small, spent creating something with a personal touch, will certainly be worthwhile and appreciated.

Gifts in the Nick of Time

When Christmas is just around the corner and you still have a few more gifts to create, look no further! We've put together a collection of our favorite quick-to-make projects especially for those last-minute gifts (and those last-minute crafters and stitchers).

Cross stitchers can choose from three charming designs for a present that you can stitch in a jiffy. First, a pair of cute, gray mice are dressed up for the holidays in ***My Gift to You***, shown at right, worked on the Aida-cloth band of a fingertip towel. Next, ***The Skaters***, shown on opposite page, features a cross-stitched couple skating on a frozen pond, attended by curious reindeer. Corner heart motifs and a red border "frame" the wintry scene, with snow falling from the sky and the moon overlooking it all. And finally, ***Holiday Happiness***, shown on page 100, will provide just the right finishing touch to a gift basket. Tie the finished cross-stitch design to a red or green basket, filled with goodies for all to enjoy.

Holiday accessories can turn an everyday wardrobe into festive attire. The ***Christmas Button Covers***, shown on page 101, will transform a plain shirt into the star of the party. No need to buy a new shirt. Just embellish one from your regular wardrobe. Patterns for the button covers include Mrs. Claus, holly leaves and berries, a wrapped package, a wreath, a Christmas tree, and a row of "ho-ho-hos."

Create different ***Postage-Stamp Pins***, shown on page 101, each year with the gorgeous Christmas stamps issued by the U.S. Postal Service. When you purchase stamps to mail your stack of holiday cards, pick up a few extras and fashion these quick-finish accessories. Your sewing box probably holds enough scraps of fabric and trim to make several pins; simply add pin backs and you'll have a super selection of jewelry.

Above—*In the background of this cross-stitch project, a little green house looks warm and inviting, while in the foreground,* The Skaters *are spending a starry, winter night gliding atop a frozen pond. Chart is on page 109.*

Left—My Gift to You, *a cross-stitch design for a towel band, shows two mice exchanging Christmas gifts. Both mice are festively dressed, right down to the red and green bows on their tails. Color code is on page 110. Chart is on page 111.*

Above—Fill a holiday gift basket with good things, then add a cross-stitch greeting. Chart is on page 110.

Among the aromas associated with Christmas are the scents of freshly cut evergreens, bayberry candles, and spicy cinnamon. The easy-to-assemble ***Cinnamon Basket***, shown on page 102, has a border of cinnamon sticks. Fill it with aromatic, cinnamon potpourri to make it an even more fragrant gift.

The ***Surprise Packages***, also shown on page 102, are truly full of surprises! We show them attached to a Christmas card and a gift card, but what you can't see are the pin backs that transform the tiny, brightly wrapped "packages" into holiday accessories—great for dressing up a sweater or blouse. Make several, attach them to place cards for a dinner party, and give them to your guests afterward as reminders of the occasion.

Grandmother, Mother, or whoever is the "pastry chef" of the family will adore the ***Christmas Pie*** ensemble, shown on page 103. The apron and pot holder feature appliquéd Christmas sweets. This project can be completed in a jiffy with machine appliqué.

Imagine the smiling face of the happy little one who receives a ***Snowman Necklace***, shown on page 104. Use woodworking skills to cut out the snowman pattern; then add painted details, such as rosy cheeks, sparkling eyes, perky nose, and a striped scarf.

***Left**—Turn a plain red, green, or white shirt into the highlight of your holiday wardrobe with these cleverly painted* Christmas Button Covers. *Instructions begin on page 111.*

***Above and left**—Use small scraps of Christmas fabric and trims, and the beautiful holiday stamps issued each year by the U.S. Postal Service, to create several different* Postage Stamp Pins. *Instructions are on page 111.*

***Above**—The* Cinnamon Potpourri Basket *is a fragrant, easy-to-make gift that will please anyone on your list. Instructions are on page 115.*

***Above**—You don't have to be an expert seamstress to whip up this colorful,* Christmas Pie *ensemble of appliquéd apron and pot holder. Instructions begin on page 112.*

***Above**—Versatile and fun to create, the* Surprise Packages *look great attached to Christmas cards or worn as holiday pins. Instructions begin on page 115.*

The ***Earth-Friendly Gift Bags***, shown on page 104, are an eco-conscious gift to Mother Nature, a welcome change from traditional wrapping paper, and a great gift holder that becomes part of the gift! Friends and family will appreciate the thoughtfulness that goes into making the gift bags and decorating them with cutouts of trees, gingerbread men, or the word *Noel*. Drawstring ribbons keep the contents safe. Change the motifs on the fronts of the bags and use them for birthdays and other special occasions, as well!

Right—*Painted details on the wooden* Snowman Necklace *include Christmas-colored hat and scarf, and coal black eyes, nose, and buttons. This "frosty" darling will become a holiday favorite for people of all ages. Instructions are on page 113.*

Below—*Give a gift to Mother Nature this year! The festively trimmed* Earth-Friendly Gift Bags *will be a nice change from wrapping paper. Use our decorative designs—pine trees, gingerbread man, and* Noel*—or create your own. Instructions begin on page 116.*

Last-Minute Decorations

Need the perfect decoration for that bare wall, but your crafting time is limited? Don't panic! Read on for eight great suggestions that won't take too much time, money, or effort.

Shown below, the ***Noel Candle Holders*** will look wonderful on a windowsill, sending a holiday glow out into wintry evenings. Or try them as a holiday centerpiece—the candlelight will add a festive atmosphere to your feast. We chose to use white candles, but feel free to try red, green, or an assortment of holiday colors. We also suggest painting your own holiday message on the blocks, such as "Merry Christmas," or, if you're really in a hurry, "Joy."

Silver Bells Garland, also shown below, is the perfect addition to this year's tree. With the children's help, you can complete yards of this garland in a short time. It's a simple combination of Styrofoam® bell and package shapes that are cut out using cookie cutters. Finish with paint and trim, string together, and you'll be set for seasonal decorating.

Get the entire family involved with the quick-and-easy ***Gingerbread Men Ornaments*** on page 106. The kids can help roll out clay, cut out gingerbread men, bake them in the oven, and decorate them with paint. Grandma will love getting these friendly guys from the grandkids this year.

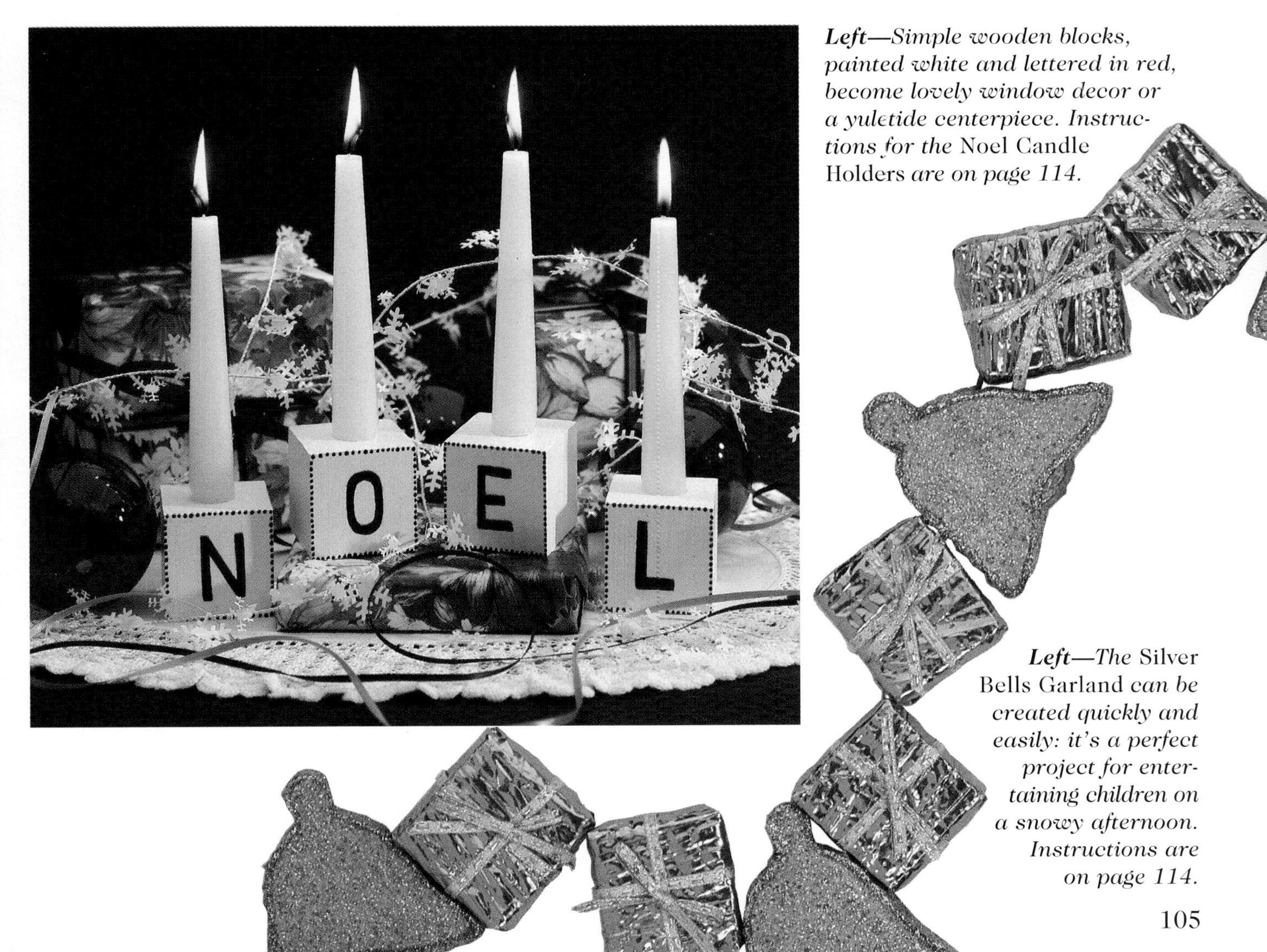

Left—*Simple wooden blocks, painted white and lettered in red, become lovely window decor or a yuletide centerpiece. Instructions for the* Noel Candle Holders *are on page 114.*

Left—*The* Silver Bells Garland *can be created quickly and easily: it's a perfect project for entertaining children on a snowy afternoon. Instructions are on page 114.*

Above—Instead of dough and icing, you'll use clay and paint to "cook up" the Gingerbread Men Ornaments. *The entire family will want to help create these adorable decorations. Instructions are on page 116.*

Here's another fun project to share with children: spend a "snow day" making ***Fingerprint Ornaments***, shown on page 107. By using poster board, ink pads, and markers, the youngsters can create mice, angels, Santas, and noel designs. Try letting your little ones experiment with their own drawings to see what they can make using their imaginations and fingerprints. Years later, you'll marvel at how they've grown as you hang their childhood fingerprints on the tree. Start this annual tradition with the grandchildren.

Everyone's office could use a quick, Christmas pick-me-up during the holiday rush. Our ***Save the Earth Computer-Paper Wreath***, shown at bottom right, is made from a wire hanger, tractor-feed strips of used computer-printer paper, and ribbon. Hang one on your office door, or make one for a co-worker. It's certain to put you in the holiday spirit, and bring a steady stream of compliments your way for your creative recycling idea.

When the detergent box is empty, don't throw away that little scoop! Save them and make the ***Laundry Detergent Scoop Decorations*** shown on page 108. Fill them with candy or silk poinsettias, paint names on them to personalize, and use them as table favors for a party. Or, place tiny Christmas figurines inside the scoops and hang the scoops by their handles for use as ornaments.

***Above and right**—What a wonderful way to spend a day with the kids: making these sweet,* Fingerprint Ornaments. *Use our designs of mice, angels, Santas, and Noel motifs, or let the young artists have free reign to create their own fingerprint fancies. Instructions begin on page 114.*

***Left**—Decorate your work area with the* Save the Earth Computer-Paper Wreath, *made of tractor-feed strips from printer paper. Instructions for this creative recycling project are on page 115.*

Below—The gingerbread house is, without a doubt, a Christmas classic. For a simplified version, try our Gingerbread House Ornaments. *Instructions are on page 116.*

Above—The Laundry Detergent Scoop Ornaments *are unusual, eco-conscious, and very cute! Use them as party favors or tree decorations. Instructions are on page 116.*

Above—The full-skirted, white, paper-twist bodies of our Angel Ornaments *will contrast prettily with the evergreen boughs placed throughout your home. Gold wings and halos, and red and green bows, add color to the heavenly angels. Instructions are on page 109.*

If your energy level this year leaves you not quite up to making an entire gingerbread house, how about trying our ***Gingerbread House Ornaments***, shown at top left. They require little time to complete and a few easy-to-find supplies, such as house-shaped cookie cutters, wooden gingerbread men, and ribbon.

The ***Angel Ornaments***, shown at left, may be the prettiest addition to your Christmas collection this year. Their metallic gold wings and full-skirted bodies are made from paper twist. Gold bells hang from the heavenly angels' crossed hands, and gold, chenille-stem halos hover over their heads.

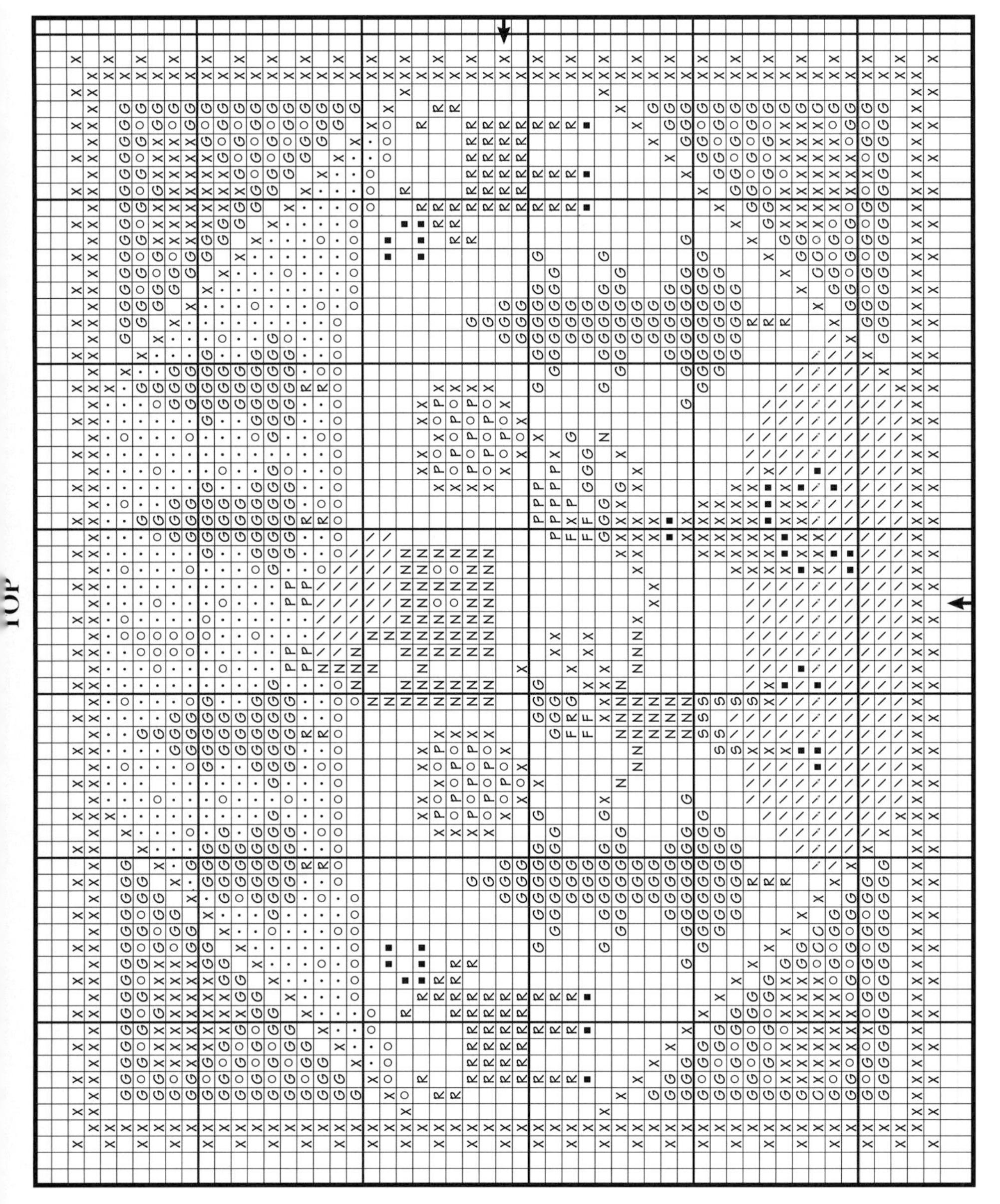

The Skaters

	DMC	Color
N	943	aqua, med.
X	666	red, bt.
G	701	green, lt.
P	604	cranberry, lt.
•	796	royal blue, dk.
F	225	pink, vy. lt.
\	519	sky blue
R	433	brown, med.
S	3032	mocha, med.
O	white	white
■	310	black

Fabric: 25-count white Lugana® from Zweigart®
Stitch count: 53H x 67W
Design size:

14-count	3¾" x 4⅞"
18-count	3" x 3¾"
25-count	4¼" x 5⅜"
30-count	3⅝" x 4½"

Instructions: Cross stitch over two threads, using three strands of floss.

Angel Ornaments

Materials:
Three 1" STYROFOAM brand plastic foam balls
3 yds. 4"-wide white paper twist cord (**Note:** Paper twist will be 4" wide when untwisted.)
⅞ yd. 4"-wide metallic gold paper twist cord (**Note:** Paper twist will be 4" wide when untwisted.)
Three ½" gold jingle bells
3 small holly picks **or** other holiday trim
Three 3mm x 12" gold tinsel chenille stems
¾ yd. ¼"-wide green double-faced satin ribbon
1¼ yds. ⅛"-wide red double-faced satin ribbon
Aleene's Thick Designer Tacky Glue
1 yd. 2-ply metallic gold thread
Clear nylon monofilament
Ruler
Scissors
Hot glue gun

Note: Materials listed will make three *Angel Ornaments*.

1. Cut two 12" lengths from white paper twist. Cut one 10" length from metallic gold paper twist. Untwist and flatten all three pieces paper twist. Cut one 7½" length from white paper twist. Partially untwist center, leaving approximately ¾" on each end tightly twisted for angel's hands.
2. Center Styrofoam® ball on one 12" length white paper and neatly shape paper around opposite sides of ball. Place second 12" length on Styrofoam® ball at center of paper and shape paper around ball, crimping paper directly underneath ball to form angel's neck. Tie monofilament around angel's neck to secure paper.
3. Slip 7½"-length white paper twist below head under back piece of white paper. Center. Crimp skirt below arms and tie tightly with monofilament. Trim bottom of skirt if uneven.
4. Cut 9" length from red ribbon. Wrap ribbon around angel's neck and tie into a small bow in front. Trim ends if necessary. Cut 9" length from green ribbon. Loop around angel's waist and knot at back, leaving ribbon ends dangling. Hot glue to paper twist at back knot.
5. To make wings, overlap short ends of gold paper twist to form wide tube. Secure ends with tacky glue. Let dry. Flatten tube slightly. Crimp center of tube to approximately 1" wide. Wrap crimped center with monofilament thread and tie. Hot glue wings to back of angel between neck and waist.
6. To make halo, fold chenille stem into a 1"-diameter circle at one end of stem. Make a hook at opposite end of stem. Place hook under wings and hot glue halo to wings and at back of head.
7. Thread 3" gold thread through bell loop. Knot thread at ends. Bend angel arms toward front of angel, cross hands, and hot glue hands together with knot in thread tucked between hands.
8. Cut 6" length from red satin ribbon. Tie ribbon in a bow and hot glue bow to holly spray. Hot glue spray and bow to front of angel's crossed hands.
9. Thread 9" length gold thread under chenille stem between back of head and wings. Tie a knot in thread ends to form hanger.

Holiday Happiness

	DMC	Color
×	321	Christmas red
✳	640	beige gray, vy. dk.
⟍	562	jade green, med.
⌐	676	old gold, lt.
Z	436	tan

Fabric: 14-count antique white Aida from Zweigart®
Stitch count: 47H x 87W
Design size:

12-count	4" x 7¼"
14-count	3⅜" x 6¼"
16-count	3" x 5½"
18-count	2⅝" x 4⅞"

TOP

HOLIDAY HAPPINESS

Instructions: Cross stitch using two strands of floss. Backstitch using one strand 640.

Finishing instructions:
Materials:
Purchased basket of your choice
½ yd. ¼"-wide satin ribbon in color of your choice
Iron

1. Complete cross stitch following instructions given.
2. Fold fabric edges under along edge of stitched design and press.
3. Tack ribbon at fabric edges along sides. Weave ribbon ends to inside of basket and tie together to secure.

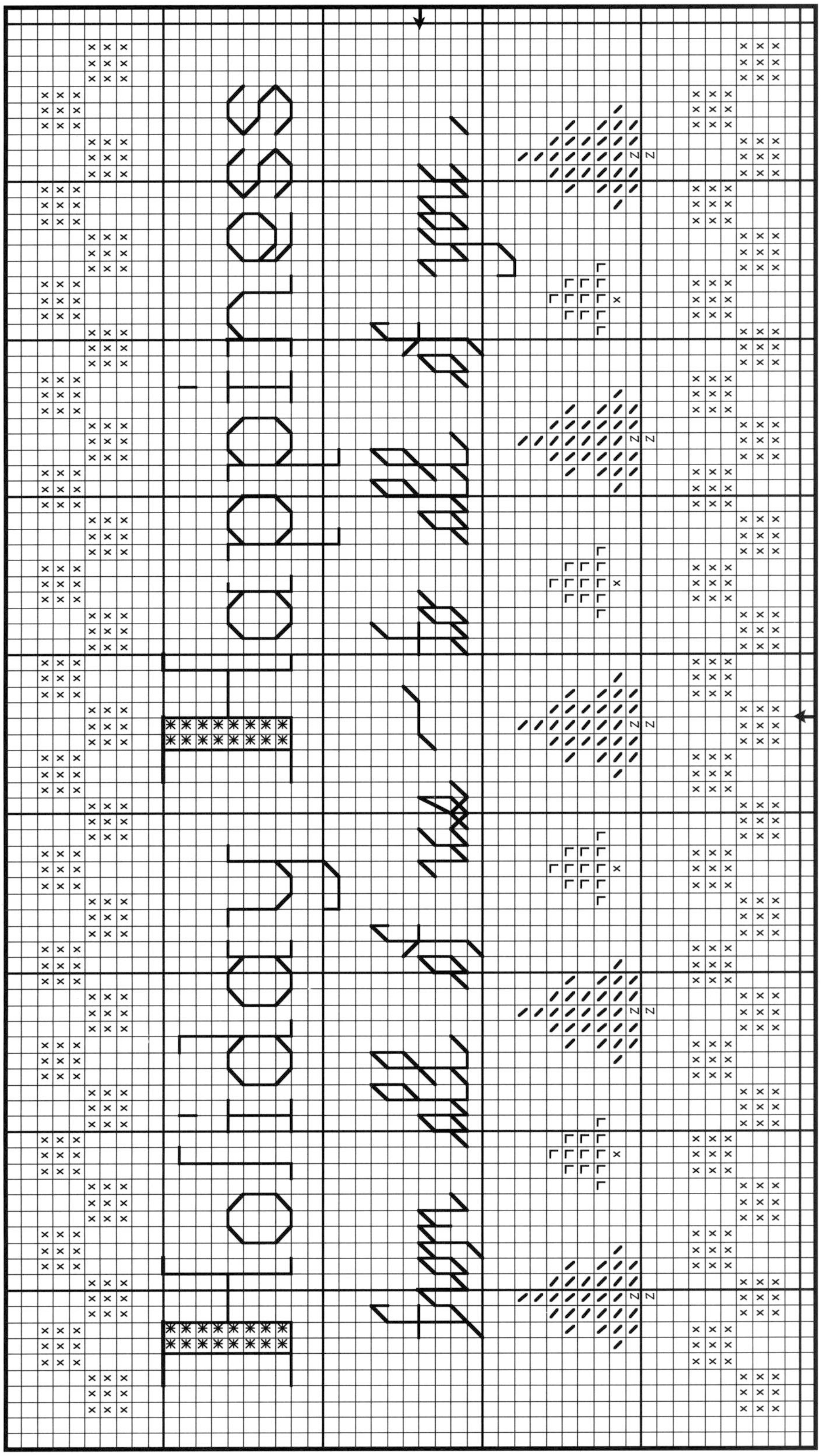

My Gift to You

	DMC	Color
•	white	white
○	3326	rose, lt.
X	321	red
Z	498	red, dk.
✳	699	green
V	700	green, bt.
6	414	steel gray, dk.
=	318	steel gray, lt.
⁄	415	pearl gray
3[	700	green, bt.
	321	red
bs	3799	pewter gray, vy. dk.

Fabric: 14-count white Park Avenue Fingertips™ towel from Charles Craft, Inc.
Stitch count: 24H x 62W
Design size:

14-count	4⅜" x 1¾"
18-count	3⅜" x 1⅜"
25-count	5" x 1⅞"
27-count	4⅝" x 1¾"

Instructions: Cross stitch using two strands of floss. Backstitch using one strand of floss. Make French knots using two strands of floss, wrapping floss around needle twice.

Backstitch (bs) instructions:

700	*Merry Christmas*
321	candy-cane stripes
3799	remainder of backstitching

French knot instructions:

3799	eyes
3326	noses
699	center of bows
700	dot on *i*

MY GIFT TO YOU

Postage Stamp Pins

Materials:

Unused Christmas postage stamp
2" x 2½" piece 300-lb. watercolor paper (for pin backing)
1" x ¾" piece 140-lb. watercolor paper (for stamp backing)
3" x 5" scrap fabric to complement stamp colors
Scraps of braid **or** ribbon and assorted trims
Small paintbrush (for applying glaze)
Delta® Jewelry Glaze
Tacky glue
Toothpick
1" pin back
Utility scissors
Low-temperature glue gun

Note: Materials listed will make one *Postage Stamp Pin*. Dimensions calculated and instructions given are for stamps measuring 1⅛" x ⅞". If using another size Christmas stamp, you will need to recalculate the dimensions of materials needed.

1. Adhere stamp to stamp backing paper. Coat stamp front with jewelry glaze and let dry.
2. Cover pin backing paper with fabric cut ½" larger all around than pin backing. Wrap fabric around paper and use glue gun to secure edges on back. Notch (cut out) corners of fabric as needed to keep back of pin flat.
Note: If unable to find 300-lb. paper, double 140-lb. paper for pin backing. Using low-temp glue gun helps prevent burned fingers when working on small projects.
3. To design pin, place stamp and scraps of braid **or** ribbon and assorted trims on front of fabric-covered pin backing as desired, experimenting with placement until design pleases you. Refer to photo for ideas. Glue stamp and braid, ribbon, or trims to front of pin backing, using tacky glue. Apply glue with a toothpick as needed for very narrow ribbon or small trims.
4. Cut piece of fabric approximately ⅛" smaller all around than pin backing. Glue to back side of pin, covering raw edges wrapped from front side. Attach pin back using glue gun.
Design suggestions: A wide band of gold ribbon can be wrapped around pin backing and under the stamp or pleated and extended past the pin backing edges. Stamp can be glued to fabric-covered backing and have ribbon or braid placed around its edges. Stamp can be used centered or placed off-center.

Christmas Button Covers

Materials:

9" x 12" sheet 140-lb. watercolor paper
DecoArt™ Americana™ acrylic paint, colors: calico red, holly green, flesh, true blue, cadmium yellow, white, glorious gold metallic
Artist's paintbrush, size: very small
Permanent fine-tip black marker
Delta® Jewelry Glaze
Small brush (for glaze)
Darice brass button covers, approximately 5 per blouse (**Note:** ⅝" button covers were used for models.)
Pencil
Tracing paper
Low-temperature glue gun

1. Make sure designs cover the size button covers you are using. Trace designs onto watercolor paper, using pencil and tracing paper.
2. Paint as follows:
Santa face: Paint face flesh, hat and mouth red, cheeks pink (by mixing red with white), eyes blue, and pom-pom gold. Outline beard and fur trim of hat, using gold paint. Add dots in beard and on fur trim of hat, using gold paint. Let dry.
Christmas tree: Paint tree green and ornaments blue, yellow, red, and gold. When paint is dry, add upside-down *V* shapes for branches, using black marker.
Wreath: Paint bow red, side bow loops gold, wreath green, and ornaments blue, red, and gold. When paint is dry, add tiny straight lines in groups of three for pine needles, using black marker.
Present: Paint bow gold and package red. When paint is dry, outline box shape, ribbon around box, and bow, using black marker.
Holly spray: Paint two leaves green, two leaves light green (by mixing green with white), and berries red. When paint is dry, outline leaves, using gold paint. Let dry. Add veins to leaves, using black marker.
Ho: Paint red stripes on *H*. Mix green paint with white paint to make light green, and paint O. Paint ornaments red, blue, and gold. Let dry.
3. When finished painting, cut out shapes. Touch up paper edges with paint as needed. When paint is dry, glue paper to button covers. Let dry. Apply Jewelry Glaze to stiffen and protect. Let dry.
(Patterns are on page 112.)

CHRISTMAS BUTTON COVER PATTERNS

Christmas Pie Apron and Pot Holder Set

Materials:
1 yd. 44/45"-wide white heavy cotton duck or twill fabric
¼ yd. 44/45"-wide red Christmas print fabric
¼ yd. 44/45"-wide tan print fabric
Small scraps beige print fabric
½ yd. fusible web
1 spool **each** Coats Dual Duty Plus thread, Art. 210, colors: 128A atom red, 155 dogwood, 177 kerry green
3 pkgs. Coats Extra Wide Double Fold Bias Tape, Art.M.890, color: 128A atom red
1 skein J. & P. Coats 6-strand Embroidery Floss, color: 5345 spice, med.
8" square fusible fleece
1 yd. ⅛"-wide green satin ribbon
36" square pattern paper
Water-soluble fabric-marking pencil
Size 5 J. & P. Coats embroidery needle
Sewing machine with zigzag stitch
Measuring tape
Straight pins　　Pencil
Scissors　　Iron

Note: Pre-wash all fabrics to prevent shrinkage and bleeding in finished project. Press.

1. Enlarge apron and pocket pattern as indicated. Trace patterns onto paper and cut out. Cut one apron and one apron pocket from white fabric. Cut one 7" square from white fabric for pot holder.
2. Fold binding in half along lengthwise edge and sew to apron, using red thread. Sew binding to top, neck edge of apron. Then sew binding down right side of apron, across bottom, and up left side, mitering the corners. To bind armhole edges and make ties, measure 30" of bias tape and mark but **do not** cut. Fold 30" length of bias tape in half along lengthwise edge and sew edges together to form left tie. Where stitching ends, sew bias tape to left, armhole edge of apron, referring to Illustration 1. **Do not** cut bias tape when you reach end of armhole. Instead, measure 25", mark, and sew edges together as for left tie to form neck strap. Where stitching ends, sew bias tape to right, armhole edge of apron. To make right tie, measure another 30" of bias tape and sew edges together as for left tie.
3. Trace one complete pie and two complete muffins onto paper backing side of fusible web. Cut out. Fuse pie and muffin bases to red print fabric and pie and muffin tops to tan print fabric, following manufacturer's instructions for fusing. Fuse steam vents to scraps of beige fabric. Center pie at top of apron and fuse. Fuse one muffin to center of apron pocket and one to center of pot-holder square. Machine appliqué pieces in place, using red thread for bases and dogwood thread for steam vents and top of pie and muffins. Use a narrow, ⅛"-wide machine satin stitch.
4. Mark steam curls with water-soluble fabric-marking pencil, using patterns provided or drawing freehand. Cut one 18" length of 6-strand embroidery floss and separate strands. Backstitch steam along markings, using two strands of floss and size 5 embroidery needle.
5. Bind edges of apron pocket, using bias tape and red thread. Position pocket on apron approximately 3½" in from left edge and 3½" down from bottom of left armhole and sew in place, using red thread. Sew along inner and outer edges of bias binding around perimeter of pocket, leaving top open. Set aside.
6. To complete pot holder, fuse fleece to back side of appliquéd square. Trim away excess fleece around edges. Cut a 7" square from red print fabric for backing. Pin layers together. Beginning at top center of pot holder, bind edges, using red bias tape and red thread and mitering the corners. Continue around pot holder to starting point and continue to sew binding, running it off the pot holder and making a 2"-long tail. Curl binding tail into a loop for hanging and sew end of bias tape to back side of pot holder. Remove pins.
7. Cut a 10" length from green satin ribbon. Hand-sew ribbon to pie plate along large dotted lines as indicated on pattern, using green thread and folding raw edges of ribbon under at

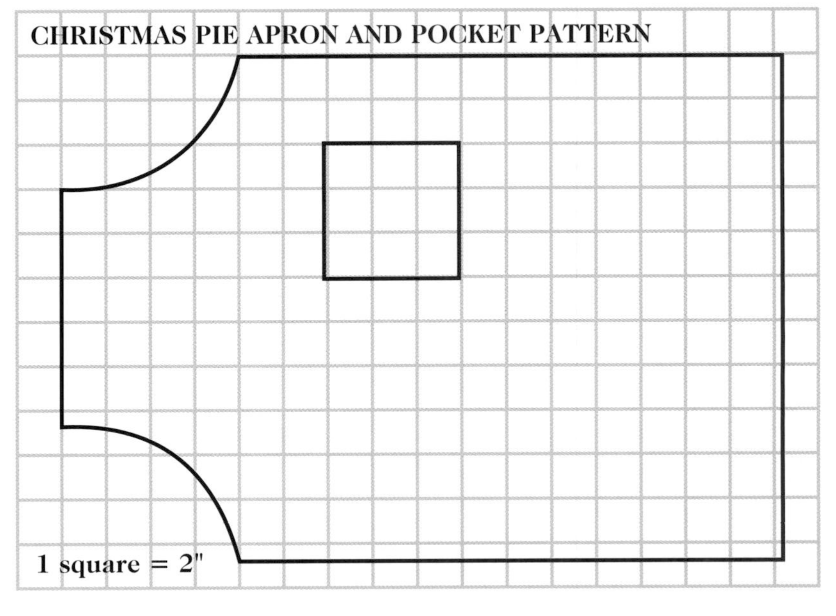

each end. Make four 2"-wide bows from remaining green satin ribbon. Tack one bow above muffin on apron pocket, one at base of loop on pot holder, and the remaining two at top corners of apron, using green thread.

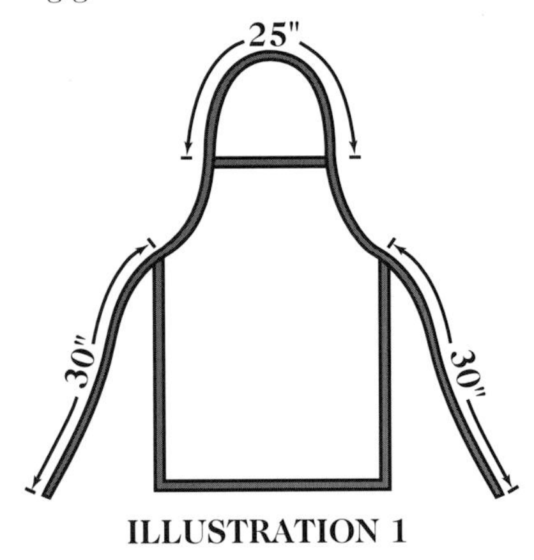

ILLUSTRATION 1

Snowman Necklace

Materials:

3" x 4½" piece 5/16"-thick wood
Eight ⅜" x 9/16" wooden beads
Tracing paper and pencil
Graphite paper
Water-base varnish
Paintbrushes: one small, one medium
Acrylic paints, colors: white, green, red, black
4 yds. 1/16"-wide red satin ribbon **or** 45" length 3/16"-wide green braid
Fine sandpaper
Drill with 3/16" bit
Jigsaw, band saw, **or** scroll saw
Tacky glue (optional)

Note: Materials listed will make one *Snowman Necklace*.

1. Trace snowman pattern onto tracing paper. Transfer outline of snowman to wood, using graphite paper. Cut out snowman, using saw. Drill hole through neck area of snowman, from side to side, for ribbon or braid necklace. Use sandpaper to smooth rough edges of snowman.

2. Paint front, back, and sides of snowman white. Let dry. Repeat with a second coat of paint. Let dry.

3. Transfer snowman pattern lightly onto white snowman. Paint hat and scarf green or red. Let dry. Paint mouth red. Paint alternating stripes on scarf red and white or green and white. Paint scarf fringe green or red. Mix red and white paint to make pink. Paint snowman's cheeks pink. Paint snowman's buttons, eyes, eyelashes, eyebrows, and nose black. Paint highlights in nose and eyes white. Mix black with white to make gray. Paint outline of snowman's arms gray. Mix white with green or red to highlight brim of hat. Let dry thoroughly.

4. Apply two coats of varnish to snowman, letting dry between coats. Paint beads with two coats white, letting dry between coats. Apply two coats of varnish to beads, letting dry between coats. Cut three 45" lengths from ribbon (if using ribbon, not braid). Thread ribbons or braid through four beads, snowman, and then four more beads. Space beads along ribbon at ¾" intervals from snowman and each other. Secure beads and snowman on ribbon or braid with tacky glue if desired.

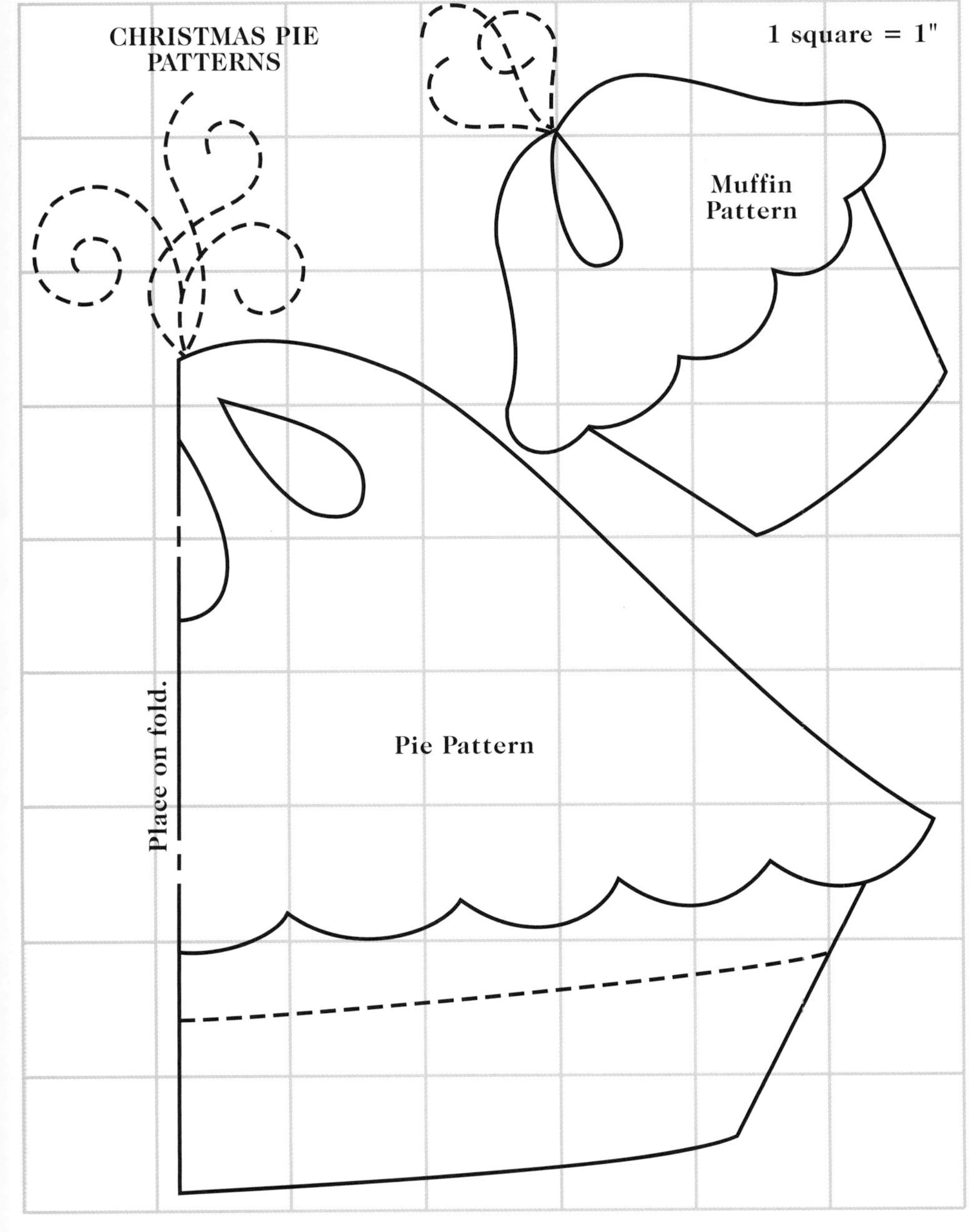

SNOWMAN NECKLACE PATTERN

Noel Candle Holders

Materials:
Four 2"-square wooden blocks
Acrylic paints, colors: white, red
Paintbrushes, sizes: fine, medium
Water-base varnish
Four candles with ⅝" bases
Sandpaper
Pencil
Drill with ¾" bit
Graphite paper

Note: Materials listed will make one set of *Noel Candle Holders*.

1. Drill hole ¾" deep in top center of each block. Sand rough edges using sandpaper. Paint each block with two coats of white paint, letting paint dry between coats.
2. Trace letter *N* onto first block, *O* onto second block, *E* onto third block, and *L* onto fourth block, using graphite paper and pencil. Paint all letters red using medium paintbrush. Let dry. Paint red dots along four edges of block, surrounding each letter, spacing evenly, and using small paintbrush. Let dry thoroughly.
3. Apply two coats of varnish, letting dry between coats.
4. Place candles in drilled holes, pressing base of each candle firmly into hole in top of block.

NOEL CANDLE HOLDERS PATTERNS

Silver Bells Garland

Materials:
12" x 18" piece ½"-thick STYROFOAM brand plastic foam
2¼" x 2¼" metal bell-shaped cookie cutter
Tulip Fine Line Glitter Paint™, color: silver
Tulip Paint Writer™, color: iridescent bronze
2½ yds. metallic blue paper twist cord (**Note:** Designer used Creative Twist™ by MPR.)
12 yds. ⅛"-wide silver ribbon
Low-temperature glue gun
4" darning needle
Paintbrush
Waxed paper
Scissors
Craft knife
Ruler

Note: Materials listed will make 68" of *Silver Bells Garland*.

1. To make presents, use ruler and craft knife to cut twenty-six 1½" squares from sheet of Styrofoam®.
2. To wrap presents, cut paper twist cord into thirteen 4½" pieces. Untwist pieces, lay flat, and cut in half, making twenty-six 3" x 4½" rectangles. Wrap each piece of plastic foam with paper twist, using glue gun to secure.
3. To decorate presents, wrap each package with ⅛"-wide ribbon, referring to photo on page 105 for placement. Cut 5" length of ribbon for each package and tie into a small bow. Glue bow to top center of each package.
4. To make each bell, press cookie cutter into sheet of Styrofoam®. Gently remove bell shape. Make twelve bells.
5. To paint bells, cover work surface with waxed paper. Squeeze silver glitter paint onto bell and paint front and edges, using paintbrush. Repeat for remaining bells. Let dry. Paint reverse side of each bell, using silver glitter paint. Let dry. Repeat, covering both sides and all edges with a second coat of silver glitter paint. Paint clappers on bells, using iridescent bronze paint. Outline each bell, using a line of silver glitter paint. Let dry completely.
6. To make garland, thread darning needle with remaining ribbon. String bells and presents as follows: two presents, one bell, two presents, one bell, etc., ending with two presents. Knot ends of ribbon and place small dot of glue on knots to secure.

Fingerprint Ornaments

Materials:
6" x 9" piece white poster board
5 small plastic frames, shapes: round, square
Non-toxic ink pads, colors: black, red, blue
Fine-line markers, colors: red, green, blue, yellow, black
Five 6" lengths ⅛"-wide satin ribbon, colors: red, green, blue

Note: Materials listed will make five *Fingerprint Ornaments*, with one 3" square of poster board leftover. Square can be used to practice making thumb prints, if desired.

1. Cut poster board into 3" squares. Set aside three and place two on table, shiny-side down. (See note above.) Press thumb into black ink pad; then press thumb on center bottom area, in a vertical position, of one square of poster board, as if pressing down a stamp. Repeat inking thumb and press thumb onto center bottom area of second poster-board square in a horizontal position. Let dry.

FINGERPRINT ORNAMENTS PATTERNS

Draw holly leaves and berries on both squares, using red and green fine-line markers. Draw mouse ears, paws, feet, face, and tail on and around thumbprints, using black marker and referring to mouse patterns on page 114. Set aside. **Note:** Wash thumb when changing from one ink pad to another to avoid mixing inks.

2. Use red ink pad to make two thumbprints on two separate squares of poster board, making first thumbprint diagonally from bottom right to top left of poster-board square. Let dry. Make second thumbprint near center bottom of second square in a vertical position. Let dry. On first square, use red marker to draw *N_EL* around thumbprint, making thumbprint the *O*. Make dot inside letters, using green marker. On second square, draw Santa arms and hat, using red marker, and color in. Draw Santa face, boots, belt, hat cuff, and ball, using black marker. Color in boots and belt, using black marker. Draw and color in mittens, using green marker.

3. Use blue ink pad to make one thumbprint in a vertical position in center of final square. Let dry. Draw angel face, hair, and wings, using black marker. Draw halo using yellow marker. Draw angel feet using blue marker.

4. When drawings are completely dry, cut poster-board squares into shapes to fit frames. Press each design into a frame. Tie ribbon around each frame hanger and tie ribbon into a bow.

Save the Earth Computer-Paper Wreath

Materials:

200 waste tractor-feed strips from used computer-printer paper
4 yds. ⅞"-wide red-and-white polka-dot ribbon
DecoArt™ Americana™ spray gloss sealer/finisher
White wire hanger
Wire cutters
12" length thin wire
Pencil

1. Cut hanger at neck. Remove hook. Bend **each** end into a small *J* shape. Shape wire into a loop 9"–10" in diameter, referring to Wire Illustration.

2. Separate paper strips at perforations. Fold each paper strip in half and thread onto wire loop, referring to Illustration 1. When all paper strips have been threaded onto wire loop, curl each strip, as shown in Illustration 2. Hook two *J* shapes in wire together to form wreath loop.

3. Spray wreath with gloss sealer/finisher to hold curls in paper. Let dry.

4. Make bow from polka-dot ribbon. Secure bow center, using wire. Wire bow to wreath loop close to where *J* shapes are hooked together.

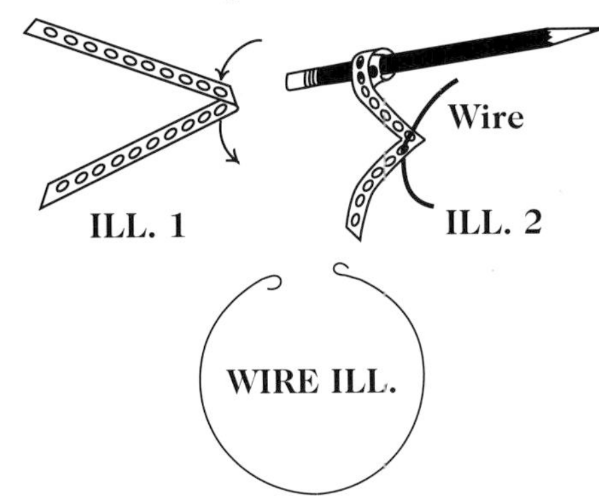

Cinnamon Potpourri Basket

Materials:

Small wicker basket of your choice (**Note:** Model basket measures 7" x 4" x 7¾" tall at top of handle)
Cinnamon sticks (See note below.)
1¼ yds. ⅞"-wide plaid ribbon
Plastic wrap
Hot glue gun
Seasonal potpourri
Scroll saw

Note: Number of cinnamon sticks needed will depend on size basket used. Model basket contains twenty-eight 2"-long sticks. Cinnamon sticks are available in longer lengths at craft stores and can be cut as needed using a scroll saw.

1. Line basket with plastic wrap.

2. Cut cinnamon sticks into 2"-long pieces, using scroll saw. Apply glue to middle of each stick and place sticks around top of basket, spacing evenly.

3. Fill basket with potpourri.

4. Cut a 6" length of ribbon and set aside. Tie remaining ribbon into a multi-loop bow. Tie bow to handle, using 6" length of ribbon.

Surprise Packages

Materials:

Two 1 x 1¼" pieces ½"-thick STYROFOAM brand plastic foam
3" x 5" plain index card
9" x 12" sheet white parchment paper (**Note:** Morilla Calligraphist Parchment was used for model.)
⅛ yd. **total** assorted Christmas-fabric scraps
¾ yd. 3/16"-wide metallic gold ribbon
¾ yd. ¼"-wide green picot-edged ribbon
½ yd. ⅛"-wide Christmas trim of your choice
Assorted sequins, buttons, **or** beads
4½" square Pellon® Wonder-Under® Transfer Web
4½" square green moiré fabric
Aleene's Thick Designer Tacky Glue
Two 1"-wide pin backs
Hole punch, awl, **or** ice pick
Ruler
Toothpicks
Pencil
Iron
Scissors
Hot glue gun

Note: Materials listed will make one gift card and one Christmas card.

1. Center foam pieces on fabric scraps and wrap pieces as if wrapping a gift. Secure ends of fabric with tacky glue. For first 1" x 1¼" package, cut gold metallic ribbon into 3¾" piece. Wrap ribbon around package length. Glue ends together on underside of package. Cut a second piece of gold metallic ribbon to fit around width of package. Wrap ribbon around package and glue in place, as before. Cut a third piece 6" long from gold metallic ribbon. Make a bow from gold metallic ribbon and glue bow in place on top of package. Repeat for second package.

2. To make gift card, use glue gun to secure pin backs to two largest packages. Set one package aside. Fold index card in half along lengthwise edge. Cut two 3" lengths and one 8" length from picot-edged green satin ribbon. Glue shorter lengths onto index card along top fold and left-hand side. Trim ends even with edges of card. Tie bow in remaining length of ribbon and glue where ribbons intersect. Punch two holes in lower-right half of card approximately 1" apart. Pin large package to index card, pinning through holes.

3. To make Christmas card, fold 9" x 12" sheet white parchment paper in half along width of paper. Fold paper in half again to form 4½" x 6" rectangle.

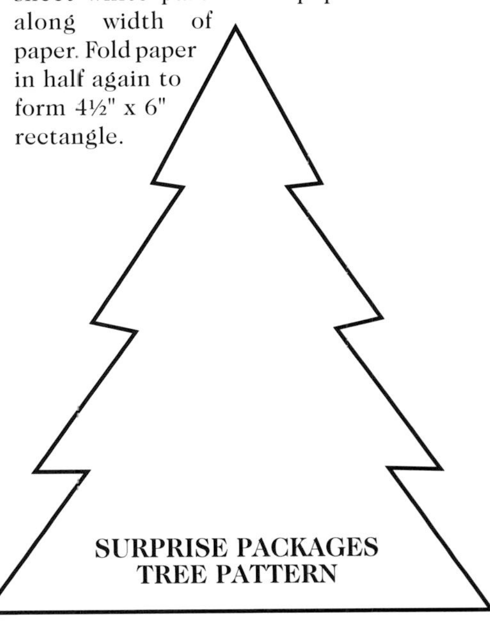

Place paper on table with folds at top and left-hand side. Trace tree pattern onto paper side of Wonder-Under®. Fuse Wonder-Under® to wrong side of green moiré, following manufacturer's instructions for fusing. Cut out tree. Center tree on card and fuse tree to card. Cut two 5½" lengths and two 4¼" lengths from Christmas trim. Glue Christmas trim in place ¼" in from edges of card to form border. Arrange sequins, buttons, or beads on tree as desired and glue in place. Punch holes in card at bottom of tree, approximately 1" apart, and pin package to tree as for gift card.

Laundry Detergent Scoop Decorations

Materials:
4 laundry detergent scoops
1½ yds. ⅜"-wide red satin ribbon
½ yd. ¼"-wide green satin ribbon
Paint pen, color: red
Acrylic spray paint, color: green
Cotton balls
3 silk poinsettia sprays
2" square white STYROFOAM brand plastic foam
Christmas miniatures **or** small ornaments
1 yd. twine
Foil- or plastic-wrapped candy
¼" hole punch
Craft glue **or** hot glue gun

Note: Materials listed will make four *Laundry Detergent Scoop Decorations*.

1. Spray one scoop green. Let dry. Leave remaining scoops white and set two aside. For green scoop and one white scoop, pull cotton balls apart and glue inside scoop opposite handle and on bottom of scoop.
2. Glue red or green ribbon along top, outside edge of each scoop, covering printing on scoop. Cut ribbon where handle protrudes from scoop side. Make bows from remaining ribbon and glue to scoop. Vary look by placing bow on handle, scoop side, etc., referring to photo on page 108 for placement.
3. Glue Christmas miniatures such as trees, houses, and Santa figures inside cotton-filled scoops.
4. Glue Styrofoam® in one empty scoop. Insert poinsettia stems into Styrofoam®. Arrange in pleasing manner and glue in place.
5. Fill remaining scoop with wrapped candy. Glue candy in place, if using scoop as an ornament. Glue Santa figure to end of handle.
6. To use as ornaments, punch hole in each scoop handle, thread 7" length twine through hole, and tie twine ends in a knot to form hanger.

Gingerbread Men Ornaments

Materials:
FIMO® polymer clay, color: caramel (2 oz.)
Delta™ Shiny Stuff paints, colors: white, black, red, green
Hand-sewing needle
2"-tall gingerbread boy cookie cutter
1 skein brown pearl cotton
Tacky glue
Aluminum foil
Waxed paper
Rolling pin
Cookie sheet
Mineral oil (optional)

Note: Materials listed will make approximately twelve *Gingerbread Men Ornaments*. Follow manufacturer's instructions when working with clay. Soften clay by warming it in your hands. Keep your hands clean, as clay attracts smudges. Clay will not dry out but should be stored away from sunlight.

1. Cover cookie sheet with aluminum foil. Set aside.
2. Roll out clay between sheets of waxed paper to 3/16" thick.
3. Cut out gingerbread men with cookie cutter and place on covered cookie sheet. Gather scraps of clay and re-roll to form more gingerbread men. Repeat until clay is completely used.
4. Bake at 260°–270°F for 20–30 minutes. Let cool.
5. Paint eyes black. Alternate using red and green paint for buttons on each gingerbread man. Fill in each gingerbread man's body with dots of white paint. Let dry.
6. Cut pearl cotton into a 3½" length for each gingerbread man. Bring ends together to form hanging loop and glue to back of gingerbread man's head. Let dry.

Gingerbread House Ornaments

Materials:
24" length ⅝"-wide Christmas ribbon
5" length ¼"-wide ribbon (for hanger)
3½"-wide metal house-shaped cookie cutter
2"-tall purchased gingerbread man wood cutout (available at craft stores)
Acrylic paint, colors: brown, white
Paintbrushes, sizes: fine, medium
Hot glue gun

Note: Materials listed will make one *Gingerbread House Ornament*.

1. Paint gingerbread man cutout on both sides, using brown paint and medium paintbrush. Let dry. Paint features on both sides of cutout, using white paint and fine paintbrush, and referring to photo on page 108. Let dry.
2. Glue ¼"-wide ribbon at top of cookie cutter, placing ribbon ends to inside of cookie cutter and forming a loop for hanging.
Note: Handle cookie cutter carefully—metal will become hot!
3. Glue ⅝"-wide ribbon to inside and outside flat surfaces of cookie cutter, referring to photo.
4. Glue gingerbread man cutout to ribbon on bottom, inside surface of cookie cutter.

Earth-Friendly Gift Bags

Materials:
14" x 16", 18" x 24", and 24" x 30" pieces wool, corduroy, **or** other heavyweight fabrics of your choice
Thread to match fabrics
3 yds. ½"–¾"-wide ribbon **or** 3 yds. rattail cord (**Note:** use rattail cord only if using wool fabric.)
1 yd. Pellon® Wonder-Under® Transfer Web
6" x 14" scrap green felt
6" square burgundy Doe Suede **or** felt
5" x 6" scrap brown Doe Suede **or** felt
Large blunt yarn needle **or** bodkin (if using rattail cord)
Delta Shiny Stuff™ fabric paint, colors: black, white
Iron
Sewing machine

Note: Materials listed make one bag of each size: 8" x 12", 11" x 16", and 14" x 22".

1. Enlarge patterns as indicated. Trace trees, gingerbread boy, and noel design onto paper side of Wonder-Under®, placing all patterns right-side up. (**Note:** Letters in noel design will be backward when traced on Wonder-Under®. This is correct; and pattern should be used right-side up, as process used for fusing with Wonder-Under® will reverse fabric design from the way it appears on paper pattern.) Fuse trees to green felt, gingerbread boy to wrong side of brown

Doe Suede, and noel design to wrong side of burgundy Doe Suede, following manufacturer's instructions for fusing. Cut out. Set aside.

2. Fold fabric pieces in half along long edges, placing wrong sides of fabric together. Center and fuse design to right side of one half of each fabric piece, following manufacturer's instructions for fusing. (**Note:** Bag decorated with trees is large. Bags decorated with gingerbread boy and noel design are medium size. Plain green bag is small.) Sew designs to bags using matching thread, if desired.

3. Fold fabric pieces in half, placing right sides of fabric together. Sew each bag at side and bottom, using ½" seam allowance and referring to Illustration 1. Hem or fringe top of each bag. To hem, fold and press top edge under ½" and then fold over 1" and press again, referring to Illustration 2. Machine sew hem. To fringe, if bag is made from wool fabric, unravel ¾" at top edge of bag.

4. Miter bottom corners of bag, referring to Illustration 3. To miter, fold across corners, aligning seams. Measure down from corner 1½" and sew diagonally across corner at this point. Turn bag right-side out.

5. To add ties, sew middle of ribbon to center back of bag approximately 4" from top edge, referring to Illustration 4. For rattail cord (if using wool fabric), thread cord into large blunt needle or bodkin and weave through bag top approximately 4" from top edge, beginning and ending at center front of bag. Tie cord tails in a bow.

6. Paint eyes on gingerbread boy, using black fabric paint. Add dots to noel design and ribbon, using white fabric paint.

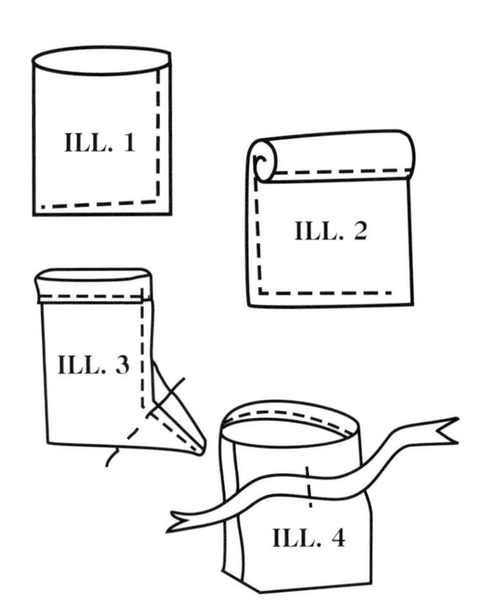

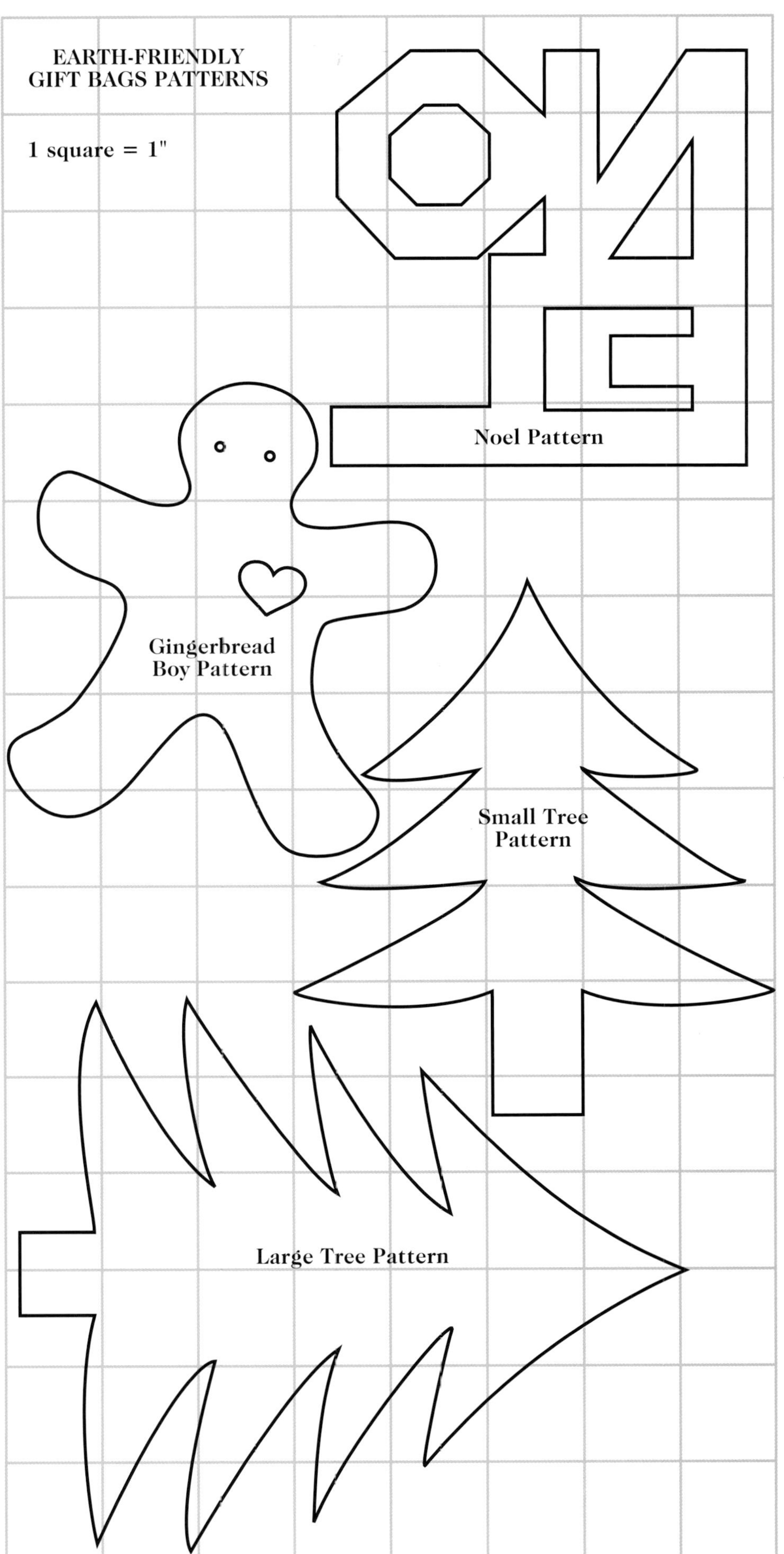

DESIGNER
Offray
RIBBONS
PATTERN:
WIDTH:

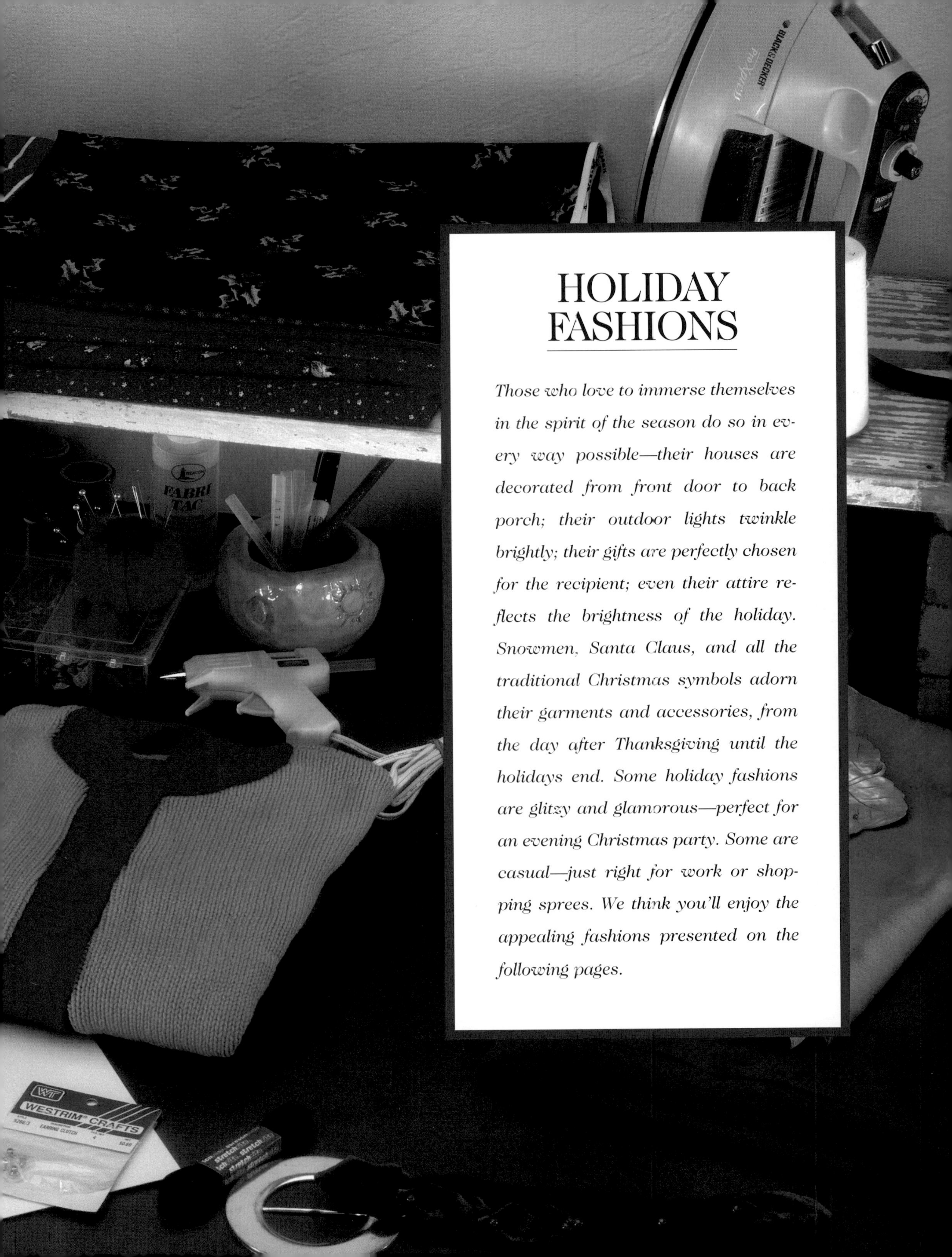

HOLIDAY FASHIONS

Those who love to immerse themselves in the spirit of the season do so in every way possible—their houses are decorated from front door to back porch; their outdoor lights twinkle brightly; their gifts are perfectly chosen for the recipient; even their attire reflects the brightness of the holiday. Snowmen, Santa Claus, and all the traditional Christmas symbols adorn their garments and accessories, from the day after Thanksgiving until the holidays end. Some holiday fashions are glitzy and glamorous—perfect for an evening Christmas party. Some are casual—just right for work or shopping sprees. We think you'll enjoy the appealing fashions presented on the following pages.

Festive Accessories

Add just the right splash of holiday spirit to your everyday wardrobe with the exciting, fun-to-wear accessories featured in this chapter. Everyone knows it would be impractical to have a totally different wardrobe for Christmas. Still, you don't want to look like Ebenezer Scrooge, so what can you do? Well, here's a practical, cost-conscious solution—work with what you have, adding festive belts, pins, earrings, hair accessories, bags, and more, all of which will dress up your usual attire for the holiday season without overextending your budget.

Take the office crew by surprise when you arrive at the annual Christmas party dressed to the nines and sporting one of the ***Fancy Holiday Belts***, shown opposite. Give sparkle to a black dress or pantsuit with the ***Holly Moiré Stretch Belt***, shown in detail at right. The stretchy, wide elastic belt is made bright with green holly leaves, coated with Liquid Sequins™, and red, acrylic-jewel holly berries.

Ask the man in your life to don his tuxedo and then provide him with a ***Christmas Cummerbund***, shown in detail at the bottom of this page. The green, Ultrasuede® accessory is decorated with expressive Santa faces, also cut from Ultrasuede®. If you're feeling especially creative, you can try using different embellishments; for example, a poinsettia instead of holly on the moiré belt or snowmen instead of Santas on the cummerbund. What a pair you will be with your fanciful, fun, holiday belts.

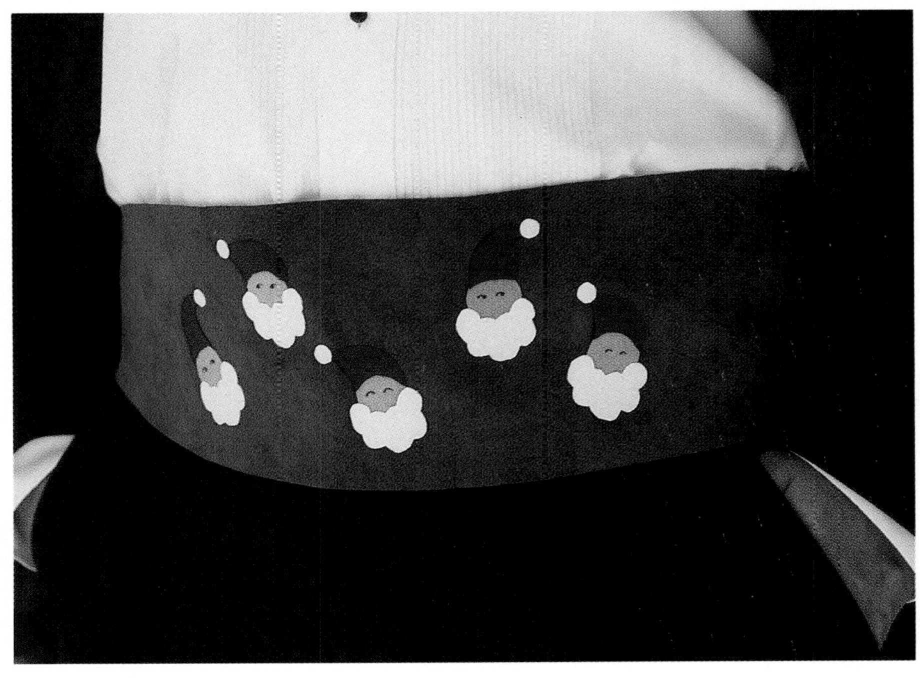

***Left**—Who says formal can't be fun? These* Fancy Holiday Belts, *also shown in detail at right and above right, will add glitz and whimsy to a dressy occasion. Instructions are on page 129.*

Above and right*—Pluck a snowflake from the winter sky to wear as a pin; then add two more for earrings. The* Crochet Snowflake Jewelry *shines with silvery blending filament, and will add a lacy, elegant touch to holiday attire. Crochet a snowstorm for yourself and others! Instructions begin on page 129.*

For any occasion—perhaps a family reunion, an afternoon of gift wrapping, the school Christmas pageant, or a day at the office—***Crochet Snowflake Jewelry***, shown at left, will be the ideal complement to any outfit. Combine white crochet thread with silvery blending filament for the snowflakes, and use pink and green thread for the rosebud trim. Finally, use stiffener on the snowflakes, add jewelry findings, and your shining earrings and pin will be ready to wear.

Make a small blizzard of these crocheted flakes and share them with special friends! Or use them as ornaments by replacing the earring findings and pin back with clear nylon monofilament hangers or ribbon hangers that complement the colors used in the snowflakes. The tiny crochet pieces will make your tree appear to have been standing in soft snow flurries.

Little girls and their moms will love donning the ***Holly Wearables***, shown at top right, and wearing them to Christmas parties and family dinners. Velvety green holly leaves and red bead holly berries are made into shoe clips, a headband, and combs. Any daughter will adore dressing like her mother, and these soft-to-touch accessories are cute enough for a young one, but grown-up enough for her mother. The combs make holiday curls even prettier, and will certainly make someone feel very grown-up on a dressy occasion. Mother's holly headband will coordinate well with a Christmas dress, flowing pantsuit in a rich fabric, or embellished sweater. The shoe clips can appear on Mother's elegant, green suede shoes, as

shown at right, or on a child's patent-leather Mary Janes. When your daughter has outgrown the ***Holly Wearables***, put them away carefully, until the day she becomes mother to a little girl. Give them to her on their first Christmas, and happily await the day that she and her daughter will continue a family tradition.

Above and right—*Mother and daughter, or even big sis and little sis, will adore this set of* Holly Wearables. *Headband, combs, and shoe clips all feature soft-to-touch leaves, and berries made of beads. Instructions are on page 130.*

Plan a special Christmas shopping spree with some friends. Invite them to breakfast on the morning of the event, then surprise them each with a bright ***Holiday Tote***. These easy-to-make bags are the perfect size to hold several small gifts, plus your wallet and other little necessities. Colorful "packages" appliquéd on the outside feature both "wrapping paper" and trim. Scraps of your Christmas fabrics from other sewing projects can be transformed into the wrapping paper; and short lengths of red, green, and white ribbons will become perky bows. Swirls of golden glitter accent the tote's bright red corduroy. If you really want to get in the spirit of the season, you can also use the tote at the grocery store throughout the holidays. You'll not only look good; you'll also be helping the environment. Why not bring out your scrap bag today and make this charmer—it'll provide a great excuse to go shopping!

Above*—Make several festive, appliquéd tote bags to share with your closest friends; then get set for a fun and fantastic shopping spree. Fellow shoppers will be sure to comment on your* Holiday Tote. *Fabric for the appliqué "packages" can probably be found in your scrap bag.* *Instructions begin on page 130.*

Winter Wearables

When the Christmas holidays come around this year, why not have a few new, hand-stitched garments ready to put on—for work, play, or just any old day? Our selections are both lovely and simple to create, and will carry you through the season in style.

The ***Christmas Jumper***, shown at left and below, is actually a transformation of a basic, blue denim jumper taken from the designer's closet. Whether your jumper is many washings old or brand new, it will become a festive favorite. With red and green fabric scraps and some basic sewing supplies, you can make this charming holly-leaves-

Left and above*—Turn a basic denim jumper into a hand-embellished, holiday fantasy of holly leaves and berries, using simple appliqué skills. Instructions for the* Christmas Jumper *are on page 140.*

and-berries appliqué to trim the denim jumper. The technique used on this project is easy and has the added benefit of not requiring a sewing machine for completion. If your jumper has buttons, try replacing them with same-size red or green buttons. If you would rather embellish a denim shirt or skirt, adapt the holly design to fit on the shirt pocket or around the skirt's hem. The result will be a finished piece you'll be proud to wear throughout the holiday season.

Welcome the arrival of Christmastime in matching mother-and-daughter ***Herald Angels Sweaters***, shown at right. If you don't have a daughter, you certainly must know a mother-daughter pair who would dearly love to have beautiful cardigans like these. Duplicate-stitch angels form heavenly "bands," down both sides of the sweater front, with a larger, trumpet-playing angel on the back (see detail below). Designs for both sweaters are coordinating, but Mom's angels are a bit larger than her little girl's. Duplicate stitching, if you haven't tried it, will delight you with its ease and simplicity. One simple stitch, worked over the stitches of a purchased, stockinette-stitch sweater, is all you'll need to learn; and you'll use six-strand cotton embroidery floss, with blending filament added in places, to complete the designs. We know these angelic sweaters will cheer you each time they are worn to a holiday event.

***Right and above**—What mother and daughter wouldn't love the matched set of* Herald Angels Sweaters? *The duplicate-stitched pair features angels playing various musical instruments on the front and back of festive cardigans.* *Charts begin on page 132.*

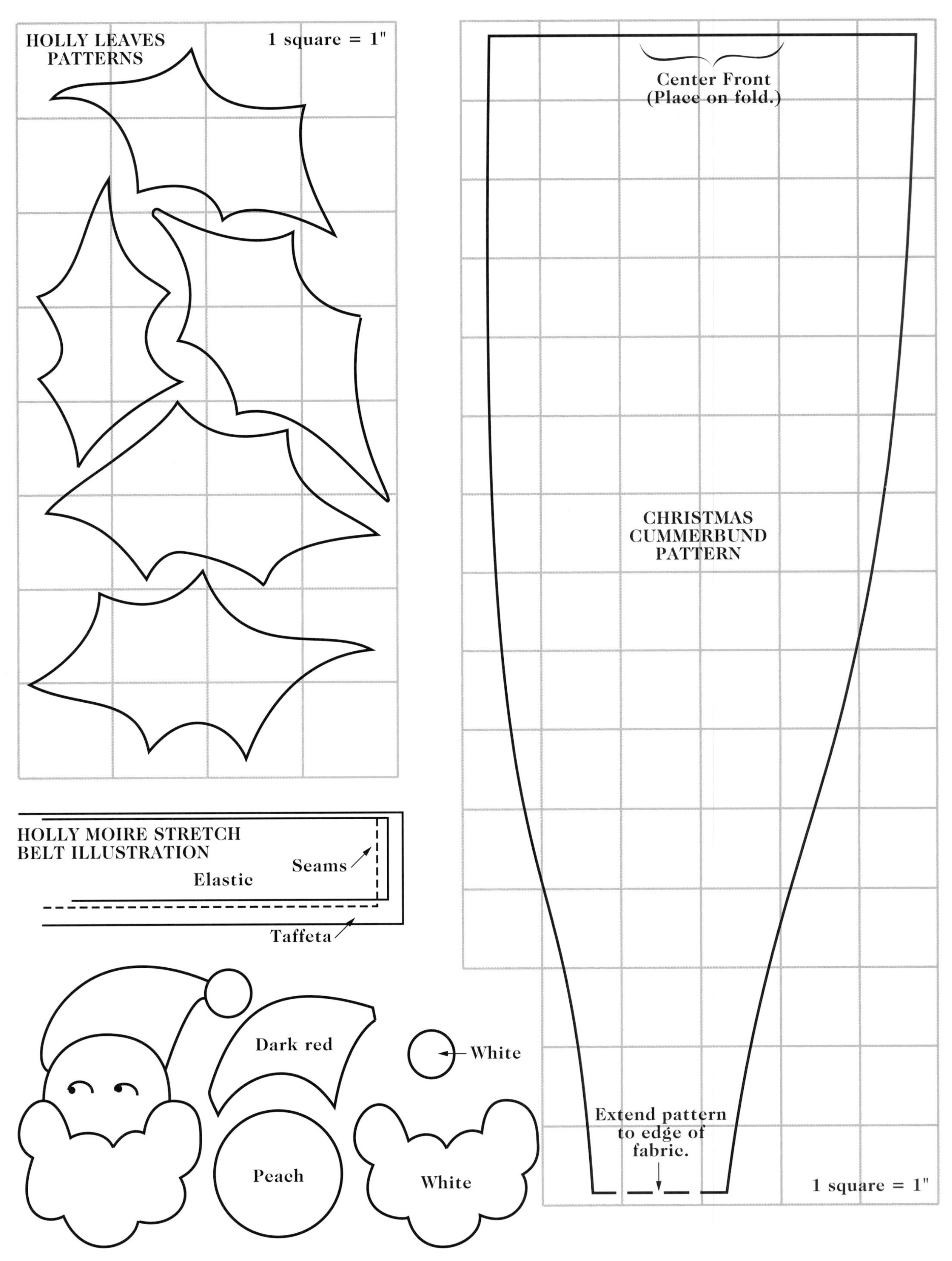
HOLLY LEAVES
PATTERNS
1 square = 1"
Center Front
(Place on fold.)
CHRISTMAS
CUMMERBUND
PATTERN
HOLLY MOIRE STRETCH
BELT ILLUSTRATION
Seams
Elastic
Taffeta
Dark red
White
Extend pattern
to edge of
fabric.
Peach
White
1 square = 1"
SANTA PATTERNS

Fancy Holiday Belts

Christmas Cummerbund
Materials:
¼ yd. 44/45"-wide dark green UltraSuede®
¼ yd. 44/45"-wide matching green **or** black felt
2" x 4" scraps UltraSuede®, colors: white, flesh, dark red
1⅓ yds. Pellon® Wonder-Under® Transfer Web
Fine-tip permanent black marker
Two 2" D rings   Scissors
Press cloth   Iron

1. Enlarge pattern as indicated. Extend small ends of pattern to use entire width of UltraSuede®. Trace cummerbund pattern onto paper side of Wonder-Under®. Fuse to felt, following manufacturer's instructions for fusing. Cut out. Fuse felt to wrong side of Ultra-Suede®. Cut out. **Note:** When working with UltraSuede®, check iron temperature frequently and use press cloth between iron and UltraSuede®.
2. To make Santa appliqués, trace five of each Santa face, hat, pom-pom, and beard onto paper side of Wonder-Under®. Fuse to wrong side of UltraSuede®, using flesh for face, white for beard and pom-pom, and dark red for hat. Cut out. Arrange on front of cummerbund, referring to photo on page 121 for placement, and fuse in place.
3. To attach D rings, fold one end of cummerbund over the two rings, folding end back 1½" toward back side of cummerbund. Use Wonder-Under® to fuse end to back side.
4. Make simple eyes on each Santa's face, using fine-tip marker.

Holly Moiré Stretch Belt
Materials:
¼ yd. 44/45"-wide black moiré taffeta
1 yd. 2"-wide non-roll elastic
9" x 10" scrap green Doe Suede, velveteen, **or** velour
⅓ yd. Pellon® Wonder-Under® Transfer Web
Thread to match fabrics
Six 9mm red round acrylic faceted stones (**Note:** Stones used for model are from The Beadery®.)
DecoArt™ Liquid Sequins™, color: sea aqua **or** green twinkle
Small fabric paintbrush
¾"-wide black hook and eye closure
Hand-sewing needle   Scissors
Straight pins   Craft glue
Sewing machine (optional)

1. Fold taffeta in half along 9" edge, placing right sides of fabric together. (**Note:** Selvage edges will be opposite each other, raw edges will be together, and fold of fabric will be opposite raw edges.) Pin elastic to folded taffeta. Sew across one end through all layers. Then sew down length of belt ⅛" away from edge of elastic. Turn right-side out, with seam at edge of elastic. Press as needed. Slide taffeta down length of elastic, gathering fabric slightly. Turn raw edges of taffeta at remaining end of belt under ½" to inside of belt. Sew across end through all layers to secure.
2. Trace leaves onto paper side of Wonder-Under®. Fuse to wrong side of green fabric, following manufacturer's instructions for fusing. Cut out. Fuse leaves to wrong side of remaining green fabric. Cut out. Sew leaves to one end of belt, sewing only one end of each leaf and leaving remainder of leaf unattached. Refer to photo for placement. (**Note:** Position one leaf to cover belt end.) Glue red acrylic stones to leaves. Let dry. Add sparkle by brushing Liquid Sequins™ onto one half of each holly leaf. Let dry.
3. Sew hook under end of belt with leaves, ½" from end. Sew eye to other end of belt.

Crochet Snowflake Jewelry

Crochet Abbreviations:
bet—between
ch—chain stitch
dc(s)—double crochet(s)
lp—loop
nxt—next
rem—remaining
rep—repeat * to *
sc—single crochet
sk—skip
sl st—slip stitch
sp—space
tr—treble or triple crochet

Materials:
30 yds. size 10 crochet thread, color: white (**Note:** DMC Baroque was used for model.)
Size 8 crochet hook
Two 35-yd. reels Kreinik Metallics Blending Filament, color: 032BF pearl
15 yds. variegated pink crochet thread
7 yds. green crochet thread
Earring findings   Tacky glue
Pin back finding   Fabric stiffener
Rustproof pins   Waxed paper
Stretching board

Note: For a frosted look that makes the snowflakes sparkle, hold two strands of blending filament together with the white cotton thread as you crochet. Add the delicate roses for a touch of color.

Earrings
(Pair requires approximately 15 yds. size 10 crochet thread.)
Ch 5, sl st in 1st ch to form ring.
Rnd 1: *Ch 3, tr in ring, ch 3, tr in last tr, ch 6, sl st in tr just made, tr in tr below, ch 10, sl st in tr just made, tr in tr below, ch 6, sl st in tr just made, ch 3, sl st in tr below, ch 3, sc in ring.* Rep * 5 times. Fasten off. (Make two.)

Pin
(Pin requires approximately 15 yds. size 10 crochet thread.)
Ch 5, sl st in 1st ch to form ring.
Row 1: *Ch 3, dc in ring, (ch 3, dc in sp just made) 5 times (= 6 spaces); sc in 4th sp from hook; ch 3, dc in same sp, (ch 3, dc in sp just made) 2 times, sc in ring.* Rep * 5 times (= 6 arms).
Row 2: Sc in 1st sp, *ch 3, sc in nxt sp, ch 3, sc in nxt sp, sc in nxt sp; ch 5, sc in same sp, ch 8, sc in same sp, ch 5, sc in same sp; sc in nxt sp, ch 5, sc in same sp, ch 10, sc in same sp, ch 5, sc in same sp; sc in nxt sp, ch 5, sc in same sp, ch 8, sc in same sp, ch 5, sc in same sp; sc in nxt sp, ch 3, sc in nxt sp, ch 3, sc in nxt sp, sc in 1st sp on nxt arm.* Rep * 5 times, except instead of final sc make sl st in 1st sc on row. Fasten off.

To Stiffen:
Saturate snowflakes in fabric stiffener or a one-to-one solution of fresh white glue and water. Gently squeeze out excess. Use **rustproof** pins to shape snowflakes individually on waxed-paper-covered stretching board. Align points of each snowflake for a balanced look. Let dry thoroughly. Remove pins.
Note: Use fan or hair dryer to speed drying.

Rosebud
Note: Make dcs and sc under 1 strand of thread in ch. Bud will curl naturally.
Rose—Leave 3" tails on both ends for tying rose to snowflake. With rose thread, ch 10, make 3 dc in 5th ch from hook, 3 dc in nxt 4 chains (= 15 dc); sc in base of rose. Cut thread and knot ends.
Leaves—With green thread, make a lp on hook and sc in base of rose. (Ch 6, sc in 4th ch and each rem ch and 1st sc; sc in base) 2 times. Cut thread and knot ends. Dab knots with glue and let dry. From right side, pull green threads through center hole of small snowflake and pink threads through spaces to left and right. Tie gently in back, dab with glue, let dry, and trim ends.

Open loop on finding, insert in ch 10 sp, and close loop.

Rose

Note: Twirl petals to shape as you make rose.

Rose—With rose thread, ch 10 loosely; in 4th ch from hook make 10 dc; (sk 1 ch, in nxt ch make sc, ch 4, 10 tr) 2 times. Sc in base of middle petal between 5th and 6th tr, sc bet 2nd and 3rd petal. Cut thread 3" long and gently tie knot at base of rose. Swirl petals into shape with fingers.

Leaves—With green thread, make a lp on hook and sc in base of rose. (Ch 9 loosely, dc in 4th ch from hook and each of nxt 5 ch, sc in base of rose) 2 times. Cut thread 3" long, tie gently, and dab knot with glue. Use crochet hook to pull threads through center hole in large snowflake and through holes in pin back. Tie and glue. Let dry and trim ends.

Holly Wearables

Materials:

1/8 yd. 44/45"-wide green velveteen fabric
1/8 yd. 44/45"-wide green taffeta fabric
Thread to match fabrics
1/2 yd. 3/8"-wide black elastic
Small pkg. 4mm red pearl beads
Tracing paper and pencil
Straight pins
2 sew-on shoe clips
Hot glue gun
2 clear plastic combs
Scissors

Note: Materials listed will make one set of hair combs, one set of shoe clips, and one headband.

1. Trace holly-leaf patterns onto tracing paper. Cut out. Layer lining right-side up and velveteen right-side down atop a flat surface. Pin patterns on top, minding grain lines of fabrics. Cut out three leaves for each comb, two leaves for each shoe clip, and six leaves for headband. Sew around holly leaves, using a 1/8" seam allowance and leaving an opening for turning. Turn right-side out. Whipstitch opening closed.

2. To make each comb, arrange three holly leaves with ends overlapping. Sew three red pearl beads onto one end of center green holly leaf on velveteen side, referring to Comb Diagram for placement. Hot glue holly leaves to comb, overlapping solid plastic edge with two of the leaves and placing third leaf with red, pearl-bead berries diagonally between two leaves so that teeth of plastic comb are slightly covered.

3. To make each shoe clip, sew two holly leaves, velveteen side up, to straight edges of shoe clip. Sew three red pearl beads to center of holly leaves where they overlap.

4. To make headband, join ends of elastic together to fit head comfortably. Find center point of elastic band by bringing ends of elastic together and pinching curve at center. Sew six holly leaves, velveteen side up, to one half of black elastic, overlapping ends of each successive leaf and using holly leaves to cover overlapping elastic ends. Sew three red pearl beads to two center holly leaves where leaves overlap. Sew one red pearl bead to each of four holly leaves where leaves overlap, spacing beads approximately 1½" apart.

Holiday Tote

Materials:

2/3 yd. 44/45"-wide red corduroy
Three 7" x 8" scraps assorted Christmas-print fabrics (**Note:** Fabrics used for model were red print, green stripe, and red-and-green floral print.)
3/4 yd. 3/8"-wide white satin ribbon
3/4 yd. 1/4"-wide green picot-edged satin ribbon
3/4 yd. 1/4"-wide metallic gold ribbon
Thread to match corduroy and fabric scraps
3 yds. 1"-wide red bias tape
1/3 yd. Pellon® Wonder-Under® Transfer Web
DecoArt™ Heavy Metals Liquid Glitter Paint™, color: karat gold
Small fabric paintbrush
Straight pins
Scissors
Iron
Sewing machine (**Option:** Use DecoArt™ Dimensions™ shiny paint, color: Christmas red, to outline, instead of sewing.)

1. Enlarge tote pattern as indicated. Cut out. Pin pattern to corduroy, following straight grain of fabric. (**Note:** Center line on pattern is included for optional placement on fold of fabric.) Cut two pieces for tote. Remove pins. Set aside.

2. To prepare appliqué shapes, trace package designs onto paper side of Wonder-Under®. Fuse to wrong side of fabric scraps, following manufacturer's instructions for fusing. Cut out. Place appliqué shapes on one side of tote, referring to photo on page 124 and pattern for placement. Fuse to tote. Cut 1/4"-wide and 3/8"-wide strips of Wonder-Under® and use to fuse ribbons

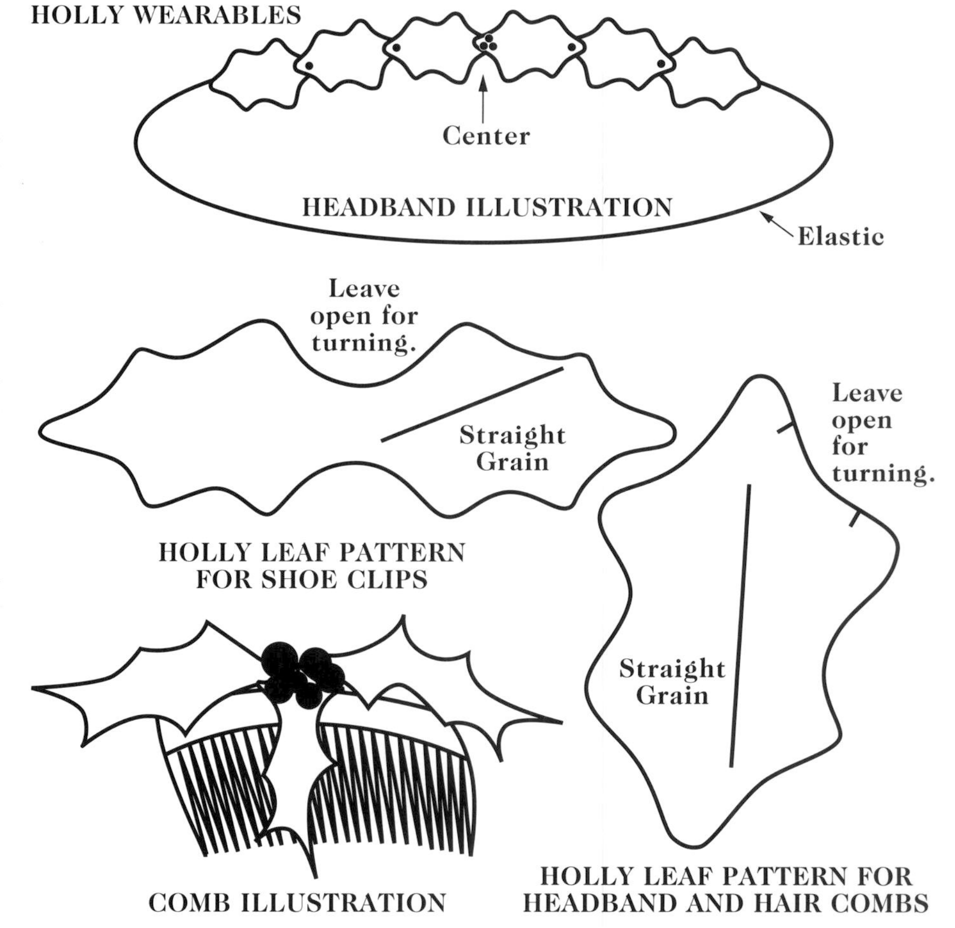

to packages. With machine set on close zigzag, satin stitch around edges of packages. Straight stitch lines on packages to suggest package edges and corners inside appliqué shapes, referring to photo. (**Note:** If desired, outline packages with red dimensional paint instead of satin stitches.) Tie ribbon bows and tack to each package at *X*.

3. To finish tote, sew sides, bottom, and across handle, placing right sides of corduroy together and using a ¼" seam allowance. Zigzag edges for a smooth finish. Miter bottom corners by pulling fabric apart at bottom corners and folding corners to form triangle with seam running up middle. Sew 2" line across corners from folded edge to folded edge, 1½" from bottom edge of corner. To finish handle, place bias tape on handle with right sides together and sew around openings, using a ¼" seam allowance. Press bias tape to inside of tote. Topstitch ¾" in from handle edge.

4. Paint swirls around packages and on knots of bows for added sparkle, using gold glitter paint.

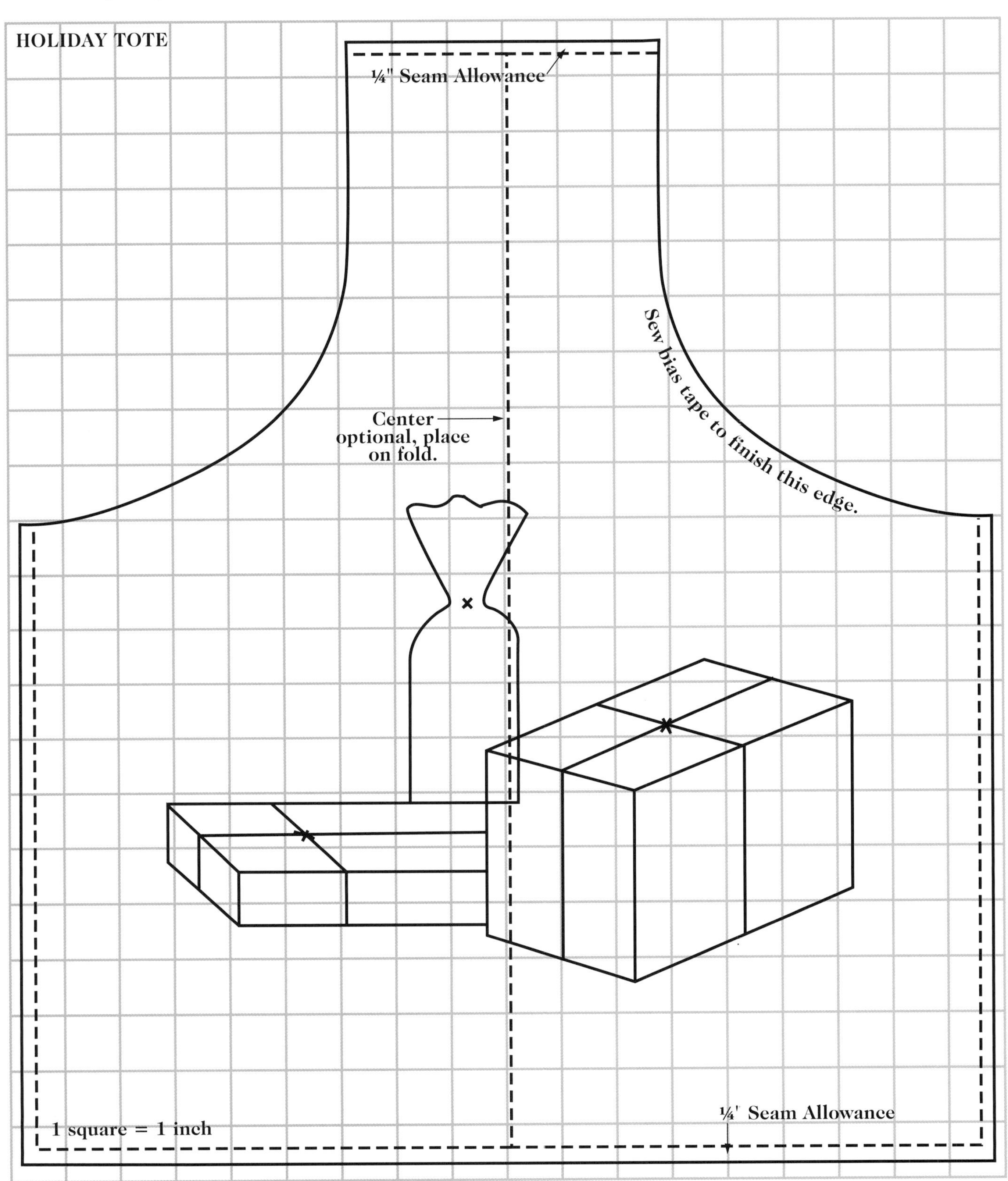

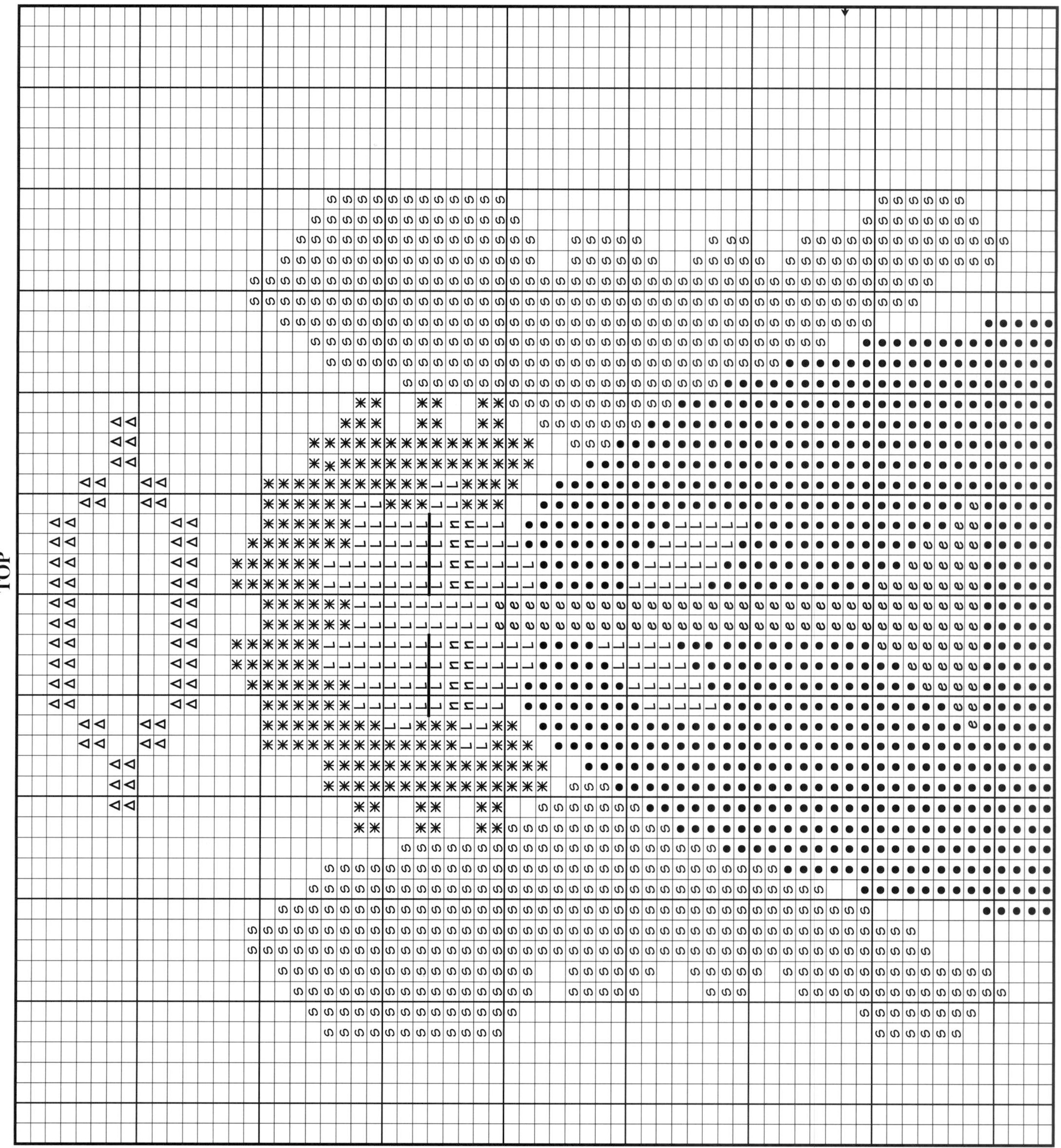

CHILD'S SWEATER—BACK PANEL

Shaded portion indicates overlap from previous page.

Herald Angels Sweaters

	DMC	Kreinik Metallics	Color
a	798		royal blue
n	3733		dusty rose
G	977		gold-brown, lt.
e	676		old gold, lt.
L	754		peach flesh, lt.
S	648		beaver gray, lt.
		001HL BF	silver, hi lustre
✱	433		brown, med.
V	799		delft, med.
▬	800		delft, pl.
●	white		white
⊙	727		topaz, vy. lt.
△	834		olive, vy. lt.
		002HL BF	gold, hi lustre
■	310		black

Additional skeins needed:

	Mother	Daughter
798	5	2
676	1	1
648	8	3
799	5	0
800	8	2
white	0	5
001 HL BF	2	0

Sweaters: red-and-green color-block cardigans (6 horizontal stitches per inch, 9 vertical stitches per inch) from *Just CrossStitch*®

Stitch count:

Mother

Left Panel	202H x 42W
Right Panel	202H x 43W
Back Panel	174H x 85W

Daughter

Left Panel	142H x 37W
Right Panel	142H x 37W
Back Panel	104H x 52W

Instructions: Work duplicate stitch using six strands of floss. (See illustration.) For best coverage, floss strands should be separated and put back together. When blending DMC and Kreinik Metallics, use four strands of floss and two strands Kreinik Blending Filament. Backstitch using four strands 310 for angel's eyes and strings on lyre and mandolin.

Duplicate-stitch instructions: Thread needle and tie knot at end of floss. Anchor floss on back of sweater, looping thread several times before beginning. Insert needle from the back and bring through to right side of sweater in center of a stitch. Slip needle under two threads of stitch above and draw through. To complete stitch, insert needle in hole where stitch began. This represents one square on the chart.

DUPLICATE STITCH

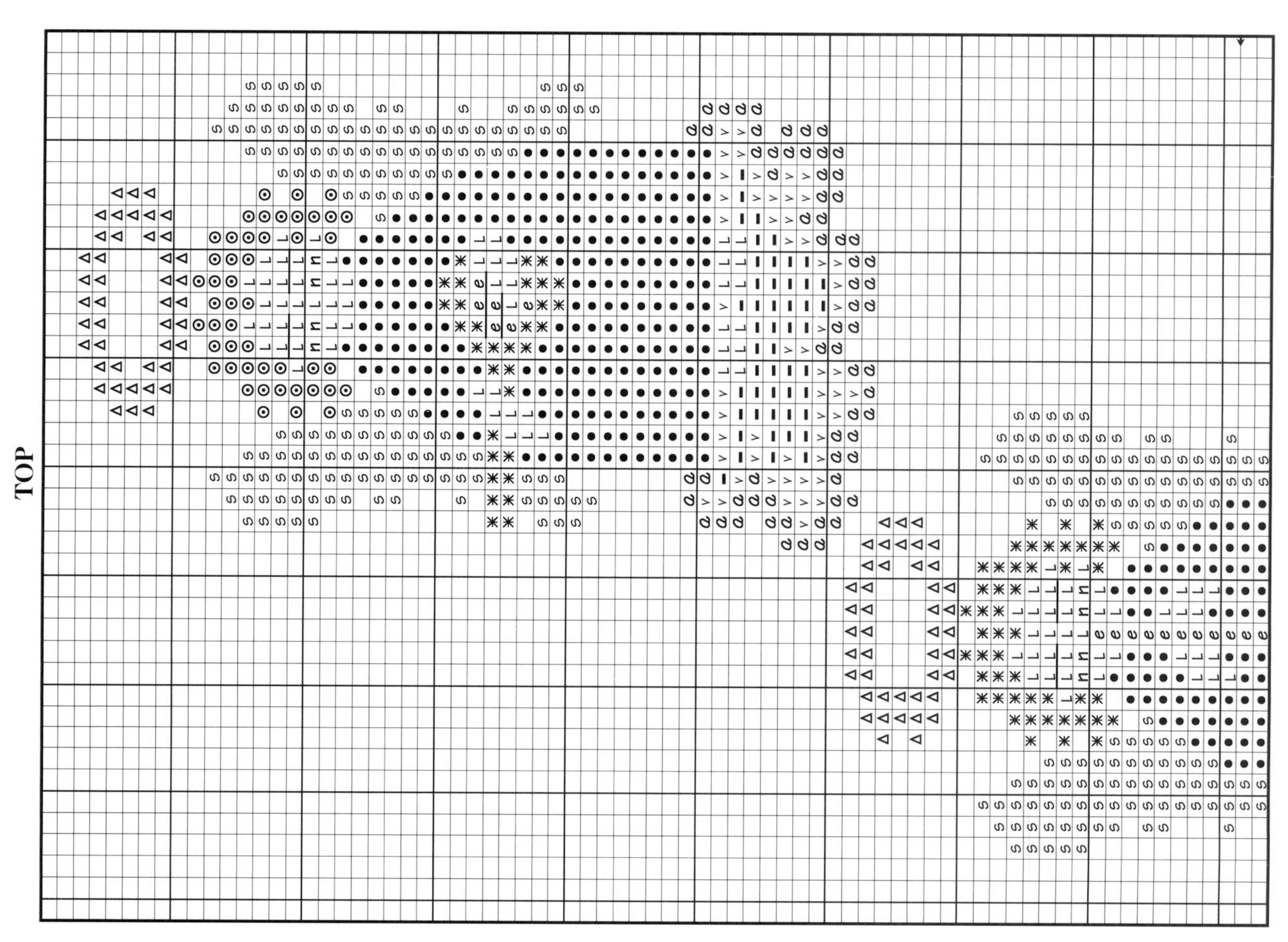

Shaded portion indicates overlap from chart above.

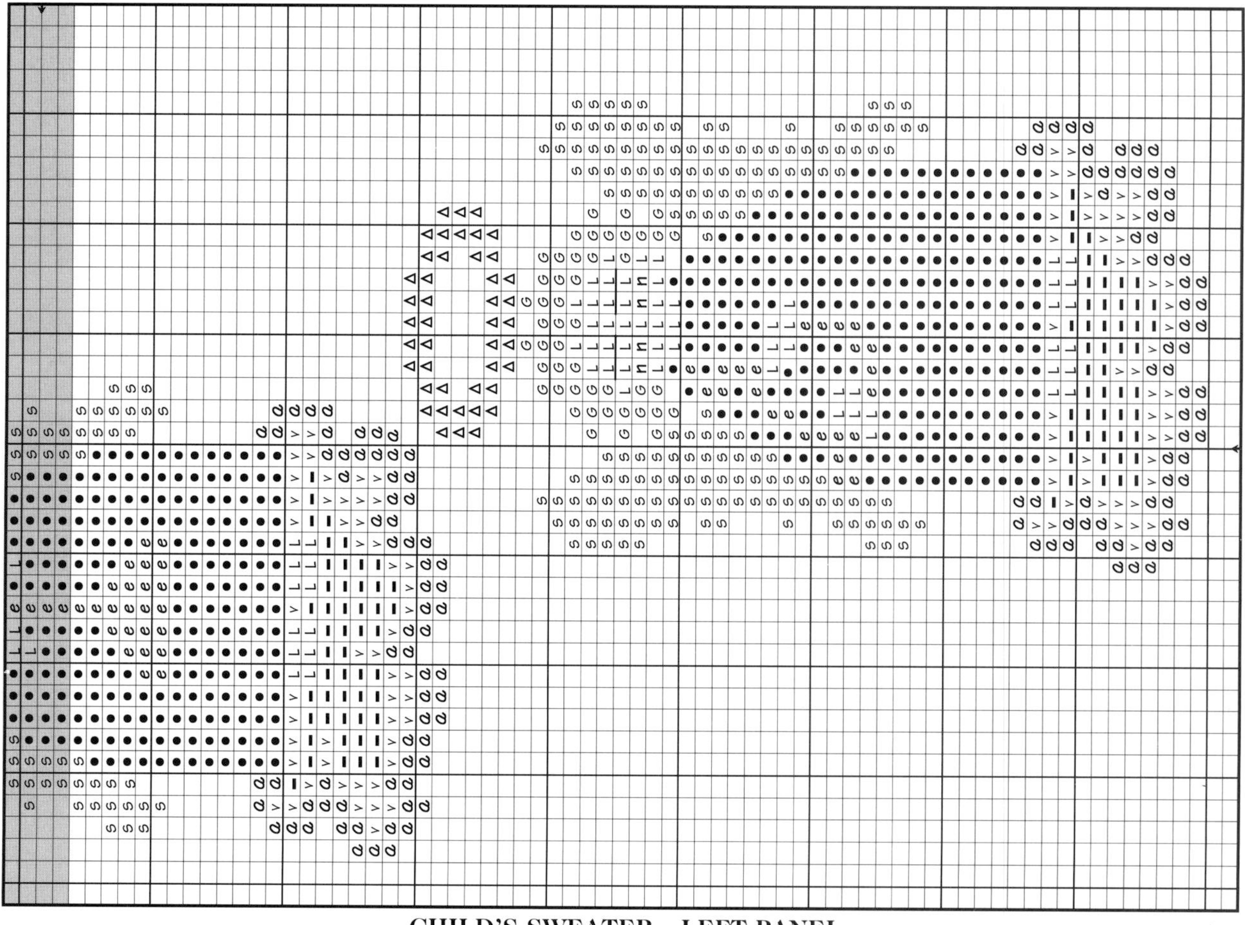

CHILD'S SWEATER—LEFT PANEL

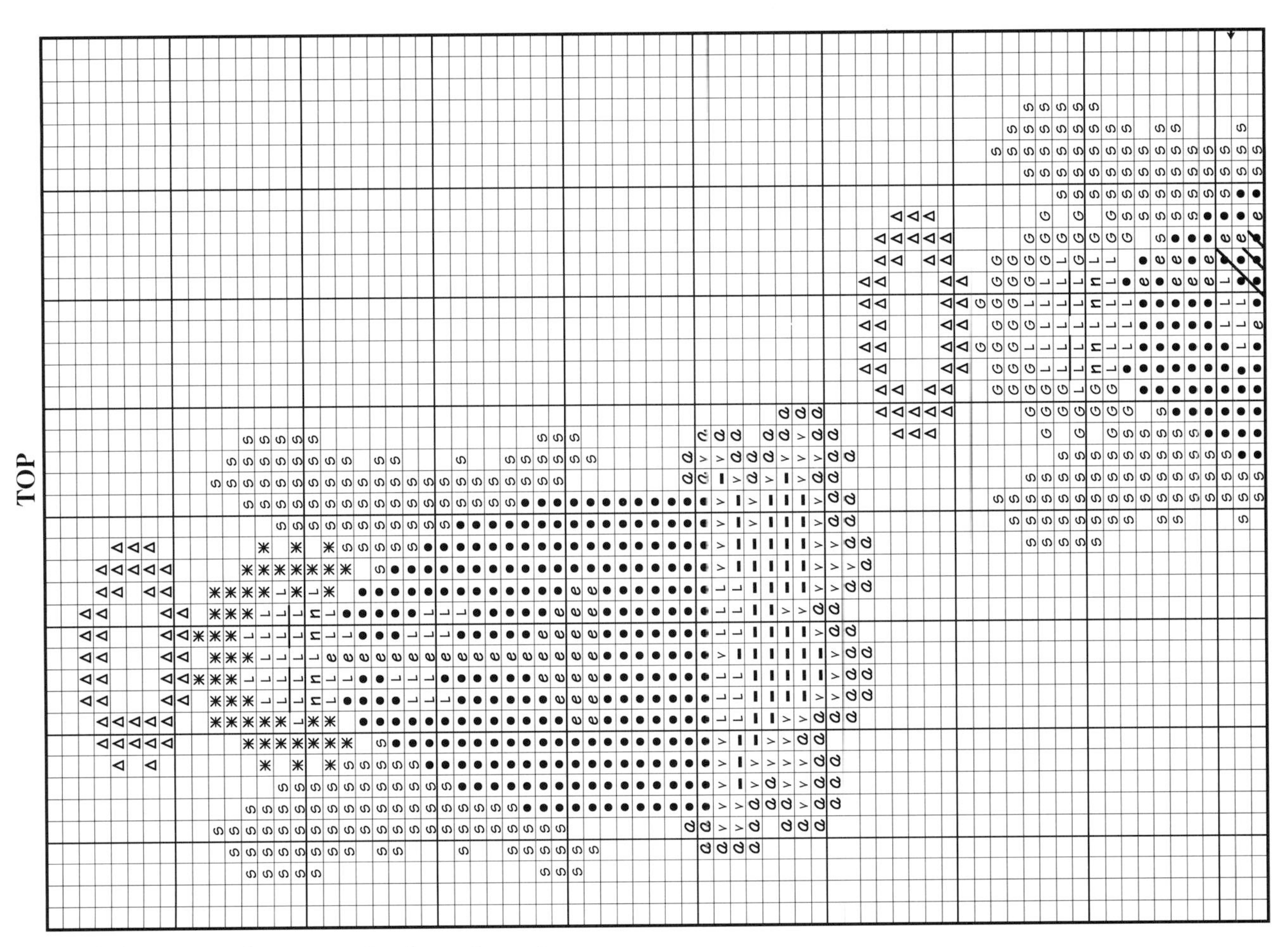

Shaded portion indicates overlap from chart above.

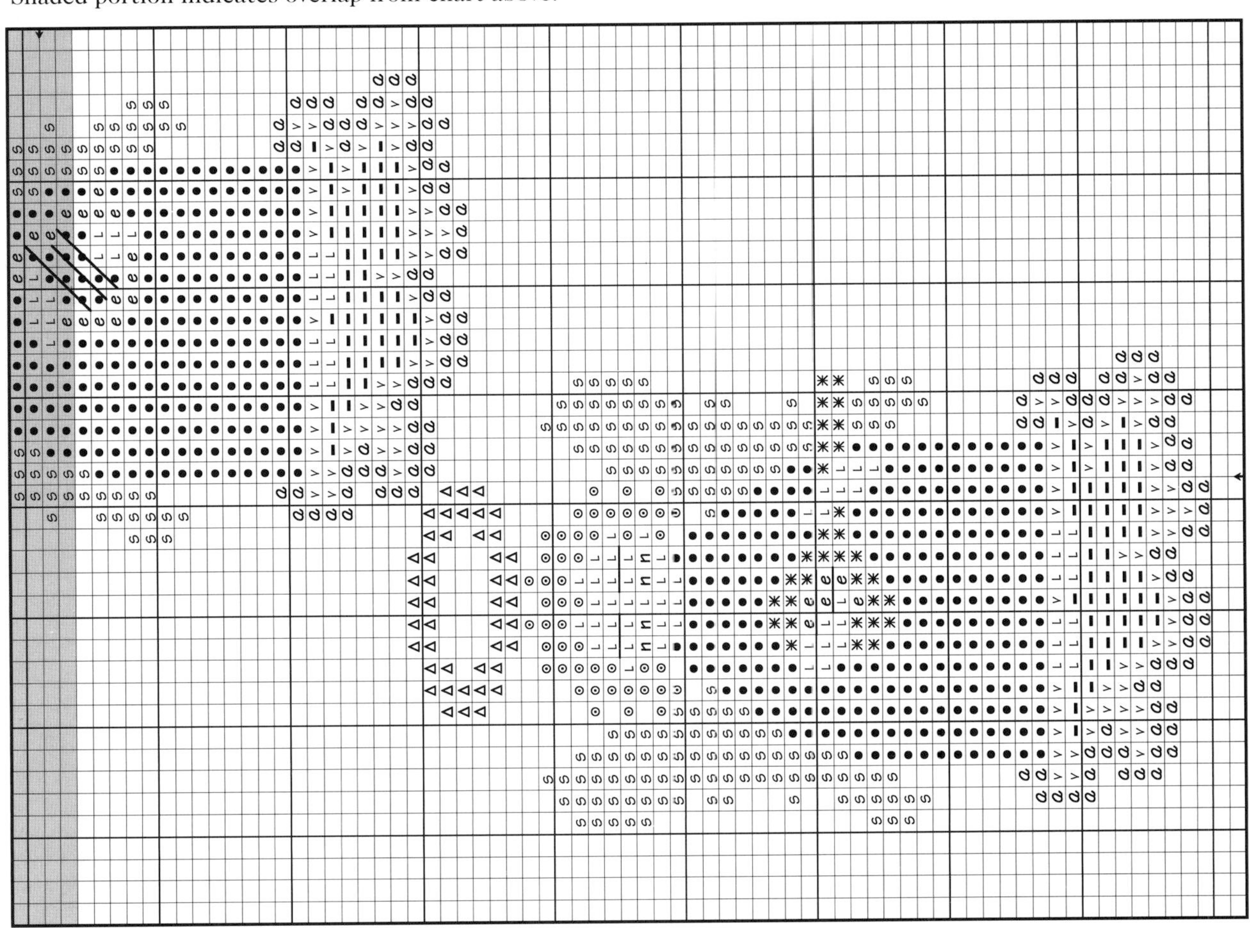

CHILD'S SWEATER—RIGHT PANEL

Shaded portion indicates overlap from chart above.

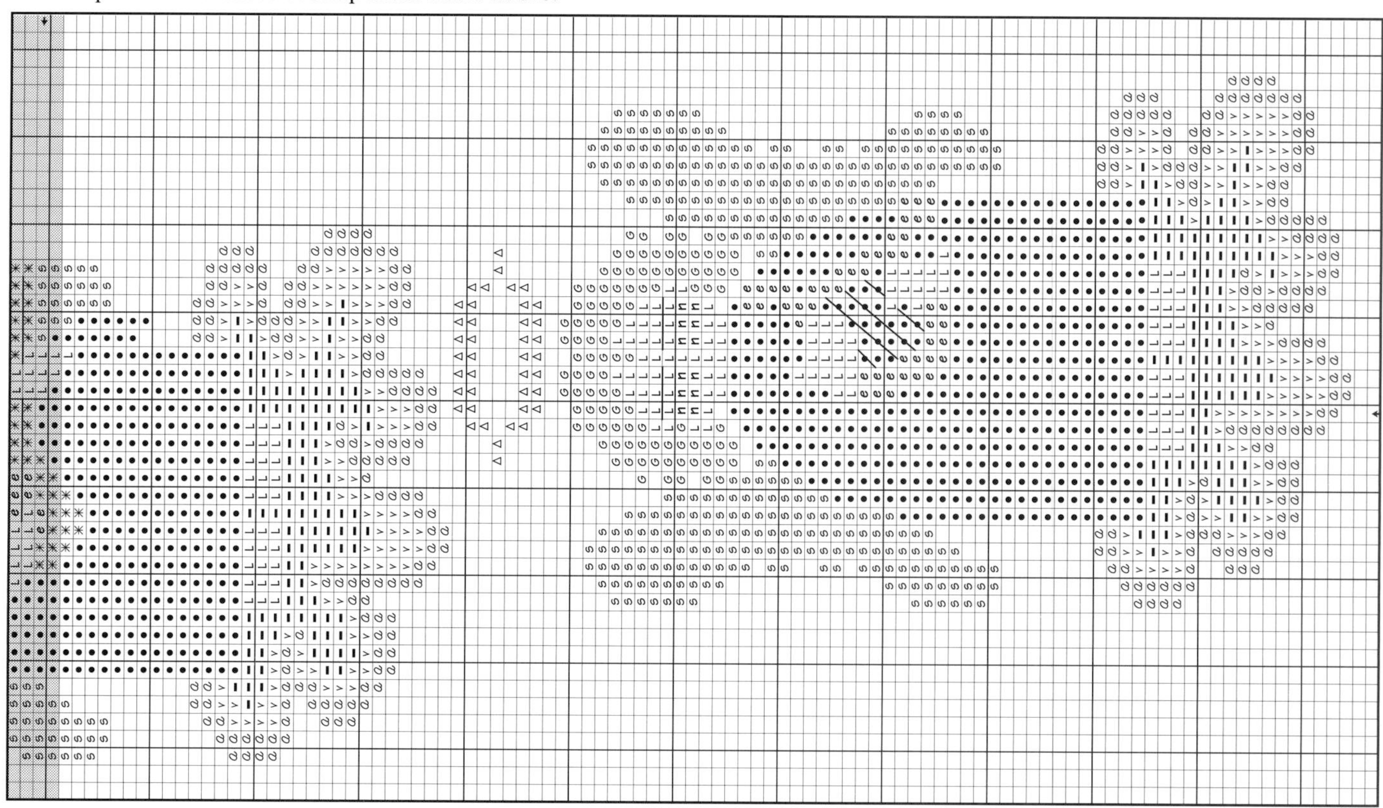

ADULT'S SWEATER—LEFT PANEL

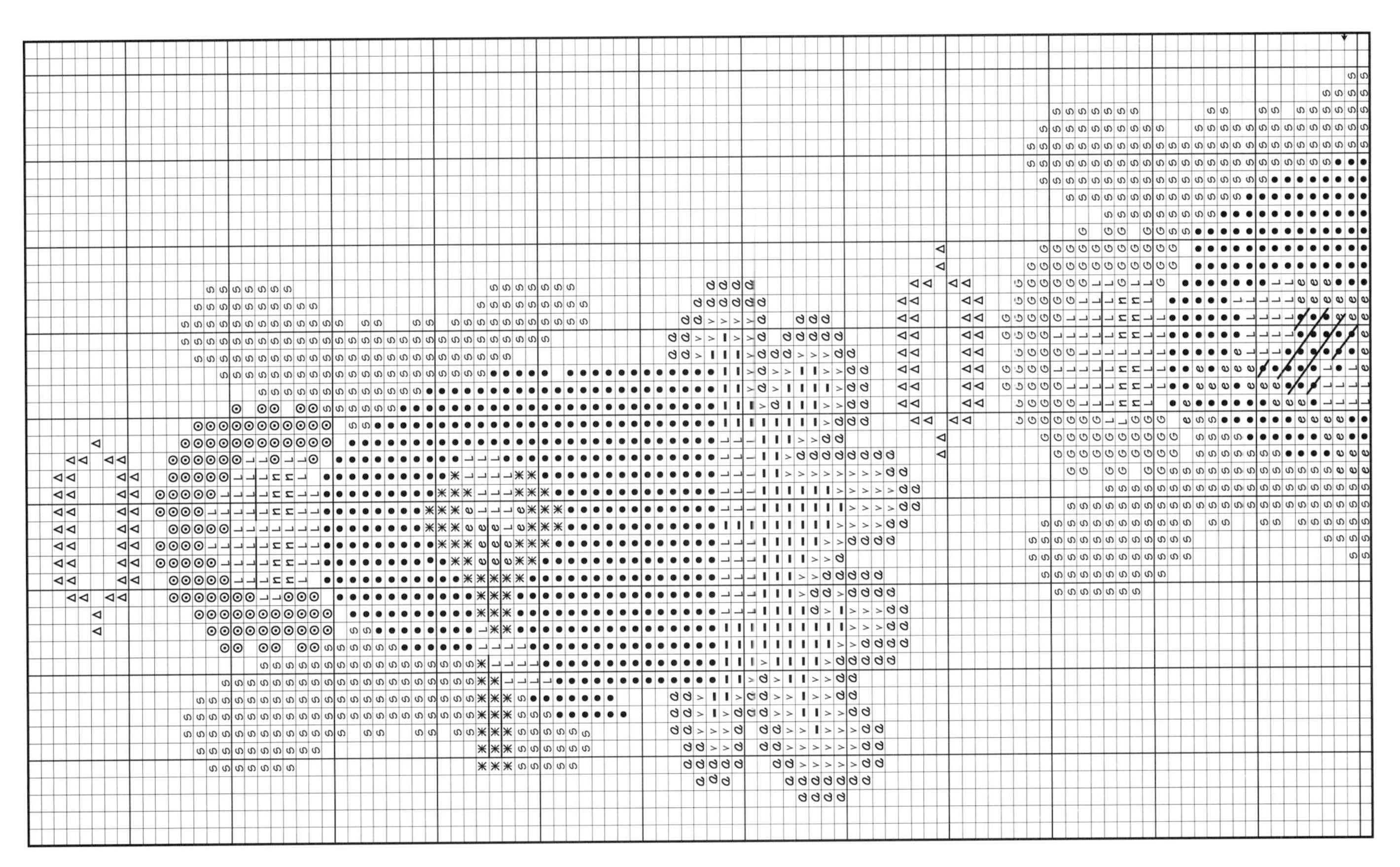

Shaded portion indicates overlap from chart above.

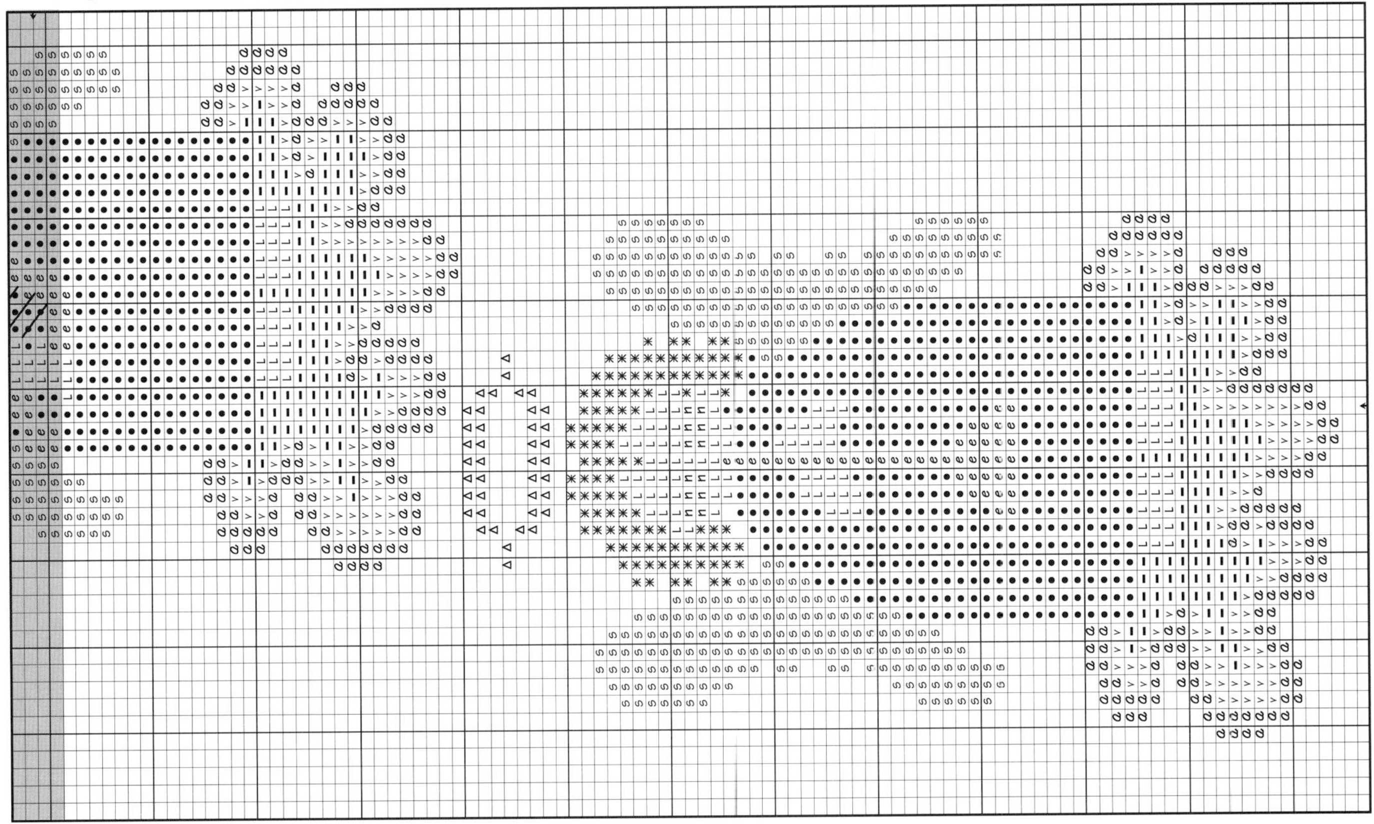

ADULT'S SWEATER—RIGHT PANEL

TOP

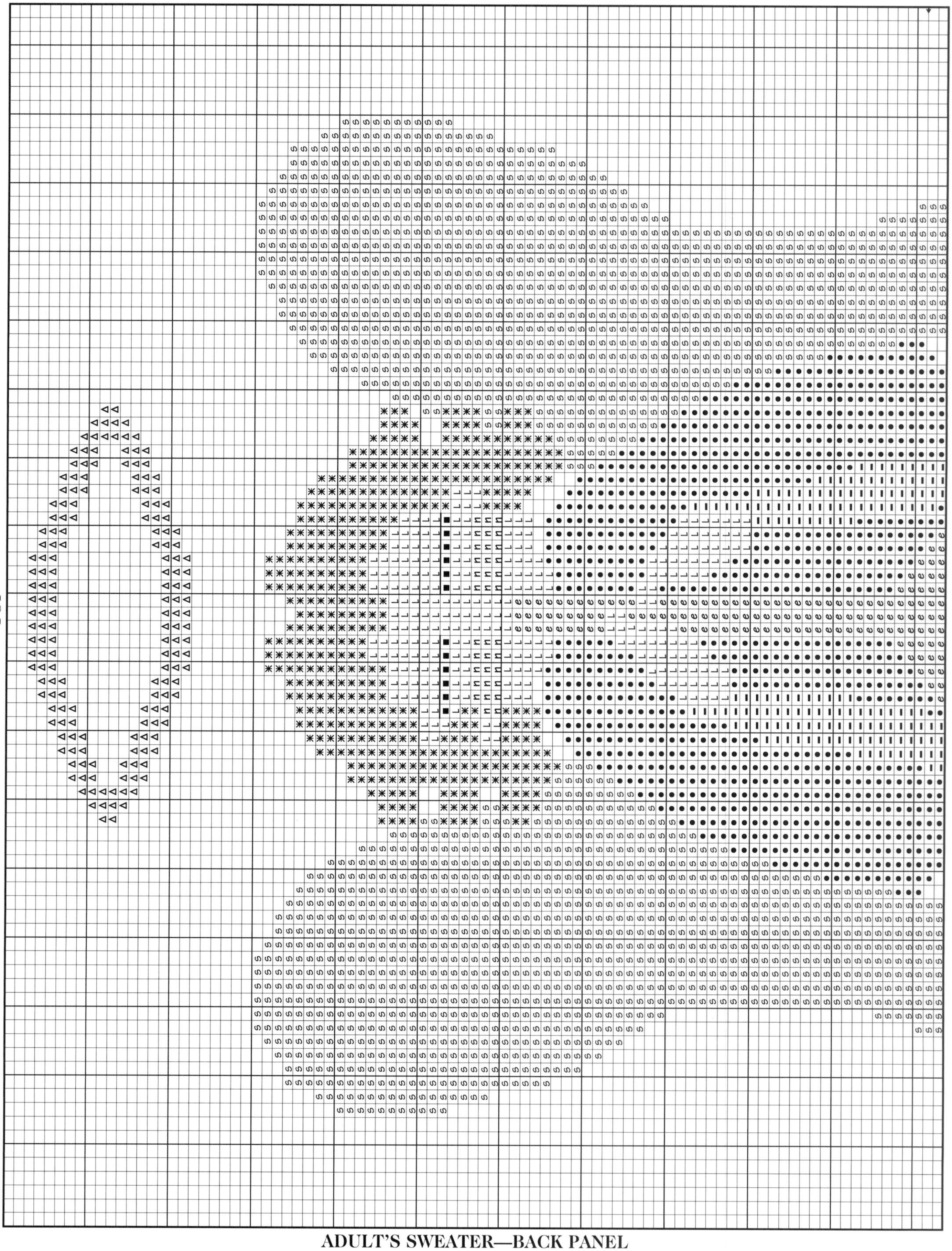

ADULT'S SWEATER—BACK PANEL

Shaded portion indicates overlap from previous page.

Christmas Jumper

Materials:

Purchased blue denim jumper
¼ yd. 44/45"-wide dark green cotton print fabric
⅛ yd. 44/45"-wide red cotton print fabric
¼ yd. Pellon® Wonder-Under® Transfer Web
Small amount polyester filling
Red buttons to replace buttons on jumper (**Note:** Purchase size and number of buttons needed for your jumper.)
1–2 skeins DMC floss, color:#320 (or shade of green to coordinate with green fabric)
Hand-sewing needle
Sewing thread, color: red
Stiff paper **or** template plastic
Water-soluble fabric-marking pen
Scissors
Pencil
Iron

1. Trace pattern pieces onto stiff paper or template plastic. Cut out.
2. Fuse Wonder-Under® to dark green fabric, following manufacturer's instructions for fusing.
3. Trace around patterns on paper side of Wonder-Under®, tracing seven large leaves, seven small leaves, and six stems. Cut out all pieces and peel off paper backing.
4. Sew small running stitches down center of each leaf, using one strand of floss. Gather large leaves to approximately 3¼" long and small leaves to approximately 2½" long. Knot floss at end of each leaf to secure gathers.
5. Cut fourteen berries from red fabric. Sew a small running stitch around perimeter of each circle, approximately ⅛" from edge, using needle and thread. Put one teaspoon-size piece of polyester filling in center of berry and pull gathering thread tightly to form ball. Secure with several stitches through gathered area.

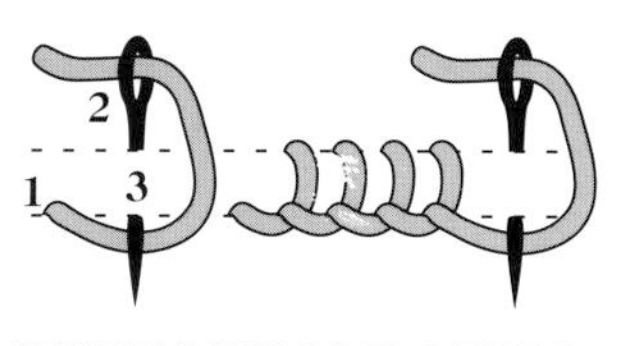

BUTTONHOLE STITCH

6. Place leaves and stems appliqué pieces on right, shoulder area of jumper, referring to diagrams and photo on page 125. Place berries as desired and mark placement of each on jumper with a small dot, using water-soluble fabric-marking pen. Set berries aside.
7. Fold and adjust gathers on each leaf for a pleasing effect. Use steam iron to fuse points of leaves in place.
8. When all leaves have been placed, use iron to steam fuse entire surface of each leaf and stem to jumper.
9. Repeat steps 6–8 for left-pocket area and jumper back.
10. Work small buttonhole stitches around each leaf and stem, using three strands green floss.
Note: When stitching in pocket area, be careful not to sew pocket closed. On jumper back, complete all stitching **under** back facing, if there is one.
11. Sew each berry securely in place from inside of jumper, using needle and thread.
12. Replace jumper buttons with red buttons.

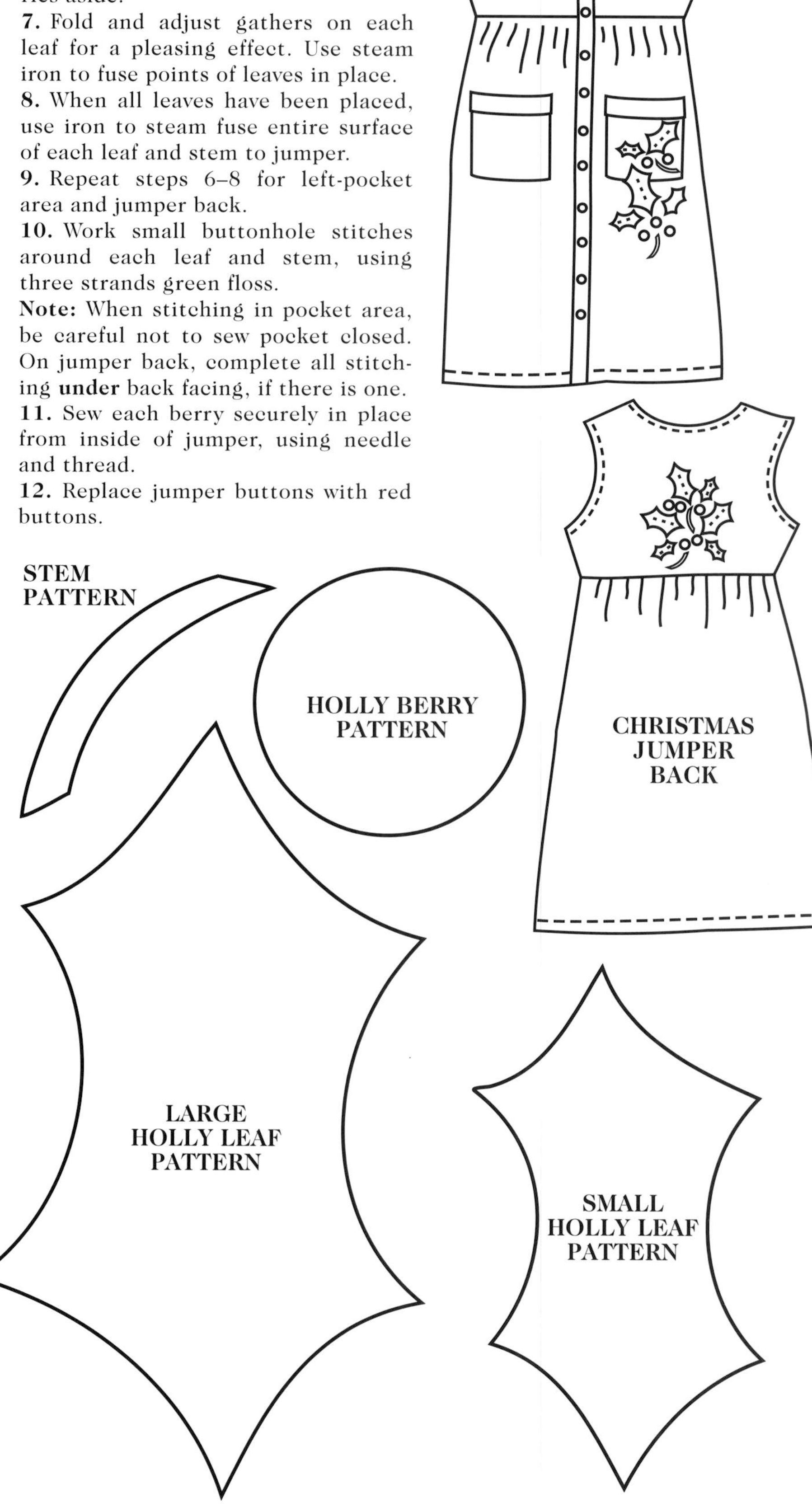

Shopper's Guide

Bells & Trees Wall Hanging
Page 17—Red-and-white striped, metal cannister set from Hickory Farms of Ohio, Inc.

Golden Angels and Kings
Page 21—Kreinik Japan Thread available in needlework shops or from The Daisy Chain, Box 1258, Parkersburg, WV 26102.

Heirloom Christmas Angels
Page 46—Angels from Park Lane Flowers, Birmingham, Alabama.

Clay Ornaments
Page 66—Sculpey clay available from Aardvark Adventures, Post Office Box 2449, Livermore, CA 94551.

Copper Ornaments
Page 66—Copper tooling foil available from Saint Louis Crafts, Inc., 7606 Idaho Avenue, Saint Louis, MO 63111-3219, (800) 841-7631.

Victorian Egg Ornaments
Page 67—Beaded cross ornaments courtesy of The Ritz Florist, Birmingham, Alabama.

Plaid Table Trimmers
Page 81—*Gold Florentine* china by Wedgwood; centerpiece basket from Pier 1 Imports; angel napkin rings from Macy's, Birmingham, Alabama.

Poinsettia Runner & Trivet Set
Page 83—*Christmas Tree* china by Spode.

Snowy Evergreens
Page 85—Glass Christmas tree mug and plate and two-tier serving tray from Rich's, Birmingham, Alabama.

Holiday Aviary
Page 87—*Christmas Tree* china by Spode.

Cinnamon Potpourri Basket
Page 102—Sled ornaments from Christmas Cottage, Birmingham, Alabama.

Holiday Tote
Page 124—SANTA Spray Snow is available in stores where craft and holiday specialty items are sold.

Christmas Jumper
Page 125—Hat courtesy of Rich's, Birmingham, Alabama.

Herald Angels Sweaters
Page 127—Adult's red-and-green colorblock cardigan (#295; $39.00 plus $4.50 shipping and handling; M, L, XL, XXL) and child's red-and-green colorblock cardigan (#296; $28.00 plus $3.75 shipping and handling; S 4–5, M 6–8, L 10–12, XL 14–16) available from *Just CrossStitch*®, 405 Riverhills Business Park, Birmingham, AL 35242, 1-800-768-5878.

Basic Stitch Diagrams

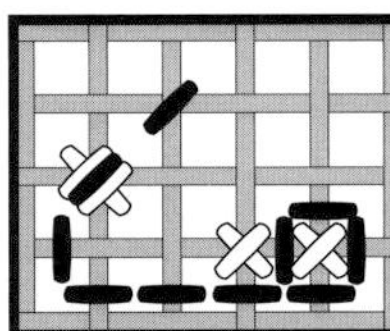

Backstitch (across two ¾ stitches and around full cross

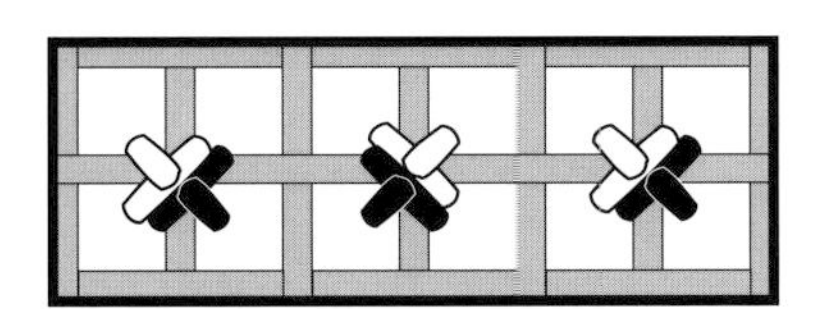

Two ¾ Stitches (in one square, using two different floss colors)

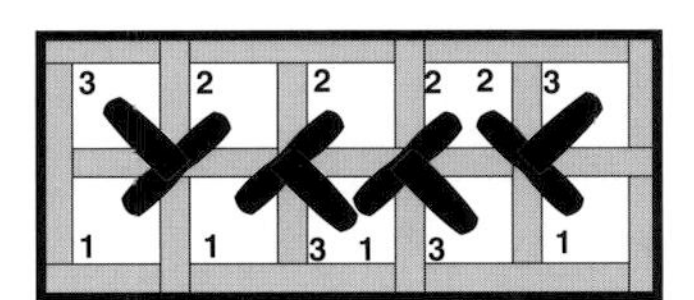

¾ Cross Stitches (over one in various positions)

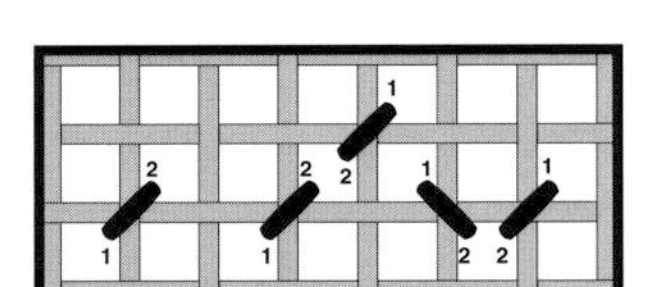

¼ Cross Stitch (over two threads)

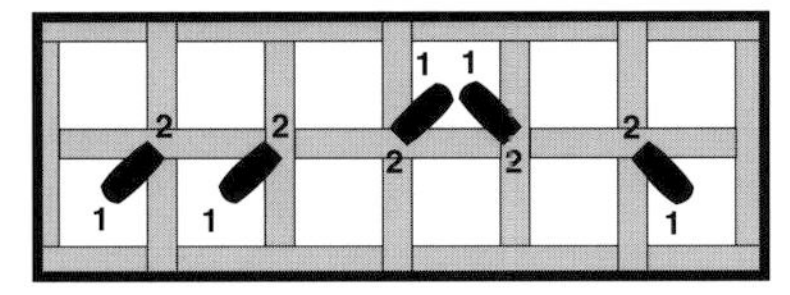

¼ Cross Stitch (over one thread)

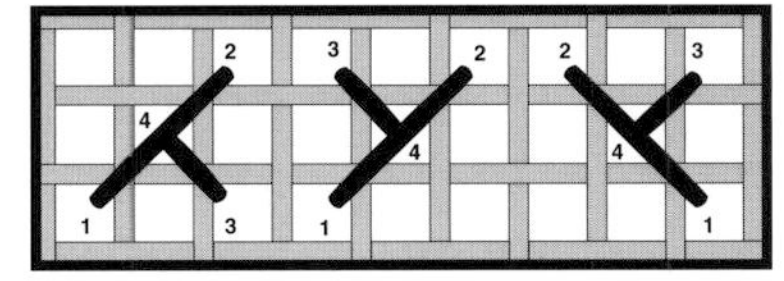

¾ Cross Stitch (over two threads)

Full Cross Stitch (over one thread)

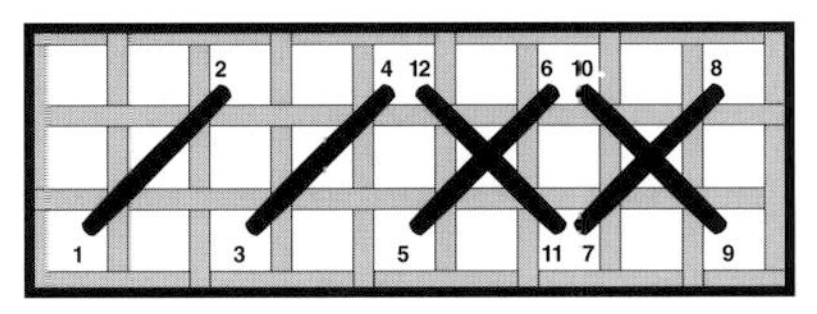

Full Cross Stitch (over two threads)

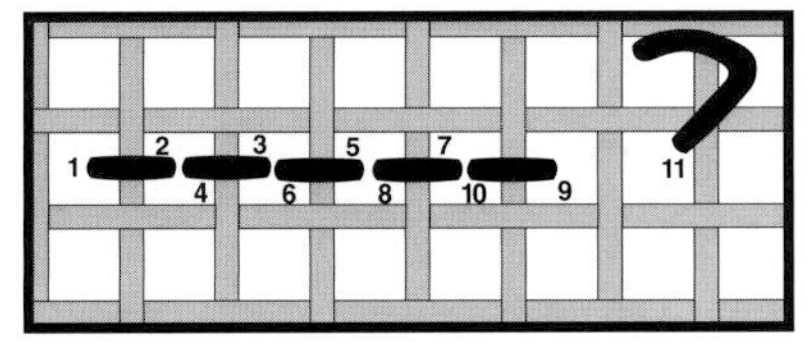

Basic Backstitch

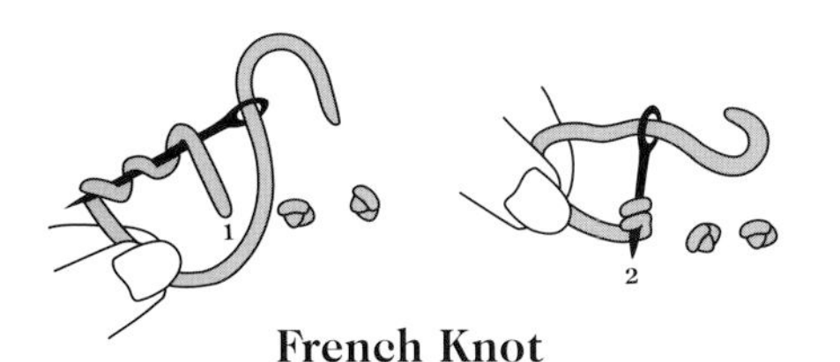

French Knot

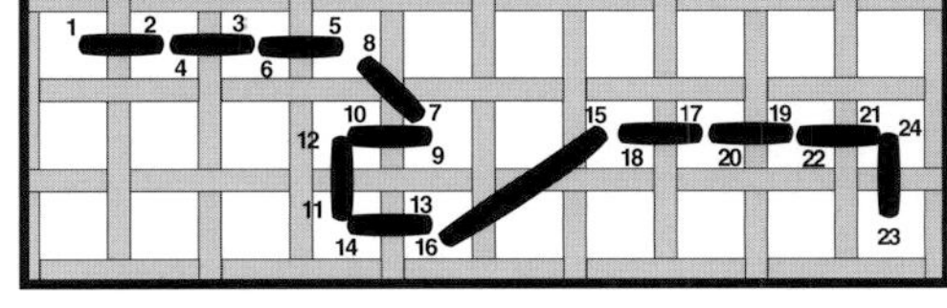

Backstitch (showing variations)

General Instructions for Cross Stitch

Basic Supplies: Even-weave fabric, tapestry needle(s), six-strand embroidery floss, embroidery scissors, embroidery hoop (optional).

Fabric Preparation: The instructions and yardage for finishing materials have been written and calculated for each of the projects shown stitched on the fabric listed in each color code. Alternate fabric choices have also been listed. If you wish to stitch a design on an alternate fabric, or alter its placement, you will need to recalculate the finished size of the project, as well as the yardage of finishing materials needed, and make the necessary dimension adjustments when finishing.

Determine size of fabric needed for a project by dividing number of horizontal stitches by thread count of fabric. For example, if a design 35 stitches wide is worked on 14-count fabric, it will cover 2½" (35 divided by 14 equals 2½). Repeat process for vertical count. Add three inches on all sides of design area to find dimensions for cutting fabric. Whipstitch edges to prevent fraying.

Floss Preparation: Cut floss into 14" to 18" lengths. Separate all six strands. Reunite number of strands needed and thread needle, leaving one floss end longer than the other.

Where to Start: Start wherever you like! Some designers suggest finding center of fabric and starting there. Others recommend beginning with a central motif, while still others work borders first. Many find fabric center, count up and back to the left, and start with the uppermost left stitch. Wherever you begin, be sure to leave allowance for all horizontal and vertical stitches so that a 3" fabric margin is left around completed design.

Should you choose to begin at the center point, find it by folding fabric from top to bottom and then from left to right. Use a straight pin to mark upper-left corner at junction of folds, and then unfold fabric. Pin will be in center of fabric.

After deciding where to begin on fabric, find same point on graph. Each square on graph represents one stitch. Those squares containing a symbol (i.e., X,T,O) indicate that a stitch should be made in that space over those threads. Different symbols represent different colors of floss for stitches. (See color code of chart.) They may also indicate partial or decorative stitches. Familiarize yourself with color code before you begin stitching. Even-weave fabric may be stretched over an embroidery hoop to facilitate stitching.

Stitching the Design: Using the diagrams on page 141, stitch design, completing all full and partial cross stitches first. Cross all full cross stitches in same direction to achieve a smooth surface appearance. Work backstitches second, and any decorative stitches last.

Helpful Hints for Stitching: Do not knot floss. Instead, catch end on back of work with first few stitches. As you stitch, pull floss through fabric "holes" with one stroke, not several short ones. The moment you feel resistance from floss, cease pulling. Consistent tension on floss results in a smoother look for stitches. Drop your needle frequently to allow floss to untwist. It twists naturally as you stitch and, as it gets shorter, must be allowed to untwist more often. To begin a new color on project, prepare floss and secure new strands as noted. To end stitching, run floss under several completed stitches and clip remaining strands close to surface. Many times it is necessary to skip a few spaces (threads) on the fabric in order to continue a row of stitches in the same color. If you must skip an area covering more than ¼", end stitching as described and begin again at next point. This procedure prevents uneven tension on the embroidery surface and snagging on the back. It also keeps colors from showing through unstitched areas. Do not carry thread over an area that will remain unstitched.

When You Are Finished: For designs using cotton or linen floss on cotton or linen even-weave fabric, hand wash piece with mild detergent in warm water. Rinse thoroughly with cold water. Roll in terry towel and squeeze gently to remove excess moisture. Do not wring. Unroll towel and allow piece to dry until barely damp. Iron on padded surface with design face down, using medium setting for heat. A press cloth will help prevent shine on dark fabrics. **Note:** Acrylics, acrylic blends, wools, or silks must be treated differently when cleaning. Check manufacturer's guidelines for special cleaning instructions.

Helpful Hints for Crafting

The instructions and yardage for finishing materials have been written and calculated for each of the projects shown and crafted from the materials listed. If you wish to craft a design using materials of different dimensions than those listed or to stitch a design on an alternate fabric or to alter its placement, you will need to recalculate the finished size of the project, as well as the yardage of finishing materials needed, and make the necessary dimension adjustments when purchasing supplies and making the projects.

Crafters and Designers

Celebrate the Season

Barbara Black
Pines in the Patches, page 14.

Hallie Downing
Joy Wall Hanging, page 16.

Cheryl Fall for Coats & Clark
Home For Christmas Wall Hanging, Pillow, and Tree Skirt, page 12.
Papercut Snowflake Pillow, page 20.

Naomi Kaplan for Coats & Clark
Bells & Trees Wall Hanging, page 17.

Inez Norton
Pinecone Basket, page 8.
Natural Sweet-Gum Wreath, page 9.
Christmas Tree Pillow, page 20.

Kay Pealstrom
Feathered Friends Stockings, page 11.

Sheryl Pittman
Joy and Noel Pillows, page 18.

Dee Dee Triplett
Victorian Fruits Wreath, page 10.
Real Reason Banner, page 15.
Golden Angels and Kings, page 21.

Christmas Favorites

Betty Auth
Wood-Burned Santa Egg, page 44.

Annabelle Keller for The Dow Chemical Company
Mr. & Mrs. Claus Ornaments, page 44.

Cathy Livingston
Heirloom Christmas Angels, page 46.
Christmas Curiosity, page 49.

Ursula Michael for The DMC Corporation
Down the Chimney, page 42.

Inez Norton
Recycled Bottle Angel, page 47.

Dee Dee Triplett
Clay Claus, page 43.
Angel to Watch Over You, page 45.
Folk-Art Bunnies Throw and Pillow, page 48.

A Memorable Tree

Lorri Birmingham for The DMC Corporation
Victorian Egg Ornaments, page 67.

Helen Haywood
Angels with Rosebuds, page 67.

Annabelle Keller for The Dow Chemical Company
Fan Ornaments, page 68.

Inez Norton
Cone Ornaments, page 64.
Holiday Bells, page 64.
Victorian Lace Eggs, page 64.

Marty Spear
Christmas Ball Ornaments, page 64.

Karen Taylor
Clay Ornaments, page 66.
Copper Ornaments, page 66.
Calico Angels, page 69.

Dee Dee Triplett
Handprint Ornaments, page 69.

Yuletide Tables

Cheryl Fall for Coats & Clark
Poinsettia Runner & Trivet Set, page 83.

Hope Murphy
Ho Ho Ho Place Mat, page 85.
Snowy Evergreens, page 85.

Inez Norton
Pineapple Centerpiece, page 80.
Plaid Table Trimmers, page 81.
Crafting Fun with Roses, page 84.
Holiday Aviary, page 87.

Dee Dee Triplett
Muslin Place Mats and Napkins, page 82.

Quick & Easy

Mary Area
Gingerbread House Ornaments, page 108.

Polly Carbonari
The Skaters, page 99.

Cheryl Fall for Coats & Clark
Christmas Pie Apron & Pot Holder Set, page 103.

Maria Filosa for The Dow Chemical Company
Silver Bells Garland, page 105.

Annabelle Keller for The Dow Chemical Company
Surprise Packages, page 102.
Angel Ornaments, page 108.

Cathy Livingston
My Gift to You, page 98.

Inez Norton
Cinnamon Potpourri Basket, page 102.
Snowman Necklace, page 104.
Noel Candle Holders, page 105.
Laundry Detergent Scoop Decorations, page 108.

Robyn Taylor
Holiday Happiness, page 100.

Dee Dee Triplett
Christmas Button Covers, page 101.
Postage Stamp Pins, page 101.
Earth-Friendly Gift Bags, page 104.
Save the Earth Computer-Paper Wreath, page 106.
Fingerprint Ornaments, page 107.
Gingerbread Men Ornaments, page 106.

Holiday Fashions

Helen Haywood
Crochet Snowflake Jewelry, page 122.

Charlotte Holder
Herald Angels Sweaters, page 127.

Dee Dee Triplett
Fancy Holiday Belts, page 120.
Holly Wearables, page 123.
Holiday Tote, page 124.

Claudia Wood
Christmas Jumper, page 125.

Index

Numbers in **bold** type indicate color photo pages. All other numbers refer to pages for charts, color codes, patterns, and instructions.